HOLDING THE LINE

How Britain's Railways Were Saved

Richard Faulkner and Chris Austin

First published 2012

ISBN 978 0 86093 647 3

Published by Oxford Publishing Co

an imprint of Ian Allan Publishing Ltd, Hersham, Surrey KT12 4RG. Printed in England.

Visit the Ian Allan Publishing website at www.ianallanpublishing.com

Front cover: In the twilight period following the Beeching report, the sun sets behind Barmouth's unusual distant signal in July 1966. The Cambrian Coast line was not included in the Beeching report, but was subsequently proposed for closure twice as well as being a candidate for bus substitution and threatened by the condition of the timber bridge over the Mawddach. The uncertainty blighted the line's development for 25 years.

Back cover: In January 1981, just two years before closure, a train from Huddersfield arrives at Clayton West. One of the few lines in the 1979 'list of 41' to close, it failed to secure support from West Yorkshire PTE – which did, however, support the Penistone line, which it joined near Shepley. The route is now used by the 15in-gauge Kirklees Light Railway.

Title page: A Cambridge to Oxford train pauses at Bedford (St John's) in July 1966, eighteen months before closure. Excluded from the Reshaping report, this line was added to the list the following year, 1964. St John's remained to serve the truncated service from Bletchley, but closed in 1984 when trains were diverted to the Midland station. Plans to restore trains to Oxford are well advanced.

Picture Credits
Chris Austin, Brian Barnsley, Frank Dumbleton, Richard Faulkner, Ian Allan Library, *The House Magazine, The Sunday Times,* CBT, Aggregate Industries, The Wensleydale Railway Association, Norfolk County Council.

CONTENTS

ACKNOWLEDGEMENTS

This book is dedicated to Sue Faulkner and Georgina Austin, whose understanding of their husbands' 'endless capacity for taking trains' (as Peter Parker once said of John Betjeman) is acknowledged with love and gratitude.

We are also grateful for the advice and information provided by many people during the book's preparation, particularly by the following:

Liz Atkins; Ron Atkins; Brian Barnsley; David Brown; Neil Buxton; Ann Carlton; Frank Dumbleton; David Faulkner; Lord Fowler; Simon Hoggart; Kelvin Hopkins MP; Lord Howell; Stephen Joseph; Lord Liddle; Alan Marshall; David Morgan (Network Rail); John Nelson; Frank Paterson; Gordon Pettitt; Lord Rodgers of Quarry Bank; Judy Raumann; Andy Savage; Lord Snape; David Spaven.

Their help has been invaluable. However, the authors take full responsibility for any errors and omissions and will not be offended if readers wish to point them out.

BIBLIOGRAPHY

The authors' research has drawn upon the following wide range of sources:

Books and magazines
Bairstow, Martin *The Huddersfield & Sheffield Junction Railway*, 1993
Britain's Growing Railway, Railfuture, 2010
British Railways Pre-Grouping Atlas and Gazetteer, Ian Allan, 1988
Castle, Barbara *The Castle Diaries 1964-70*, Weidenfeld & Nicolson, 1984
Crosland, Susan *Tony Crosland*, Cape, 1982
Crossman, Richard *The Diaries of a Cabinet Minister*, Hamish Hamilton, Jonathan Cape, 1977
Daniels, Gerald and Dench, L. A. *Passengers No More*, Ian Allan, 1974
Dow, Andrew *Dow's Dictionary of Railway Quotations*, John Hopkins University Press, 2006
Ellis, C. Hamilton *British Railway History*, George Allen & Unwin, Volume One 1954, Volume Two 1959
Fiennes, G. F. *I Tried to Run a Railway*, Ian Allan, 1967
Fowler, Norman *Ministers Decide*, Chapman's, 1991
Gourvish, T. R. *British Rail 1974-97*, Oxford University Press, 2002
Gourvish, T. R. *British Railways 1948-73*, Cambridge University Press, 1986
Greville and Spence, *Closed Passenger Lines of Great Britain, 1827-1947*, 1974
Griffith, E. C. *The Basingstoke & Alton Light Railway 1901-1936*, 1947
Hall, Peter and Smith, Edward *Better Use of Railways*, Department of Geography, University of Reading, January 1976
Hardy, R. H. N. *Beeching, Champion of the Railway?* Ian Allan, 1989
Henshaw, David *The Great Railway Conspiracy*, Leading Edge, 1991
Hillman, Mayer and Whalley, Anne *The Social Consequences of Rail Closures*, Policy Studies Institute, 1980
Hoole, K. *Railway Stations of the North East*, David & Charles, 1985
House Magazine, The
Kidner, R. W. *The Mid-Wales Railway*, Oakwood Press, 2003
Lipsey, David *In the Corridors of Power*, Biteback Publishing, 2012
Madge, Robin *Railways Around Exmoor*, Exmoor Press, 1971
Marsh, Richard *Off the Rails: An Autobiography*, Weidenfeld & Nicholson, 1978
Mitchell, Sir David *From House to House: The Endless Adventure of Politics and Wine*, Memoir Club, 2008
Modern Railways (magazine)
Morgan, John Scott *The Colonel Stephens Railways*, Ian Allan, 1999
Morris of Aberavon, Lord *Fifty Years in Politics and the Law*, University of Wales Press, 2011
New Scientist (magazine)
Nock, O. S. *Branch Lines*, Batsford, 1957
Parker, Sir Peter *For Starters*, Jonathan Cape, 1989
Penistone Line Trail, The Penistone Line Partnership, 2003
Perkins, Anne *Red Queen*, Macmillan, 2003
Pryke, Richard and Dodgson, John *Rail Problem – An Alternative Strategy*, Robertson, 1975
Railnews (magazine)
Railway Magazine, The
Rolt, L. T. C. *Railway Adventure*, David & Charles, 1961
Sellick, Roger *The West Somerset Mineral Railway*, David & Charles, 1970

Stott, Richard *Dogs and Lampposts*, Metro Publishing, 2002
Towler, James *The Battle for the Settle and Carlisle*, Platform 5, 1990
Tramlink User Guide, Transport for London, January 2010
Vole, The (magazine)
Wardroper, John *Juggernaut*, Temple Smith, 1981
Weighell, Sidney with Taylor, Robert *On the Rails*, Orbis, 1983
Whitelaw, William *The Whitelaw Memoirs*, Headline, 1989
Wolmar, Christian *Fire and Steam*, Atlantic Books, 2007

Official Publications
Community Rail Development Strategy, Strategic Rail Authority, November 2004 (available on DfT website)
Connecting Communities, Association of Train Operating Companies, 2009 (available on ATOC website)
Development of the Major Railway Trunk Routes, The British Railways Board, 1965
Everyone's Railway: The Wider Case for Rail, Strategic Rail Authority, 2003
Future Rail, British Railways Board, 1991
Hansard (Lords and Commons)
Opportunity for Change, An British Railways Board, 1976
Railways Acts 1974/1993
Realising the Potential of GB Rail (McNulty Report), Department for Transport, May 2011
Reorganisation of the Nationalised Transport Undertakings, Cmnd 1248, HMSO, 1960
Report of the Railway Pay Committee of Inquiry, HMSO, 1960
The Reshaping of British Railways, HMSO, 1963
Steer Davies & Gleave *Northern Rail Review*, March 1966 (available on DfT website)
Transport Acts 1962/1968/2005
Transport of Freight, Cmnd 3470
Transport Policy, Cmnd 3057, July 1966
Transport Policy, a consultation document ('orange paper'), HMSO, 1976

Archives and libraries consulted
BBC Archive, Caversham, Reading
Bodleian Library, Oxford
Crosland, Anthony – private papers at the London School of Economics
Foot, Michael – private papers at the People's History Museum, Manchester
Heritage Railway Association website
National Archives
National Archives of Scotland
National Newspaper Library
Railway trade union papers at the University of Warwick
Search Engine, National Railway Museum, York
Sherman, Sir Alfred – private papers at Royal Holloway, University of London
Transport 2000 papers
West Somerset Railway papers

FOREWORD

*'Most men who have really lived have had, in some shape,
their great adventure. This railway is mine.'*

JAMES HILL, AMERICAN 'EMPIRE BUILDER',
WRITING TO GREAT NORTHERN RAILWAY EMPLOYEES
ON HIS RETIREMENT IN 1912

This book is about the British people's love affair with their railways – and also about the repeated attempts made during the second half of the twentieth century to destroy them. The main threats lay in starving them of financial investment and drastically reducing the size of the network by extensive programmes of closure, which would have reduced it to little more than a small number of intercity routes and commuter services in conurbations – a similar outcome to what had occurred in most of the United States.

There were also bizarre proposals to concrete over rail lines in order to create new roads and busways. Other such 'solutions' included a widespread programme of substituting buses for trains and passing to local authorities the decision as to whether lines should close or stay open. The possibility of death through starvation was ever present, as Government funding levels were cut and insufficient finance made available to carry out essential railway renewals and maintenance.

There was no single conspiracy to destroy the railways, but individuals from various parts of the political spectrum were drawn to the supposed holy grail of a much smaller network and a profitable 'core'. They included right-wing free-market ideologues opposed to the concept of public transport, well-meaning but misguided social democrats who saw rail subsidies as regressive, beneficial only to the middle classes, and a variety of lobbying interests who would benefit from the expansion of road building, car ownership and road haulage – including trade unionists opposed to the development of rail freight services.

From the 1950s onwards, there was a widespread view that the nationalised railway was both badly managed and wasted vast amounts of money. The maximum threat to the integrity of the network occurred when at least two (or more) of the negative forces cited above came together, as in the period leading up to the Beeching Report and the subsequent implementation of its closure proposals in the 1960s.

In this book, we examine the way in which closures were handled, the determination of officials to ensure that they took place (albeit in many cases these were thwarted) and the attempts made in more recent years to repair the damage that they caused.

Both authors were involved in the management of the railways during much of the period covered by this book. Chris Austin joined British Rail in 1967, his career taking him through operations, investment and business planning – where he was able to convince managers and ministers of the value of restoring an obscure piece of abandoned railway running from Blackfriars to Farringdon, now known as Thameslink. He was later responsible for the BR board's relationship with parliamentarians, his remit covering the fraught period in the run-up to privatisation. Chris subsequently worked for the Strategic Rail Authority, where he instigated the Community Rail Development Strategy, and the Association of Train Operating Companies, for which he wrote a report on connecting communities who had lost their direct rail access.

Richard Faulkner was a public affairs adviser to the British Railways Board from February 1977 until 1998. He and his business colleague, William Camp[1], were initially engaged as outside consultants by Sir Peter Parker, shortly after Parker's appointment as BR Chairman. Earlier, they had been commissioned by the three railway trade unions – the NUR, ASLEF and TSSA – to mount the 'No Rail Cuts' campaign of 1975 (see Chapter 8).

---

1   See endnote on page 66.

INTRODUCTION

'The railways will do as much for mankind as the monasteries did.'

BENJAMIN DISRAELI, IN HIS 1845 NOVEL *SYBIL*

Monsal Dale viaduct
Monsal Dale, described by Ruskin as 'divine as the vale of Tempe', is crossed by an attractive viaduct.
Seen here, a Class 46 heads the 08.05 St Pancras to Manchester on 1 June 1965.

Somerset & Dorset – busy train at Sturminster Newton
A popular day at Sturminster Newton as a train from Bournemouth arrives.
The line remained unchanged until the end came in March 1966.

The railways are part of Britain's social fabric, one of the most important building blocks of the nation. Their beneficial contribution has been incalculable, but they have also generated controversy – whether it was art critic and polymath John Ruskin's concern about their impact on the landscape or difficulties with politicians, harking back to the day in 1830 when the President of the Board of Trade (then responsible for the railways) was knocked down and fatally injured by the *Rocket*.

Railing against the building of the railway through Monsal Dale in the Peak District, Ruskin wrote:

> You think it a great triumph to make the sun draw brown landscapes for you! That was also a discovery, and some day may be useful. But the sun had drawn landscapes before for you, not in brown, but in green, and blue, and all imaginable colours, here in England. Not one of you ever looked at them; not one of you cares for the loss of them, now, when you have shut the sun out with smoke, so that he can draw nothing more, except brown blots through a hole in a box. There was a rocky valley between Buxton and Bakewell, once upon a time, divine as the vale of Tempe; you might have seen the gods there morning and evening – Apollo and all the sweet Muses of the Light, walking in fair procession on the lawns of it, and to and fro among the pinnacles of its crags. You cared neither for gods nor grass, but for cash (which you did not know the way to get). You thought you could get it by what *The Times* calls 'Railroad Enterprise'. You enterprised a railroad through the valley, you blasted its rocks away, heaped thousands of tons of shale into its lovely stream. The valley is gone, and the gods with it; and now, every fool in Buxton can be at Bakewell in half-an-hour, and every fool in Bakewell at Buxton; which you think a lucrative process of exchange, you Fools everywhere![1]

In more recent times, however, with the exception of the recent opposition to High Speed 2 by middle-class groups in the Chilterns, it is only when Government attempts to *deprive* people of their railway that the debate becomes most heated. It is 50 years since the Beeching Report was published, yet still the arguments rage. The report left an indelible mark on Britain's corporate memory and still resonates today. The wilful destruction of a great British investment, the permanent loss of mobility entailed in being taken 'off the network', the lack of public consultation or scrutiny and the obduracy of officials combined to create a viewpoint whereby closures were not only unjustified, but unfair. They offended the British spirit of fair play and disrupted the British way of life – particularly in a rural or seaside setting.

The railway continues to touch everyone's lives. About half of the population travel by train during the course of one year, while most of the other half benefit in terms of reduced road congestion or delivery of goods by rail – whether the white goods in their kitchen, the food in their fridge or the coal that produces the electricity they use.

Most people hold a view about the railways and many long to see them play a greater role in meeting Britain's transport needs. After a period of decline the network is now busier than ever, with levels of passenger use never before seen in peacetime. Indeed, the railway has been transformed over the space of 20 years, both in the way it is run and in the levels of service provided. However, while opinions are both vocal and varied, politicians, policymakers and economists all tend to agree that it costs too much.

This, in essence, has always defined the 'branch line' problem from the time that BR first moved from profit to loss in 1956. It led to the largest disinvestment in transport infrastructure ever seen in Britain, the consequences of which remain with us today in terms of miles of abandoned earthworks and thousands of redundant viaducts, bridges and tunnels, as well as communities denied access to a sustainable transport system.

In some cases this disinvestment has proved irreversible, with roads, offices or houses now standing where the trains once ran. In other cases the trains have been reinstated to meet the needs of today, but at a high cost in terms of laying new track or upgrading lines formerly reduced to carrying freight at low speed.

Blackpool Central station site as car park (view from the Tower)
The railway served Blackpool superbly until Central station closed in 1964. This picture shows the extent of railway land in the town and hints at how a central location might have been maintained, funded by development of the huge surrounding area.

Most surprisingly, this disinvestment took place without any real debate on how the railway could best support the country's economic, social and environmental objectives, alongside its key transport needs. It was carried out on the basis of very thin evidence of the actual costs or benefits of line provision, still less of the level of cost escapement following closure. There was an erroneous collective consensus for many years that branch lines and secondary routes were unprofitable; that their closure would result in net financial benefits large enough to solve the 'railway problem'; that there was an inherently profitable 'core' railway; and that the roads could accommodate all those for whom rail provision was supposedly uneconomic (as well as all the goods traffic). All these assumptions have proved to be largely or wholly false.

This 'collective consensus' resulted in pressure by successive Governments (and particularly the Treasury) for BR to make short-term savings and, latterly, to avoid investment in rolling stock or major infrastructure. Oscar Wilde's famous comment about cynics who 'know the price of everything and the value of nothing'[2] could be applied to Governmental policymakers, except that their knowledge of costs turned out to be pretty inadequate too.

For many it was easier to accept the proposition rather than challenge it, as there were always bigger issues at stake. Railway managers wanted to secure investment in rolling stock or electrification; trade unions sought to secure better pay and conditions. At various times, it was easier to accede to closures than to challenge them at the expense of these other priorities. At some point in this process, governmental determination to make radical and irreversible changes in the railway, and the clandestine way in which they were executed, gave them the appearance of a conspiracy.

Some senior railwaymen (and until recently they were all men) were also part of this conspiracy, working hard to implement the closure programmes once they had been agreed. The management of closures was both ruthless and effective in delivering the objectives set by Government. A cadre of managers, particularly at board level under Fred Margetts[3], were so committed to the objective that they saw off attempts by regional managers to retain lines that were not significant loss-makers or could have been of value as alternative routes. It was even suggested that, in the aftermath of Beeching, local managers were obliged to operate a quota, so that a proportion of lines would be closed in their regions regardless of whether an economic case had been made.

There was no attempt to operate much of the railway more efficiently, with many operating methods and train service patterns remaining unchanged for years before closure. The classic example was the Somerset & Dorset line which remained steam-operated to the end, with mechanical signalling retained throughout, virtually all stations staffed and an operating regime that required trains to reverse direction once at Bath and twice at Templecombe. No attempt was made either to reduce costs or to increase earnings, with the line remaining in a time warp until its closure in 1966.

Local authorities were also complicit, often because they wanted town centre developments, particularly road schemes, to make use of the railway land that would be released. One notorious example is Blackpool, where the council shamefully turned its back on the railway that had created its prosperity. In the 1960s, in the interests of building the M55 extension into the town by following the formation of the most direct railway line into Blackpool from Preston, it was happy to turn over the sites of Central station and the line to the South station to car parking. Even North station was cut back to the former excursion platforms to accommodate a traffic scheme and a supermarket. Other cities that lost large sections of railway to road and retail schemes include Gloucester, Cheltenham, Nottingham, Glasgow and Lancaster.

Most importantly, future projections were limited in scope and relatively unsophisticated. In the event, much of it has been proven wrong. Of all the scenarios that informed Government or BR planning from the 1950s to the 1990s, none gave a hint of the levels of growth that have actually been experienced since the mid-1990s, particularly in the remarkable resurgence of demand for local and regional services.

The disinvestment which saw the closure of almost half the rail network was carried out in a ruthless and determined manner, inevitably drawing comparisons with BR's vandalism in demolishing the Euston Arch. While this may seem unfair to some, it reflects the strength of feeling and resentment of the systematic destruction of a much-loved institution, via a juggernaut process pushed relentlessly by an organisation that would not listen to any proposed alternatives – even from its own passengers.

1. John Ruskin, *Praeterita 1871-77*.
2   Lord Darlington in *Lady Windermere's Fan*, Act III.
3   Frederick Chilton Margetts CBE (1905-89) was assistant operating superintendent for LNER Scotland, 1946, and for BR Scotland, 1949; chief operating superintendent, BR Scotland, 1955; chief traffic manager, BR York, 1958 – followed by assistant General Manager, 1959, and General Manager, 1961; BR committee member, 1962; operating member, BR board, 1962–67.

I

EARLY CLOSURES 1827-1947

The Wantage Tram, all steam and smoke,
Was beat by Arthur Hitchcock's moke.

ANONYMOUS POEM QUOTED IN *THE RAILWAY MAGAZINE*, VOLUME LXIII, 1928

Severn Bridge.
The two missing spans are clearly visible in this picture, brought down after collision with two oil barges in 1960.
The signals are at 'danger', protecting the obstruction, but would never be cleared again as the bridge was subsequently
demolished. A GW 2-8-0 is seen passing under the line with a goods train heading for Gloucester and the next river
crossing upstream. £45,000 had recently been spent to strengthen the bridge for 'Castle'-class locomotives, so that it
could be used for diversions when the Severn Tunnel closed for repair. £175,000 had also been authorised by the Western
Board for the replacement of the missing spans, but the BTC's decision was to close the line. Although the Lydney school
train ran from Sharpness via Gloucester for a year after the accident, the Sharpness branch closed in 1964.

Railway closures are as old as the railway itself. In the early days, lines built to carry coal would be taken up and re-laid as required. This was true for many of the early collieries, as well as the ironstone railways of Northamptonshire, the potato railways of Lincolnshire and the peat railways of the Somerset Levels. However, the focus of this book is not upon transient private railways such as these, but rather the permanent public railways that carried passengers and were part of the warp and weft of British society.

Some lines were replaced by later constructions toward the same traffic objective and their original alignment abandoned. Early tramroads and canals were converted to railways, and the sinuous alignment of some early lines – suited to short-wheelbase locomotives and four-wheel carriages – were straightened to meet the needs of larger locomotives travelling at higher speeds. For example, when travelling west from Newbury towards Taunton on the Berks & Hants line, the embankments of an older railway can still occasionally be seen today – though it was replaced when the Great Western upgraded the line in 1906, in order to create a faster route to the West Country.

There were many cases where the parliamentary powers to construct a railway were not exercised because the rail company was unable to raise the necessary capital. There were also a few where work started but was abandoned before a viable section of railway had been completed. The remains of one such line can still be seen at Llangurig in Powys. The line had been completed from a junction with the Mid-Wales Railway near Llandinam but stopped at this point when capital ran out for the section further west, intended to take the line to Pencader via a long and costly tunnel. This was part of a visionary scheme, the Manchester & Milford Railway, which was authorised in 1860 but never completed. The line to Llangurig, although signalled, would never carry regular trains and the powers to abandon it were secured in 1876, with the track being recovered in 1882.

In the case of Waltham on the Wolds in Leicestershire, a passenger station was built in 1883 but was never served by regular passenger trains throughout its existence, being used only by race specials for nearby Croxton Park, special trains for meetings of the local hunt and, latterly, by railway enthusiast specials, before its closure in 1961.

The earliest withdrawal of a passenger service was probably from the Oystermouth Railway, the first public passenger railway in the world, opened in 1807. This is where the horse-drawn passenger service from Swansea was withdrawn in 1827, once a turnpike road had been built parallel to the railway and a competing horse bus introduced. Around 1855, the line was rebuilt to standard gauge as a conventional railway rather than a tramroad and the passenger service, still horse-drawn, was reinstated. Steam replaced horses in

1877 and the line was electrified in 1928, using double-deck tramcars which continued to run until closure in 1960.

The first permanent closure of a passenger service appears to have been on a branch line, three quarters of a mile in length, built from the Stockton & Darlington Railway to serve Yarm. In 1833, a station had been built at the junction and steam trains introduced, with the horse-drawn branch passenger service discontinued on 7 September that year, only seven years after its introduction.[1]

The earliest significant closure was that of the Newmarket & Chesterford Railway in Cambridgeshire, on 1 July 1850. The first line to Newmarket left the Cambridge main line at Great Chesterford and followed the route of today's A11. However, only three years after it opened in 1848, an alternative line was opened by the Eastern Counties Railway from Cambridge to join the N&C at Six Mile Bottom, providing a link to the county town and good connections for London. The line between Great Chesterford and Six Mile Bottom was subsequently closed to all traffic.

Industrial changes

Other lines prospered or declined according to the fortunes of the industries they were built to serve. The West Somerset Mineral Railway originated at the port of Watchet in Somerset to serve iron ore workings on the Brendon Hills, the ore being shipped to Newport and then taken by canal and tramroad for smelting in the blast furnaces at Ebbw Vale. When overtaken by cheaper Spanish ore, the Brendon Hills mines were closed in 1879; they restarted later but were finally closed in 1883, although the railway did not close until 1898. Attempts were made to revive both the mines and the railway in 1907, but these were unsuccessful. After being used to demonstrate an automatic train control system in 1911/12, the line fell into disuse and was finally removed in 1917 to fulfil wartime requirements.[2]

Wartime requirements

The need for railway workers to serve in the armed forces was coupled with a requirement to release track and rolling stock for use at the Western Front, as well as in Egypt and elsewhere, during World War 1. This led to the closure of a number of lines, with 36 stations and 41 halts closed between 1915 and 1917 to release staff from the Great Western Railway alone, entailing the temporary withdrawal of some suburban services such as that between Gerrards Cross and Uxbridge High Street.[3] Some of the more lightly used branch lines were also closed or singled to provide track, including lines that were subsequently re-laid such as Titley to Eardisley in Herefordshire and Bearley to Alcester in Warwickshire, the latter of which closed on 1 January 1917. Some lines, however, were never restored after the war, such as the Great Western's line from Wyesham Junction to Coleford in the Forest of Dean and the independent Bideford, Westward Ho! & Appledore Railway in Devon. (The ship carrying the track for the latter was said to have been torpedoed and is believed to lie today on the seabed off Lundy Island.)

Other requisitions for wartime use included the Basingstoke & Alton Light Railway, which closed on 30 December 1916. This was eventually, and reluctantly, reopened by the Southern Railway on 18

Oystermouth Railway: the earliest closure, 1827.
A replica of the horse-drawn carriage for the earliest public passenger railway in the world, produced in 1954 for the 150th anniversary of the parliamentary Act that authorised the building of the line. Within six years, this popular and historic route would be swept away to avoid the replacement costs of electrical supply equipment.

West Somerset Mineral Railway – Watchet Quay with iron ore wagons.
Foreign imports of iron ore killed off business on the West Somerset Mineral Railway, forcing closure of the line in the 19th century. The station house at Watchet remains to this day, however, and the line can be seen clearly from today's steam trains on the West Somerset Railway, which ran parallel to the mineral line as far as Washford.

August 1924, only to lose its passenger service eight years later (as we will see). The Rillington Junction-Grosmont line (today's North York Moors Railway) was singled at this time, as were the Woodhall Junction-Bellwater Junction line in Lincolnshire and Clarbeston Road-Neyland in Pembrokeshire. The GWR sent 49 miles of track, 15,000 tons of rails and 50,000 sleepers to aid the war effort.

Acts of God
In other cases, it was randomly cataclysmic events that triggered the closure of a line – such as the depot fire in St Helier that destroyed the rolling stock fleet of the Jersey Eastern Railway in 1929, or the 1948 floods in the Scottish borders that spelled the end of the Jedburgh branch and the line between St Boswells and Duns. The collision of a barge with the Severn Bridge in 1960 brought a premature end to the Berkeley Road-Lydney Town line, as well as its use as an alternative route when the Severn Tunnel was closed for maintenance.

Rerouting
In other cases, new lines replaced older sections of routes. An early example is the Scotland Street tunnel running north from Waverley station in Edinburgh, at right angles to the main line. This was the original railway from Leith which was diverted via Abbeyhill in 1868 to run into Waverley from the east, when the direct route under Princes Street was closed. The old tunnel meets today's railway alongside platform 20 at Edinburgh, just to the west of Waverley Steps.

When the Great Western built its direct main line to South Wales in 1903, it crossed the branch line from Dauntsey to Malmesbury near Little Somerford. A spur line from the branch to the new route allowed the southern half of the branch to be closed in 1933. The London & South Western Railway's original line from Guildford to Farnham ran direct, but a later spur allowed trains to be routed via the important military town of Aldershot. Subsequently, in 1937, the original route

lost its passenger service when the lines to Aldershot were electrified, after which it was served only by goods trains to Tongham until its eventual closure in 1960.

More recently, in 1979 a 20-mile deviation of the East Coast Main Line was opened between Doncaster and York, to protect the route from subsidence in connection with a new drift mine built to extract coal near Selby. As a result of this rerouting, the line between Selby and Challoner's Whin Junction at York was closed.

Rail competition
Many competing lines were built in the 19th century. Competition was never fiercer than in Kent, where the South Eastern and London, Chatham & Dover Railways fought for access to every part of the county, until their amalgamation into the South Eastern & Chatham Railway in 1899. Many of the routes had by this time established their own local demand, which explains why today there are separate lines to Bromley, Sevenoaks, Maidstone, Ashford, Canterbury and Dover. Some duplicate routes were closed, however, including Chatham Central (1911), Ramsgate Beach and Margate, together with the route between Margate Sands and Ramsgate Town (all in 1926), Greenwich Park (1929) and Gravesend West (1954).

In Scotland, similar fierce competition between the Caledonian and Glasgow & South Western Railways resulted in duplicate routes to Ardrossan, Irvine and Kilbirnie, where the Caledonian routes were closed between 1930 and 1932, and to Greenock, where the GSW route was eventually cut back to Kilmacolm in 1959. The line from here to Shields Junction in Glasgow closed as late as 1983, but Strathclyde PTE subsequently reopened the line as far west as Paisley Canal just seven years later.

Tram/bus competition
While horse-drawn tramways had posed little threat, the growth of electric tramways in the first decade of the 20th century resulted in the loss of thousands of passengers from inner suburban steam trains in many British cities. Some early closures resulted from this, although there was usually a secondary trigger such as the need for wartime economies. Electrification of the Metropolitan Railway and the Metropolitan District Railway in London, as well as deep-level tube construction, also resulted in a few closures. Examples include:

- Victoria-Moorgate (London, Chatham & Dover Railway), 1916.
- Blackfriars-Richmond via Kensington Olympia and Turnham Green (London & South Western Railway), 1916 – including complete closure of the line from Olympia to Hammersmith, the viaduct piers of which can be seen today between Barons Court and Hammersmith.
- Haverstock Hill station (near Kentish Town), 1916.
- Spa Road & Bermondsey (near London Bridge), 1915.
- Halts between Westbourne Park and South Ruislip, 1947.
- Ilford-Newbury Park, 1947.

Tram competition was particularly strong in Glasgow, where 'one could travel by electric tram from Clydebank to Airdrie, a distance of over 20 miles, for twopence. People did so, sometimes, when they had plenty of time, but over shorter distances they used the tram without a second thought. The railway companies never recovered the traffic they lost in Glasgow.'[4] Tram competition on Tyneside led to the North Eastern Railway's early electrification scheme of 1904.

Railmotors and auto trains

Elsewhere, tram and bus competition was met by the introduction of steam railmotors, a combined engine and carriage with retractable steps that allowed passengers to board and alight at level crossings or low-level halts, as well as at conventional stations. 'Bell punch' tickets were sold on the train by the guard and were generally limited to stations on the route. One early successful example was the Stroud Valley line of the Great Western, where a railmotor service was introduced in 1904 between Stonehouse and Chalford, and six halts at level crossings were added to the two intermediate stations.

Growth in ridership overpowered the small railmotors, which lacked the power to haul more than one trailer coach, and so railways

Ramsgate Beach station
This was closed as a result of Southern's decision to combine the competing lines of the South Eastern and London, Chatham & Dover where they overlapped between Margate and Ramsgate. Part of the branch was subsequently used for a narrow-gauge electric railway owned by leisure operator Pleasurama, but it closed in 1965. The tunnel remains.

adapted small tank engines to handle up to four coaches (two either side of the locomotive), driven from the forward cab while the fireman stayed on the locomotive. The Great Western had a hierarchy of halts and platforms, which in descending order of importance was:

1. Staffed station handling parcels and goods traffic.
2. Platform – a simple station, with platforms raised to the level of carriage footboards – usually staffed, handling parcels but not goods traffic.
3. Halt or Halte – an unstaffed stopping place, which might have a low-level timber or gravel point from which passengers would climb up, using the steps on the railmotor. Confusingly, some of these had high platforms, and some were staffed – at least later in their existence.

The Great Western added 414 halts or platforms to its system from 1903 onwards, with a peak of 52 opened in 1905 alone. Some, like Penmere on the Falmouth branch or Dilton Marsh, as immortalised in verse by John Betjeman[5], survive to this day. The Stroud Valley service was extended to Gloucester, providing a fast and efficient service to the county town until withdrawal in 1964. Most other railways followed a similar pattern and many had delightful local nicknames, reflecting their place in the heart of the local community: the 'Tivvy Bumper' (Tiverton Junction-Tiverton), the 'Skem Dodger'

(Ormskirk-Rainford Junction) and the 'Tutbury Jinnie' (Tutbury-Burton upon Trent) are still part of local folklore.

Early closures were, however, comparatively rare. Prior to 1922, only about 400 miles had been closed out of a total of 21,700, including the railways of Ireland.

Capacity
In a few cases, stations were closed to free up capacity for longer distance services. The Metropolitan Railway stations at Lord's, Marlborough Road and St John's Wood, for example, closed when the Stanmore branch of the Bakerloo Line (now the most northerly section of the Jubilee Line) was extended north from Baker Street to Finchley Road. London, Tilbury & Southend inner suburban stations were replaced by the extension of the District Line to Upminster. In one exceptional instance in Yorkshire, intermediate stations between York and Scarborough (except Malton and Seamer) lost most of their passenger services as early as September 1930, in order to free capacity to meet the demands of holiday traffic to Scarborough. The stations remained open for goods and parcels traffic and occasional passenger services, including excursions, while Strensall found a new purpose during World War 2 by serving a nearby army camp, but more frequent local services were never reinstated.[6]

Light Railways Act 1896
Only 20 years before the first local train services fell victim to tram competition, the Government had actively encouraged the expansion of the rail network into rural areas with the Light Railways Act, particularly to assist farming and improve accessibility for rural communities. The Act simplified the process of railway construction as light railways could be approved by ministerial order, avoiding the full and costly parliamentary process. They were generally constructed with lighter track and less ballast than conventional lines, open level crossings were commonplace and some of the onerous requirements on lineside fencing could be relaxed (as was the case on the Fraserburgh & St Combs light railway, where locomotives carried 'cow catchers' until closure in 1965). These economies came at the cost of a lower speed limit, usually 25mph. A number of light railways were built as late as 1925, in the case of the line to Fawley in Hampshire (still open for freight today) and the Torrington-Halwill Junction line in North Devon and Cornwall (closed in 1965). On many, however, like the Wrington Vale light railway in Somerset (1904-31) or the Derwent Valley light railway in Yorkshire (1913-26), passenger services lasted barely a generation.

Closures in the 1920s
After the end of World War 1 in 1918, a large number of army lorries were sold. Many of these were bought by demobbed soldiers who set up as local carriers or converted the lorries to buses. Some of these operations undermined local railway stations and lines, throwing into question rail's predominance over all inland transport needs for the first time. Improved vehicle technology, metalled roads and changing patterns of land use all combined to encourage road haulage and increase the popularity of buses. Consequently, closures of lines where the economic base was very weak followed. These included:

- Brampton Town branch (Cumberland) — 1923
- Wantage Tramway (Oxfordshire) — 1925
- Hallatrow-Limpley Stoke (Somerset) — 1925
- Derwent Valley Light Railway (York-Cliffe Common) — 1926
- Wolverton-Stony Stratford Tramway (Bucks) — 1926
- Southwold Railway (narrow gauge, Suffolk) — 1929

- Lydney Town-Coleford/Cinderford (Gloucestershire) — 1929
- Mansfield-Southwell (Nottinghamshire) — 1929

Closures in the 1930s
In May 1932, *The Times* published a series of six thoughtful feature articles and two leaders about the state of Britain's railways, recognising that, since the Grouping of 1923 and the Depression that began in 1929, the railways' status as a safe investment had been undermined by economic circumstances and competition from lorries and buses. The latter was unfair in that road transport enjoyed the benefits of state-funded road developments for which it did not pay, neither did it share the burden of the common carrier obligations that hampered the railways. In the event, it was to be another 30 years before these obligations were removed, but the articles revealed the extent of the problem even at this early stage. The leader of 12 May summed up the position:

> What the country needs is not cheap road transport for selected commodities at competitive rates subsidised at the expense of the ratepayers and taxpayers, but a properly co-ordinated system of transportation which would afford the cheapest and most convenient facilities for the community as a whole.

This was an early call for an integrated transport policy – one which has never been subsequently delivered. The value of the network as a whole was clearly appreciated, however, which helps to explain why the pre-war closures were quite limited in scope. Noting that closure of lightly used intermediate stations was justified as road transport provided a more convenient door-to-door service, the feature of 16 May continued:

> On the other hand, except in certain cases, these branch lines have not been closed altogether to passenger traffic because they still pay as feeders to the main lines.

Selsey Tramway
This Colonel Stephens line had a chequered history which was brought to an abrupt halt on 19 January 1935, when the last train ran just a few hours after notices of closure were posted that morning. No time for consultation in this case! *Ringing Rock* **is seen heading a train at Chichester: apart from the quaint tank engine, note the four-wheel carriage – archaic even when this picture was taken – and the lightweight track, all typical of the Stephens lines.**

The London & North Eastern Railway did in fact start trimming some of its quieter branch lines and smaller intermediate stations in the late 1920s. In 1930 alone it closed nine lines and 35 intermediate stations, including those between York and Scarborough (see above). Of the others, many were in the north-east of England or Scotland, where no fewer than 15 stations were closed.

Other closures in the 1930s were of peripheral lines which were quite lightly used, including 10 narrow gauge lines such as:

- Leek & Manifold Light Railway (Staffordshire) 1934
- Lynton-Barnstaple (Devon) 1935
- Jersey Railway (Channel Islands) 1936

Some standard gauge independent local railways closed too, including:

- Shropshire & Montgomeryshire 1933
- Bishop's Castle (Shropshire) 1935
- West Sussex Light Railway (Selsey Tramway) 1935

Other lines were deeply rural or highly vulnerable to bus competition:
- Hurstbourne-Fullerton Junction (Hampshire) 1931
- Basingstoke-Alton (Hampshire) 1932
- Isle of Axholme (Lincolnshire) 1933
- Spean Bridge-Fort Augustus (Inverness-shire) 1933
- Chichester-Midhurst (West Sussex) 1935

(Midhurst was also served from both Petersfield and Pulborough.)

The unfortunate Basingstoke & Alton Light Railway[7] had been opened in 1901 to protect the London & South Western Railway's competitive position in this part of Hampshire from incursion by the Great Western, as was threatened in the 1890s. By the start of World War 1, this little line had enjoyed a service of six trains each way daily, from 7am until 7pm. Trains were withdrawn at the end of 1916, however, with track removed for the war effort and not reinstated until as late as 1924, by the Southern Railway which had absorbed the LSWR. The Southern tried to keep costs low by running the line on a single shift, but this offered only half the number of trains running between 10am and 5am – of little value to those travelling to work or school, let alone those on a day's business in London. Passenger trains were finally withdrawn in September 1932. The investment in building the line had hardly lasted a generation – a net 23 years. The Basingstoke & Alton Light Railway would be immortalised (and moved to Ireland!) in the 1937 Will Hay comedy produced by Gainsborough Pictures, *Oh, Mr Porter!*

Elsewhere, the adverse effects of closure were experienced by the communities they served, even if not as serious as those resulting from the closure of trunk routes and suburban lines 30 years later. When the Lynton & Barnstaple line closed at the end of the summer season in September 1935, not only did the resort lose business due to its lack of rail connections but the price of coal in Lynton rose sharply as well.

While the branch lines run by the 'Big Four'[8] had the financial backing of large joint stock companies, the small, independent, mainly light railways, such as those run by the remarkable Colonel Stephens[9], were vulnerable to closure when the money ran out. Indeed, a number would run in receivership for many years before the end came. The last passenger train on the Selsey Tramway (Chichester-Selsey) ran on the day the closure notice was posted: 19 January 1935. In the rather sad case of the Weston, Clevedon & Portishead Light Railway, a receiver was appointed as early as 1909 and recruited Stephens to run the line, which remained in receivership for the next 30 years. In 1939, the insurance company which had triggered the appointment of the receiver withdrew its petition. By that time, however, the original owning company could not be traced and the receiver had no powers to operate the line. In an early example of asset stripping, it was promptly bought by its creditor, the Excess Insurance Company, and closed down the following year, its assets sold to the GWR.

Common carrier liability

One of the constraints on early closures was the railways' common carrier liability, illustrated by a test case against the Cheshire Lines Committee following closure of its branch line between Cuddington and Winsford. As early as 1891, the CLC had tried to withdraw the passenger service on the branch to avoid re-signalling costs of £7,500 required by the latest safety standards, but the Railway and Canal Commission made an order requiring its continuation to provide 'reasonable facilities', in order to meet its common carrier obligations. Forty years later, the CLC withdrew the passenger service on 1 January 1931. This was challenged by Winsford Urban District Council, while at the same time the CLC applied to have the 1891 Order rescinded. The CLC gave evidence that passenger numbers had dropped 32 percent to 68,000 per annum over the previous six years, although costs had been reduced by a quarter to £3,700 p.a. by the use of Sentinel-Cammell steam railcars. The court dismissed the council's application and rescinded the order, saying it was up to the CLC to decide for itself, with regard to economic conditions, whether it would resume passenger services on the branch. Providing a 'reasonable facility' did not require that a railway undertook to maintain an unprofitable passenger service.[10]

World War 2

Heroic efforts were made by railway staff to keep trains moving during the Blitz, but a few lines and stations succumbed to bomb damage. Shoreditch station on the North London line closed as a result, as did

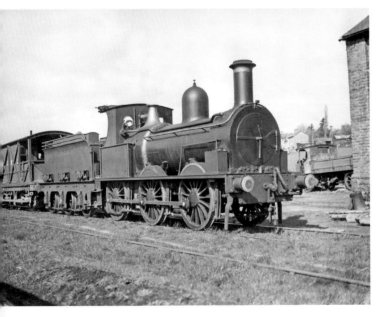

Bishop's Castle Railway
This was one of the independent railways that escaped the 1923 Grouping, but did not survive the 1930s. The condition of the much-loved locomotive *Carlisle* is very different from the track in this picture at Bishop's Castle. Note also the competition in the form of a Sentinel steam lorry in the goods yard.

the connection between the Hammersmith & City and West London lines, which carried the 'Outer Circle' service from Willesden Junction to Mansion House. Millbay station in Plymouth also closed following bomb damage in April 1941.

The little Rye & Camber Tramway 3ft-gauge line in East Sussex was taken over by the military and some of its track encased in concrete, as part of the defence of this vulnerable section of the Channel coast. In 1945, the line was returned to its owners, but it had been so heavily damaged that the cost of repair was prohibitive. The company went into liquidation.

The railways' contribution to the war effort was huge and required that some new construction take place. In preparation for D-Day, the capacity of the Didcot, Newbury & Southampton line was increased during 1942/3 by doubling the Didcot-Newbury section, with extended crossing loops between Newbury and Winchester and the construction of an up spur by the GWR between the Southern main line at Winchester Junction and the DN&S, the latter lasting only until

Winsford (CLC) branch
A rare picture of this branch of the Cheshire Lines Committee, which remained open after an 1891 tribunal concluded it was required to meet its common carrier obligations. In 1931, the High Court concluded that the LMS's obligations did not require it to maintain an unprofitable passenger service, and the line closed.

1951. Perhaps the most impressive project was the construction of a new line, one and a half miles long, and a four-platform station at Cold Meece in Staffordshire, opened by the LMS in 1941 to serve the ordnance factory at Swynnerton. Designed to handle major daily flows of staff and contractors, it could turn around five trains in 25 minutes. In 1943, it handled 200 trains daily and three million passengers over the course of the year. For reasons of national security the service was not publicly advertised, but it lasted until June 1958[11], by which time the factory was closed and production transferred elsewhere.

1   *Closed Passenger Lines of Great Britain, 1827-1947*, Greville and Spence, 2nd edition, 1974.
2   *The West Somerset Mineral Railway*, Roger Sellick, David & Charles, 1970.
3   *History of the Great Western Railway*, E. T. MacDermot, revised by C. R. Clinker, Ian Allan, 1964.
4   *British Railway History*, Volume II, C. Hamilton Ellis, Allen & Unwin, 1959.
5   *Was it worth keeping the Halt open,*
    We thought as we looked at the sky
    Red through the spread of the cedar-tree,
    With the evening train gone by?

    Yes, we said, for in summer the anglers use it,
    Two and sometimes three
    Will bring their catches of rods and poles and perches
    To Westbury, home for tea.

    There isn't a porter. The platform is made of sleepers.
    The guard of the last train puts out the light
    And high over lorries and cattle the Halt unwinking
    Waits through the Wiltshire night.

    O housewife safe in the comprehensive churning
    Of the Warminster launderette!
    O husband down at the depot with car in car-park!

    The Halt is waiting yet.
    And when all the horrible roads are finally done for,
    And there's no more petrol left in the world to burn,
    Here to the Halt from Salisbury and from Bristol
    Steam trains will return.

6   *Railway Stations of the North East*, K. Hoole, David & Charles, 1985.
7   *The Basingstoke & Alton Light Railway 1901-1936*, E. C. Griffith, 1947.
8   The 'Big Four' were the railway companies formed as a result of the amalgamation of scores of smaller railways after the Railways Act of 1921. They were the Great Western Railway, the London Midland & Scottish Railway, the London & North Eastern Railway and the Southern Railway. The grouping came into effect on 1 January 1923.
9   Colonel Holman Fred Stephens (1868-1931) was a civil engineer and manager involved in 16 light railways in all parts of England and Wales, including the Festiniog and Kent & East Sussex railways. The son of pre-Raphaelite artist and critic Frederic George Stephens, he was first apprenticed in the workshops of the Metropolitan Railway and later attained the rank of colonel in the Territorial Army during World War 1. Material from the 16 railways with which he was associated can be viewed at the Colonel Stephens Railway Museum at Tenterden station, on the Kent & East Sussex Railway.
10 *Railway Magazine*, April 1938.
11 *Railway Magazine*, July 1958.

II

BTC CLOSURES 1948-62

The Reverend Sam Weech: They can't close our line, it's unthinkable.
Squire Gordon Chesterford: What about the old Canterbury-Whitstable line?
They closed that.
Weech: Perhaps there were not men of sufficient faith in Canterbury.

THE TITFIELD THUNDERBOLT[1]

The Rail bus era
This bold experiment by the Railway Executive reduced train operating costs dramatically, its single saloon and many stops providing a friendly community service. In today's terms it would be deemed a success, providing value for money, but in 1958 it was seen as lacking the alchemy to turn branch-line losses into profits. The Cirencester car is seen here at Kemble, ready to return, having brought passengers and parcels to the main line station where a 'Hymek' waits with a London-bound train.

The British Transport Commission was established in 1948 as an integrated transport authority for Britain's nationalised transport system. Its politics were visionary, but the politicians clearly had no respect for the industry they had taken over. The Chancellor of the Exchequer, Hugh Dalton, told the House of Commons on 17 December 1946:

> This railway system of ours is a very poor bag of physical assets. The permanent way is badly worn. The rolling stock is in a state of great dilapidation. The railways are a disgrace to the country.[2]

This perception of a run-down and declining industry epitomised the views of the post-war Labour Government and those that followed. It led to the opinion that closure was a preferable outcome for much of the network rather than renewing the assets worn out over the previous six years, in which the railways had been an essential part of the defence of Britain. Integration might have been expected to lead to plans to substitute buses for lightly loaded passenger trains, and British Road Services lorries for local goods trains. In the event, no such plan was developed. Indeed, no strategy was developed by the BTC or the Government for the role that the railway should play in meeting Britain's transport needs. By 1955, the newly re-elected Conservative Government had relieved the railway of its obligation to provide a universal public service, in the expectation that station and line closures would follow as the BTC sought to reshape the railway to meet changing needs. This did not happen, however.

Modernisation plan

The British Railways modernisation plan was also published in 1955. Here, at last, was an attempt by government to make good the depredations of war that had occurred under its control and to give Britain a railway of which it could be proud. In practice, the opportunity was squandered because no clear vision of the kind of railway post-war Britain required was articulated by either government or the commission. The principal criticisms of the modernisation plan are well known: the continuation of steam traction; huge investment in marshalling yards; poor management of the huge resources available. The result was that neither the Government nor its Treasury trusted BR to handle its own major investments for the remaining 42 years of its existence, introducing onerous procedures to control expenditure.

The BTC, however, ignored that change in remit which would have enabled them to change the nature of services provided. Indeed, included in the modernisation plan were investment proposals for significant numbers of lightweight diesel units for local and rural lines, and four-wheel rail buses for the most lightly used rural lines. The experimental services that utilised rail buses on the Tetbury and Cirencester branches, and single railcars[3] on the Buckingham to Banbury (Merton Street) branch, were very successful, typically reducing costs to a third of those of steam trains and increasing revenue by up to 400 percent. But they were not enough for the hawks in government and at the BTC, who were either looking to turn losses into profits (without support payments that recognised rail transport's social value) or else to close the lines.

The BTC did, however, plan to reduce network size, in spite of the fleet of lightweight diesel trains in the modernisation plan. In a letter to the Stedeford Committee (see Chapter 3) dated 3 June 1960, Sir Brian Robertson[4] stressed that the Commission was well aware that the transport picture was undergoing drastic change:

Demolition train at Culkerton (Tetbury branch)
Sadly, the use of lightweight trains did not save the two branch lines from Kemble. Just four months after the last rail bus had passed, the track of the Tetbury branch was removed rail by rail at Culkerton.

> Although they did not announce it at the time, their plan provided for closing some 3,000 miles of track and widespread reduction in stations and other installations and a considerable reduction in stopping train mileage.

It is not clear whether the figure for closures was aspirational, or whether it was underpinned by plans to withdraw specific services. The letter goes on to say that the previous year (1959) had seen further change, not only in a decline in coal traffic but also a dramatic increase in the Government's road building plans.[5]

The Branch Line Committee

The first passenger service was withdrawn by the new administration on 30 October 1948. It was Shepherdswell-Canterbury Road on the East Kent Railway, a colliery line that struggled to carry any passengers on its roundabout route linking a few small villages in Thanet. However, a more structured process was to follow and, under pressure from Sir Cyril Hurcomb[6] (BTC Chairman) and Geoffrey Wilson (financial controller), as early as March 1949, the Railway Executive established a committee of senior officers, jointly chaired by Arthur Pearson and J. L. Harrington, to accelerate closures. One of its members from Railway Executive HQ was S. E. Parkhouse, the masterful and imperturbable operator who featured in the classic British Transport Films production *Train Time* in 1952.

Each region established its own committee, with full-time staff from the operating, commercial and engineering departments. The chairman was also a member of the Railway Executive's committee and the remit was broadly drawn: 'An investigation of every branch line whose earning capacity may be in question.' Station closures were not considered at this juncture, only branch lines.

At the outset, the committee approached their work cautiously and professionally. The minutes of the initial meeting of 7 July 1949 recorded:

It was considered that the matter should not be approached solely from the negative point of view of railway expenditure. The main object was to increase or maintain net revenue, and this could not be considered without regard to the wider aspects now opened up by transport integration, in which the fundamental economy of rail transport was of great importance. Therefore, it was considered that in the examination of branch lines, these principles should be given due weight. Possibility of developing passenger traffic by intensification of service, perhaps by light units, and the results that may be expected from a future adjustment in fares also to be assessed before a recommendation is made for closing.[7]

However, the regional representatives were quick to respond that further development of traffic in some rural areas was a 'practicable impossibility'.

Two years later, the Railway Executive initiated a re-examination of the potential cost savings from diesel railcars and 'modernised push and pull steam units' on branch lines, but this appeared to have had little effect on the momentum of the committee's work.

The committee was thorough, but only relatively modest proposals came up from the regions for the Executive to endorse and the Commission to decide. At the initial meeting, the schemes considered were closure of the Thaxted branch in Essex and the Alford branch in Aberdeenshire, while the Western Region offered only the prospect of cutting back the Golden Valley line (goods only at this stage) from Hay to Dorstone, and a 42-chain truncation of the Old Ynysybwl branch in Glamorganshire, following closure of a colliery some five years before.

Initially, the process was simple, and there was no requirement to consult the local authority or the Transport Users' Consultative Committee. As the programme increased, however, the committee agreed that consultation should be undertaken in contentious cases. As they got into their stride, their workload increased. At their meeting of 5 June 1951, for example, they considered 14 lines for closure. In 1952, in order to speed up the process, it was agreed that detailed financial justification for closure did not have to be completed prior to consideration by the committee, provided that the outline figures made the case. Detailed figures only had to be provided within six months of closure.

Once approved by the Commission, closure could follow quickly. The Old Ynysybwl auto train from Abercynon and Pontypridd was withdrawn

on 28 July 1952, just six weeks after approval had been noted by the Branch Line Committee. Similarly, the line from Leominster to Bromyard closed on 15 September that same year, just three months after approval.

Some closures took longer, in some cases up to 18 months to implement. By the summer of 1952, the Commission was becoming impatient with the slow rate of progress and the focus on what they saw as relatively minor schemes. A letter of 14 July to the Executive indicated that the closures achieved or in prospect 'will not amount to the "streamlining" of the railway system, which has been described as the long term objective'.[8]

In their reply of 24 September, the committee recommended that they should move on to looking at secondary routes once the branch line review had been completed. However, they pointed out the social obligations fulfilled by some of the lines – supporting businesses and agriculture via the increased accessibility of remote rural areas such as those on the Kyle and Mallaig lines – and the value of others as diversionary routes, including Peterborough-Spalding, Redhill-Tonbridge (both still with us) and Berwick-St Boswells (closed in 1964).

There were three main problems in pursuing a closure programme:
1. There was a concern that it risked conflict with the railway's common carrier obligations (see Chapter 1).
2. Information on the actual costs and revenue of individual branch lines was limited as the railway's accounting systems were not designed to produce this.
3. The Transport Users' Consultative Committees ran the appeal process for objectors and were initially opposed to closures, reflecting a long tradition of public antipathy to loss of services.

In the absence of detailed information on costs and income, the Executive saw its main objective as increasing or maintaining net revenue, which implied maximising income (including that from the branches) and hoping that, in aggregate, it would exceed costs. The duties of the 1947 Act in terms of transport integration led the Executive to believe it could not reasonably consider closures unless alternative services could be provided by its own buses and lorries, as operated by British Road Services. The Branch Line Committee saw replacement bus services as a problem, however, when road transport was denationalised following the 1951 election.

Indeed, it was expected that transport integration would be required to provide the proper balance. As John Elliot[9] said, 'Branches can be made to pay as much as possible, and this may be the best solution pending the integration of nationalised transport.'[10]

As early as 1951, it became known that the Railway Executive was to be abolished but, despite this, the Branch Line Committee continued their work. In October 1951, BTC's traffic costing services were established under A. W. Tait, with a particular remit to look at the Rail and Road Haulage executives. Earlier work by Tait had enabled him to report to the Commission in June 1951 that, while all the main categories of rail traffic covered their direct costs, there was a £17m shortfall on total costs for passenger and freight traffic. To give a clearer picture for individual lines, a passenger train census was held for the

Thaxted Branch train

The first closure put forward by the Branch Line Committee: the 1.43pm Elsenham-Thaxted runs into Sibleys on 26 May 1951. Its high costs, lack of passengers and stations situated a long walk from the villages they served may all be gleaned from the picture. Today, this spot is just 1.5 miles from the end of Stansted Airport's runway.

week ending 11 October 1952, with the results processed and available the following year. Overall, it indicated low load factors (30 percent nationally) and major variations between main line and local services, or between commuter services around London or other cities.

During the four years up to June 1953, the Branch Line Committee considered 200 cases and recommended complete closure of some 500 route miles with withdrawal of a further 88 passenger services, giving estimated savings of £890,000. In 1951, no fewer than 54 branch lines were closed along with 46 stations on other lines.

Table A: Closures during the period that the Branch Line Committee met (1949-1953)

Year	Route miles closed	Stations and Goods Depots closed
1948	1	31
1949	11	46
1950	112	92
1951	117	156
1952	90	122
1953	56	113
1954	72	98

Source: BTC Annual Accounts

The Branch Line Committee's approach to its task was that of professional railwaymen trying to fulfil their remit responsibly: sorting out some of the worst financial performers and a number of goods lines where traffic had actually ceased; very aware that some lines could be run more efficiently and attract more passengers; anxious to fulfil the social obligations they carried. They took proper account of the needs of passengers and freight forwarders, whereas the Commission was looking for a far more radical approach without setting its Executive a clear remit, and with no strategic view from Government of the railway's objectives.

For example, closure of the Kent & East Sussex line was approved at their meeting of 4 December 1952, with the section from Headcorn to Tenterden Town to be closed completely. However, the committee also recommended that the line from Tenterden Town to Robertsbridge be retained for goods traffic and maintained to passenger standards to allow the running of hop

Hop Pickers special on the Hawkhurst branch
A two-coach 'motor train' was usually enough for the number of passengers on this Kentish branch, where the stations were a long walk from the little Wealden towns they served. But the railway was the key link in the chain that brought families from inner London to a working holiday in the Kentish hop fields. Two engines are needed for this long train arriving at Goudhurst to collect families returning to London Bridge in 1950. The hops they have picked are already drying in the oast house beyond the station.

pickers' specials, a major social obligation of Kent's railways at that time. The line was closed on 4 January 1954 but the hop pickers' specials ran until 1958. The goods service was finally withdrawn in 1961, while the line between Tenterden and Bodiam is now a successful heritage railway.

Similarly, in considering closure of the Ashchurch-Great Malvern branch, the committee wanted to maintain services to Tewkesbury because of its tourism potential and were most concerned that passengers from Ripple would have to walk a mile to the main road for their replacement bus. Consequently, their recommendation of December 1952 resulted in the line being cut back only from Great Malvern to Upton on Severn, with a passenger service continuing on the rest of the line (including Ripple) until August 1961.

Five years on from the end of the committee, the BTC policy on closures was still tactical rather than strategic. It was set out by Henry Johnson[11], then General Manager of the Eastern Region, at a meeting with the NUR on 27 May 1959 relating to closure of the Midland & Great Northern Line:

> The policy of the Commission is to close all branch lines which are uneconomic and which have no hope of being worked as economic propositions. Only after the most thorough investigation is this course decided upon.

Transport Users' Consultative Committees

Major closures of the period made quite an impact both locally and nationally, inevitably seen as 'progress' in an age when motoring was still an enjoyable experience and steam trains were regarded as old-fashioned.

Prior to the 1947 Act, and after the Winsford Case referred to in Chapter One, there was no statutory protection for users of the lines

Railway ships
Ships, as well as trains, were vulnerable to cutbacks and representations to the TUCC. A BR container is loaded aboard the *Villandry* at Dieppe in 1966. Behind the linkspan is the main competitor, a truck running direct. 'Roll on/roll off' took most of rail's cross-channel traffic and, despite the Channel Tunnel, little has been regained.

that would close (sometimes summarily and with little ceremony). Generally though, the major railway companies did go through due process and hold a local inquiry. Indeed, the Southern Railway officer chairing the 1935 public hearing into closure of the Lynton & Barnstaple noted wryly that most of the objectors had come by car.[12]

Closures of both passenger and goods services were considered by the regional transport users' consultative committees after 1950, but required endorsement by the Central Transport Consultative Committee. The CTCC and regional committees had taken some time to set up after the 1947 Act but, in the committee's report for 1950, Chairman Egbert Cadbury[13] commented:

> The committee are glad to note the Commission are closing unremunerative branch lines and other sections of railway track, etc., no longer required for the movement of traffic, and hope this form of economy will continue.

The first closure considered by the new committees was Newburgh-St Fort in the Scottish Region which, according to their report, was used by just 47 passengers daily, or 11 per train. This was a new procedure for the Executive, which thought initially that it need not wait for the TUCC hearing before implementing the closure planned for 5 June 1950. It agreed to postpone for a month to allow the TUCC to report, but was then challenged by Fife County Council which had unearthed an agreement on the takeover of the North of Fife Railway by the North British, enshrined in statute in 1897, in which the NB agreed to provide train services on the line in perpetuity. The council then sought an interim interdict in the Court of Sessions in Edinburgh, on the basis that the Executive was not going to secure a replacement bus service, as recommended by the TUCC, at the time it withdrew the rail service. This was granted on the Friday prior to closure, with the judge taking the view that 'We cannot have nationalised bodies taking the law into their own hands.'[14]

In fact, the Executive had secured the provision of buses to run from the following Monday but its advocate was not aware of this at the time of the hearing.[15]

As a result of this farce, both the buses and the withdrawal of the train service were postponed and the North Fife line enjoyed a passenger train service for a further seven months, until closure came in February 1951.

The Scottish committee had no difficulty in deciding that there was no justification for retention of this line and the CTCC supported their decision. This became a familiar approach, to the extent that many users and campaigners assumed the role of committees was to rubber stamp the decisions already taken by the Commission. In its 1951 report, the CTCC went as far as to claim that closures were providing people with a better service, in which replacement buses went through villages served by a more remote branch line station. The first questions of hardship were also raised in this report, in relation to farmers having to take their produce further by road, following the closure of local goods yards.

Initially, decisions on the future of branch lines were wholly at the discretion of the Commission. In formulating its view, it looked at the alternative road services available (much of the bus and haulage industries was also nationalised) and consulted with local authorities. In the Commission's 1951 annual report, it was noted that, 'with the setting up of area transport committees, all important proposals are now referred to these bodies for their views'.

The Commission was represented on the area committees and was also responsible for their pay, rations and accommodation. Commission staff were seconded to run committees and it is therefore unsurprising that most decisions on closures were an endorsement of those put forward by the Commission. Even where the area committees thought the train service should be maintained, the central committee could be relied on generally to support the Commission's decision. In 1954, the East Midlands committee recommended retention of the Horncastle branch in Lincolnshire, but the central committee overturned this decision. In their view:

> There existed so strong a preference on the part of residents and workers in the area for the road facilities that there was no reasonable expectation that passenger rail services would be supported to an extent which would enable them to be operated without substantial loss.

The central committee's approach appears strange to us now, quite the opposite of the strong consumer culture that frames much decision making today. In 1958, they endorsed the Commission's decision to withdraw winter ferry services between Newhaven and Dieppe. Challenged by Newhaven Urban District Council, the committee's response was adamant and brusque. Not only was there a 'need for the commission to withdraw a service which is uneconomic and wasteful of the nation's resources', but the committee was also 'under no obligation to have to justify their recommendations to your council, nor do they intend to do so'.[16]

As the number of closures grew (see Table A above), busier lines were closed and opponents gained in both numbers and expertise, the TUCC hearings and reports became a significant bottleneck in the processing of closure cases. (The next chapter will show how this was tackled in preparation for the first Beeching Report.) Nevertheless, a substantial number of closures were considered by the TUCC during the life of the Commission, as shown below:

Table B: Closures Considered by TUCCs 1950-61

	Branch lines	301
Mileage	Passenger only	2179
	Freight only	781
	Passenger and freight	658
	Total	3618
	Estimated savings p.a.	£4,311,863

Source: CTCC Annual Report, 27 March 1962

The 1955 strike by drivers in the Associated Society of Locomotive Engineers and Firemen (ASLEF) resulted in a loss of £12m and of passenger and goods traffic, some of which never returned to rail. The Pontypool Road-Monmouth branch was closed prematurely as a direct result of the strike, indirectly serving to demonstrate that, for a time at least, people could get by without their railways. It helped set the scene for the more extensive cutbacks of the following decade and, later, for the intense debate about the future of rail in Britain.

The Southern was particularly active in closing lines during the 1950s. On the Isle of Wight, the network of lines was cut back in 1952-3, leaving just the principal routes from Ryde to Ventnor and

Closure of a network

The closure of most of the Midland & Great Northern in 1959 sent shockwaves throughout the industry. This was not just a branch line but a network of 176 miles. The centre of this network had four lines originating from Melton Constable station, as well as a goods yard, carriage sidings and workshops. The town was almost entirely dependent on the railway and would hang onto its passenger service for another five years. Here, in July 1958, the rear portion of a fast train from Birmingham heads towards Cromer. The front portion has already left for Great Yarmouth while the middle portion can be seen under the bridge, waiting to go forward to Norwich City. Six months later, the through route had gone.

Cowes. Branch lines to Bulford, Bisley, Bordon, Gosport, Gravesend West and Allhallows were closed during this period, as was the Kent & East Sussex, the Meon Valley line (Alton-Fareham) and Petersfield-Midhurst-Pulborough. Local stations between Salisbury and Warminster were also closed during the 1950s, including Codford, which had seen huge troop movements during World War 2. The historic Canterbury & Whitstable line closed in 1952, reopening briefly the following year when the main line to Whitstable was washed away by the devastating 1953 floods. Also notable was the closure of the electrified suburban line to Crystal Palace High Level, in 1954.

Closure by stealth

From the 1950s, and throughout the substantial programme of closures that followed Beeching, it has been argued that services were deliberately run down to make the case for withdrawal absolutely clear cut and that costs were inflated to prove the point. On the cost side, using the crude methodology available at the time, the shortfall of income compared with expenditure was all too apparent. In practice, the financial analysis was too crude to register money spent on track renewals or station painting as a cost on a specific branch line.

The abiding argument is not so much that many services were unprofitable (they were), but that the gap between income and costs could have been reduced through efficient operation, reinforced by proper marketing and promotion of the services. Under those circumstances, a number of routes – such as Oxford-Cambridge, Lewes-Uckfield or Bury-Rawtenstall – might have produced a subsidy per passenger mile figure which would have provided reasonable value for money, in terms of the wider social and economic benefits delivered.

For the most part, however, the railways were merely responding to the loss in traffic and trying to stem their losses. This was accentuated by the nature of funding for BR as a nationalised industry, constrained by annual cash limits.

The Commission cut train mileage to save costs, reflecting low levels of demand on some of the routes, but in some cases these cuts

made using the service for business trips or commuting impractical, and it seemed very much like sabotage. The Meon Valley line (Alton to Fareham and Gosport), for example, lost its Sunday services in 1951 and the weekday service was cut from five trains each way to four, with the last departure from Alton at 4.30pm, practically ruling out any day trips to London. The line closed on 5 February 1955.

There is limited evidence that some of the lines proposed for closure were deliberately run down, with key services withdrawn, affordable fares removed and connections broken. There are also various later examples, from the 1950s and 1960s, of apparent short-term measures to save money at a time when the pressures on BR to make economies were intense.

However, some of BR's economies simply had the effect of destroying demand and added fuel to a conspiracy theory that implied managers were running down services to a point at which closures would become inevitable. In 1956, the former Midland & South Western Junction Railway had a somewhat sparse service of three through trains between Cheltenham Spa and Andover Junction (with two running through to Southampton). Two years later, the service had been cut to just one train each weekday, removing opportunities for travel to work or education, and shopping or day trips.

The first steps were also taken toward 'rationalising' (singling or closing some main lines), notably the Great Central. The work was initiated by Gerry Fiennes[17], who admitted that they 'set out to close' the route, 'aided and abetted by some under-cover agents in operational research and costing offices'. He also started to look at the five trans-Pennine routes and the three routes to Scotland.

The Great Central first lost its express services in 1958, then its stopping train services in 1963, leaving the semi-fast service that ran throughout to be withdrawn in 1966, before the remaining truncated section between Rugby and Nottingham finally succumbed in 1969. The Settle & Carlisle lost its local stations in 1970 and the 'Thames-Clyde Express' in 1975, while the St Pancras-Glasgow sleepers disappeared in the following year, although closure proposals for the line did not appear until 1983. As we will see in Chapter 17, the Huddersfield-Penistone service was also cut back from 11 trains a day each way (including the 'South Yorkshireman' to and from Marylebone) to about half that figure, with few trains running outside the peak periods. This was after the line had been reprieved by Barbara Castle[18], however.

Elsewhere, it was perhaps remarkable that on so many country lines, the train services had changed little over the preceding 30 years despite demographic changes and the growth in car ownership. But it is still easy to see how this might have been perceived as a conspiracy to kill off the Great Central line, for example. In some cases, it may even have been true.

Sunday services

Many lines lost their Sunday services prior to closure. This was a relatively easy saving to make and required no prior consultation. Sunday costs were always higher (staff were paid at time and a half, with a minimum payment of eight hours) than those for the normal working week. In the days before Sunday trading and before weekend breaks became affordable, there was also less demand. The Penistone line, for example, lost its Sunday trains in 1961, but got them back in 1988 when the patterns of demand were very different.

The trauma of the M&GN

Elsewhere, some of the larger networks built to compete with older

Great Central: the final phase

Express trains over the route had been withdrawn in 1958 and local stations were closed in March 1963. In August of that year, a 'Royal Scot' locomotive heads the 5.15pm Nottingham Victoria-Marylebone semi-fast train on the section now run as a heritage railway.

established lines were closed – including the Stratford on Avon & Midland Junction (1952), Hull & Barnsley (1955) and the Great Northern/London North Western joint lines from Leicester (Belgrave Road) to Market Harborough and Bottesford (1953), although summer excursions continued to run from the terminus at Leicester to the Lincolnshire coast until 1962.

The most traumatic event was to come at the end of the 1950s, however, with closure of the Midland & Great Northern, a complete network of lines in East Anglia. This covered 176 miles, stretching from Peterborough and Saxby near Oakham to Great Yarmouth, Cromer and Norwich. Apart from local passenger and goods trains, the line also carried holiday expresses from Leicester to the Norfolk coast resorts.

The line had been built to allow the two railways which operated it to compete with the Great Eastern, which already served the key towns of King's Lynn, Fakenham, Cromer, North Walsham and Great Yarmouth, as well as the city of Norwich. Much of the route was single track and there were many staffed level crossings throughout Norfolk. The growth of private motoring in the 1950s had made big inroads into local and holiday traffic, and the case for closure appeared unanswerable to the Eastern Region when they put it forward. The line employed 1500 people, however, and at Melton Constable (which had not been served by the Great Eastern) it was the town's main employer – with a wagon workshop and locomotive depot, as well as a major junction station, goods yard and sidings. As a joint line, its character was different from the other lines in East Anglia, being somewhat idiosyncratic in its own proud traditions, with intensely loyal staff. (While it used the BR rule book and operating principles, the line's rolling stock had been traditionally controlled from Derby and its stations from King's Cross, unlike the nearby Great Eastern Lines where Liverpool Street's traditions were observed.)

Closure of so large a network, with main line pretensions, came as a shock to the communities it served and the staff it employed. It was also a worrying precedent for others watching elsewhere. This sense of shock was compounded by the way the closure was handled. Proposals were announced in July 1958; the TUCC hearing was held in November; the line was closed within six months of the first announcement. The last 'Leicesters' (the fast Leicester-Yarmouth trains) ran on Saturday 28 February 1959. Two days later, the first 25-yard section of line was removed by the Cambridge crane from the line just to the east of Sutton Bridge, severing it as a through route for ever.

Although some sections remained for freight, and the line from Sheringham to Melton Constable lingered on with a passenger service until 1964, demolition of the rest of the network was swiftly and brutally executed. Shockwaves went round the industry. Ernest Bartram, a signalman at Cromer with 45 years' service and a Norfolk County Council alderman, refused his long-service gold watch from BR as a protest against the way the M&GN staff were treated.

Even today, the M&GN lives on in local memory and has surprisingly strong support from people who want to keep that memory alive, with a number of books published about the line. It is particularly evident in the creation of the successful North Norfolk heritage railway which operates the section between Holt and Sheringham, reconnected to the national railway network in March 2010.

1 Ealing Studios, 1953.

2 *Hansard volume 431*, columns 1808-9.

3 One of these survives and works on the Ravenstor branch of the Ecclesbourne Valley Railway in Derbyshire, having previously worked as BR test coach *Iris*.

4 General Sir Brian Robertson (1896-1974) was the British army general who became Chairman of the British Transport Commission from 1953-61. Ennobled as Baron Robertson of Oakridge in 1961, he had formerly been Deputy Military Governor in occupied Germany from 1945-7 and promoted to Commander-in-Chief and Military Governor from 1947-9. After the formation of an independent West German Government, he was the first UK High Commissioner in Germany, from 1949-50. D800 – the first of BR's Class 42 'Warship' diesel locomotives – was named after him.

5 National Archives MT 73/385.

6 Sir Cyril Hurcomb (1883-1975) was head of the Ministry of War Transport and the first Chairman of the British Transport Commission, from 1948-53. He was also a keen ornithologist and conservationist. Ennobled in 1950, the BR 'Britannia' class locomotive 70001 was named after him.

7 Minutes of the Branch Line Committee 1949-53; National Archives AN 97 19/19.

8 British Transport Commission Files; National Archives.

9 Sir John Elliot (1898-1988) was the Southern Railway's first public relations officer, before becoming Chairman of the Railway Executive and later of London Transport. Born John Elliot Blumenfeld, son of the *Daily Mail*'s news editor, he changed his name to John Elliot in March 1923 and was knighted in 1954.

10 *Railway Magazine*, May 1951.

11 Sir Henry Johnson (1906-88) was the first career railwayman to become Chairman of British Railways Board. He joined LNER as a traffic apprentice in 1923, rising through the ranks to become General Manager of the Eastern Region of British Railways in 1958 and of the London Midland Region in 1962. Appointed vice-Chairman of the BRB in 1967, he was knighted in 1968 and served as Chairman from 1968-71. Class 86 electric locomotive 86 227 was named after him. See Chapter 6.

12 *Railways Round Exmoor*, Robin Madge, Exmoor Press, 1971.

13 A member of the eponymous chocolate family, Air Commodore Sir Egbert Cadbury DSC, DFC (1893-1967) was a World War 1 pilot who shot down two Zeppelins over the North Sea. He later became managing director of Cadbury Brothers Ltd.

14 *The Scotsman*, 1 July 1950.

15 BR records in the National Archives of Scotland, DD17/534.

16 Letter from J. C. Chambers, CTCC, to Newhaven UDC, dated 29 October 1958. National Archives MT 124/17.

17 Gerard Francis Gisborne Twistleton-Wykeham-Fiennes OBE, MA (1906-85) was a career railwayman who became General Manager of BR's Eastern Region and later chief operating manager at BRB. He was fired from British Rail in 1967 for publishing the book *I Tried to Run a Railway*, which was outspoken about the management of British Rail and particularly critical of the frequent management reorganisations it had gone through since nationalisation.

18 Barbara Castle (1910-2002) was the Labour Government's Minister of Transport from December 1965 to April 1968. The MP for Blackburn 1945-79 and Member of the European Parliament 1979-89, she was ennobled as Baroness Castle of Blackburn in 1990. She was described in *The Guardian's* obituary (4 May 2002) as 'Labour's Red Queen, the woman Michael Foot called "the best socialist minister we've ever had"'. However, the author Anne Perkins also said, 'Her career foundered on an inability to master the key political skill of building support where it counted, in the parliamentary party. She claimed to find making political alliances demeaning; her critics found her wearisomely egocentric. Even her friends distrusted her temper.'

III

BEECHING 1960-65:
THE RESHAPING REPORT

No one departs, no one arrives From Selby to Goole,
from St Erth to St Ives.[1]
They've all passed out of our lives On the Slow Train,
on the Slow Train.

'THE SLOW TRAIN', FROM *AT THE DROP OF ANOTHER HAT* (1964)
BY FLANDERS AND SWANN

Dumfries and Galloway
Just a month before closure of the Port Road in 1965, *Clan Mackintosh* (without nameplates) heads a troop train to
Stranraer near Gatehouse of Fleet at the summit of the Galloway main line. After closure, a lengthy detour via Kilmarnock
and Troon was required for the London-Stranraer boat train (the 'Paddy') and specials such as this.

There was no Chairman of British Railways better known – or more reviled – than Dr Richard (later Lord) Beeching.[2] Even today his name is in everyday parlance, with phrases such as 'doing a Beeching' used to describe implementing a widespread closure programme, often in the face of public opinion. There are almost 20 'streets', 'ways' or 'closes' in English towns and villages named after him by local authorities demonstrating a sense of humour (or perhaps irony), generally on housing developments built on former railway land made available as a consequence of Beeching-inspired closure.

But who was he? And how did he come to be appointed? Was he really part of a Government-inspired anti-railway plot?

We have already seen how relatively major programmes of railway closures were implemented in the 1930s (by the Big Four railway companies) and in the 1940s and 1950s (by the British Transport Commission, as a result of its Branch Lines Committee). Indeed, more stations were closed before 1963 than as a result of the Beeching Report. None of these closures, however, made any real contribution towards reducing the railways' deficit, which was the result of a high capital debt arising from nationalisation and the 1955 modernisation plan, rapidly rising staff costs and declining revenue. There was also a lack of strategy and objectives which served to ensure that assets were old, resource utilisation poor and management information on costs and revenue weak. Private motoring was taking off and road haulage was beginning to benefit from technological improvements and rising investment in the road network, for which it did not have to pay.

Ernest Marples

In 1959, the Conservatives had secured their third successive election victory, increasing their majority in the House of Commons to 100 seats. The Government subsequently appointed a new Minister of Transport, Ernest Marples[3], who since 1957 had been Postmaster General. Even in the more relaxed climate of the 1950s and 1960s, this was a controversial appointment. In 1948, he and an engineer called Reginald Ridgway had started a construction company (Marples Ridgway) which specialised in big civil engineering projects. The Hammersmith and Chiswick flyovers on the A4 and M4 in west London were their most celebrated contracts, but there were many others where HM Government was the client – including the M1 from London to Nottingham, Britain's first city-to-city motorway. Not only was the contract won by Marples Ridgway, Marples himself had taken the decision to build it.

On 28 January 1960, Robert Mellish MP[4], speaking from the Opposition's front bench, asked about a press report 'that the Minister of Transport was in fact the senior partner of a firm of contractors which has obtained a contract worth £250,000'. Was it not most improper that any minister of the Crown should be associated with the company with which such a contract had been placed?

R. A. Butler[5], speaking for the Government, replied, 'The general principle is that ministers must so order their affairs that no conflict arises, or appears to arise, between their private interests and their public duties'[6], and Marples himself made a personal statement that same afternoon:

> When I became Minister of Transport, last October, I realised that there was a risk of a conflict of interest appearing to arise in consequence of my holding a controlling interest in the company. I immediately took steps to effect a sale of my shares. It has taken some time to arrange this as the company is a private one engaged in long-term contracts in civil engineering, but I hope that it will be completed very soon. Then I shall have

General Sir Brian Robertson
Sir Brian's military bearing and his pleasure at being with the staff is evident from this picture of the launch of Glasgow's Blue Trains on November 1960. He is with the Lord Provost of Glasgow, Mrs Jean Roberts, as well as driver J. McPherson and guard E. Hodson, who worked the inaugural train.

> no financial interest in the company. But I think that I should tell the House that the prospective purchasers have required me to undertake to buy the shares back from them at the price they are to pay if they ask me to do so after I have ceased to hold office. I myself have no option to buy the shares back.
>
> I have not, of course, had anything whatsoever to do with any tenders put in by the company while I have been a member of the Government.[7]

Marples was not the only member of the 1959 Conservative Government determined to reduce the size of Britain's railway system. As Prime Minister Harold Macmillan[8] said to the Commons on 10 March 1960:

> First the industry must be of a size and pattern suited to modern conditions and prospects. In particular, the railway system must be remodelled to meet current needs, and the modernisation plan must be adapted to this new shape.[9]

The road lobby saw its chance, with the Road Haulage Association quickly entering the debate on the Government's side. In April 1960, its journal, *The World's Carriers*, had this to say:

> It is understood that the Government have already settled the principles of reorganisation, and it will be for the board to work out their detailed application ...
>
> We should build more roads, and we should have fewer railways. This would merely be following the lesson of history which shows a continued and continuing expansion of road transport and a corresponding contraction in the volume of business handled by the railways ...
>
> A streamlined railway system could surely be had for half the money that is now being made available ... We must exchange the 'permanent way' of life for the 'motorway' of life ... road transport is the future, the railways are the past.

Closure notice – Chipping Norton.
The line from Banbury to Chipping Norton had lost its passenger service in 1951, leaving a school train service between Chipping Norton and the junction with the Cotswold line at Kingham which lasted until the end of 1962. This notice was posted at nearby Ashton under Hill (on the Evesham to Ashchurch line), itself closed six months later.

Announcing the formation of the special advisory group, Minister of Transport Marples told the House of Commons on 6 April 1960[14]:

> … the task of the advisory body will be to examine the structure, finance and working of the organisations at present controlled by the commission and to advise the Minister of Transport and the British Transport Commission as a matter of urgency *how effect can best be given to the Government's intentions as indicated in the Prime Minister's statement.* [our emphasis]

The Road Haulage Association realised they had a golden opportunity to redraw the transport map of Britain in their favour. In their evidence to the committee, they said:

> … no permanent subsidy should be granted to the railways before it is established exactly what services, passengers and freight are conducted at a loss … the railways' subsidisation would retard the natural evolutionary process in transport by which road services are replacing rail …
>
> The railway system has a fairly long history of failure, and the decline in the importance of rail can no longer be concealed.

The RHA had been massively encouraged by a speech made at their annual dinner in May 1960 by John Hay, Parliamentary Secretary at the Ministry of Transport:[15]

> I know that our idea of getting advice on the detailed application of Government policy towards the railways from a group of businessmen … is a sensible approach which will commend itself to those present at this dinner.
>
> We were very glad to know what you thought … and the views of your association have been brought to the attention of Sir Ivan Stedeford's group.
>
> … in the search for transport efficiency, the Government is prepared in a most practical way to do what it can to help. I refer of course to the road programme. It would be too optimistic to expect you to say that what we are doing is enough. No Ministry of Transport spokesman will ever expect that from his friends in the industry.
>
> You and we worked together against the threat of nationalisation of road haulage. We won that battle. Now we must show that we were right to win it …
>
> We in the Government will back you all we can … we shall try to make sure that the roads we have and the new roads we build give the best possible dividend … sometimes in this we shall be forced to require some sacrifices by individuals or by groups in the interests of the many. Road haulage will enjoy many of the benefits …

The Stedeford committee

Like many administrations before and since, the Government decided that their best chance of delivering a new policy lay in establishing an apparently independent committee and telling it to report on the state of British transport, recommending what part the railways should play in the future economic life of the country and how they should be administered. It was abundantly clear that ministers had no intention of leaving matters to chance and marked the committee's cards from the outset. From the first, they resisted any suggestion that there should be even one representative from the railways – let alone from the trade unions. Instead, it was chaired by a British industrialist with a background in the motor industry, Sir Ivan Stedeford.[10] The other members were Frank Kearton[11], joint managing director of Courtaulds, Henry Benson[12], chartered accountant and partner in the accountancy firm Cooper Brothers and Co, and Dr Richard Beeching, technical director of ICI. There were, however, two appointed representatives of Government departments – the Treasury and the Department of Transport. The Treasury's civil servant was Mr M. Cameron, while the Department of Transport was represented by D. R. Serpell[13], who will reappear in this book as Chairman of the infamous Serpell Committee in the 1980s (see Chapter 12).

While some have assumed that the Stedeford Committee focused on reducing the network, it was actually formed as a special advisory group to make recommendations on the structure for the management of all transport in Britain, then seen as beyond the capabilities of the British Transport Commission. Closures represented only one issue among many addressed by the group, which was mainly concerned about structures and financing.

The findings of the Stedeford Committee were never published, the decision not to publish confirmed in a Cabinet committee minute of 14 November 1960, when Marples told its members the Government had made it clear to their witnesses that findings would remain confidential. BTC, he assured the committee, were 'strongly of the opinion that the recommendations should not be published'.[16]

The report was extremely critical of the BTC itself and recommended that it be broken up, coming to these conclusions within six months of starting work. There were also rumours that Stedeford and Beeching had clashed over the extent to which the railway network should be reduced.

In his book *The Great Railway Conspiracy*[17], David Henshaw writes:

According to Henry Benson, the only member of the Stedeford Committee to make any sort of public pronouncement on the report's contents, the committee had failed to reach unanimous agreement. Beeching and Benson had recommended the course of action that the Government favoured, and Stedeford and Kearton had taken a different, and unspecified, line. In the event, there was a damaging and divisive split, and Beeching was left to write the majority of the report.

However, the recommendations of the group were closely reflected in the White Paper of December 1960, which proposed abolition of the BTC. This would come about through the Transport Act of 1962.

There was a question in the House of Lords from Lord Morrison of Lambeth[18] on 30 November 1960, in which he asked the Government when they proposed to publish the report of the Stedeford advisory group on British Railways. The initial reply from Government minister Lord Chesham[19] was, 'It is not intended to publish the recommendations of the group.' Pressed further by Lord Morrison, he then said that 'this group have produced recommendations. They have not made a report at all.'

Lord Morrison of Lambeth: Well, well.
Lord Chesham: There seems to have been a good deal of rather inaccurate thinking about this group, which was set up in order to advise my right honourable friend and the British Transport Commission. As they made recommendations from time to time they sent them to the British Transport Commission and to my right honourable friend at the same time. What matters to Parliament, it seems to me, is the proposals which Her Majesty's Government, after considering the recommendations and after consultations, including consultations with the British Transport Commission, will put to Parliament; and those will be forthcoming in due course.
Lord Morrison of Lambeth: My Lords, does it matter what the right honourable gentleman the Minister of Transport said when he appointed this body? Is it not most unusual publicly to announce the appointment of a body to inquire and report and then, afterwards, to refuse to publish what they have recommended? The noble lord says that they are making recommendations: but how could they make recommendations without a report? Does the noble lord not think it is setting aside the public interest and, indeed, legitimate parliamentary expectations if, after an investigation of this importance and character takes place in regard to the British Railways system, a matter which is of profound public importance, Her Majesty's Government refuse to publish their report – or observations, if the noble lord prefers it – and their recommendations? Is that not contrary to the public interest and is it not an extraordinary state of affairs?

Somewhat unwisely, Lord Chesham then elaborated on his earlier answer:

My Lords, it matters extremely what my right honourable friend said when he announced the setting up of this inquiry, because he made it perfectly clear at the time that the findings, the recommendations of this group, were to be confidential to Her Majesty's Government and to the British Transport Commission. The group undertook their work in that light and witnesses gave evidence to the group on that understanding; therefore what my right honourable friend said is of extreme importance.

This was untrue. Nowhere in Marples' statement of 6 April that year was there any assertion that the report, or the recommendations, would remain confidential. The authors have, however, unearthed some previously unpublished material about the Stedeford Committee in the National Archives at Kew.

The Stedeford Committee recognised the need to consider rail in the context of other transport developments (particularly the developing motorway programme) and recommended further study in that area. Apart from reorganisation, the second target of the committee was the modernisation plan, including the Euston-Manchester electrification, and the BTC clearly fought hard with the committee to maintain momentum on this project. One retired railwayman told the authors that, at the time, his job as junior engineer was to calculate the scrap value of material purchased for electrification in case the project were cancelled. The heart of the problem identified by the committee was not the branch lines, but the financial structure of the industry:

The heart of the financial problem is in the railways .... The book value of the railways is now unrealistic: and the burden of debt upon the railways is greater than they can carry. (Recommendation 4, September 1960)

The truth was that the BTC had no idea of the profitability of the railways below the aggregate national level:

Large parts of its organisation, including the railway regions, have no separate accounts and no systematic financial yardsticks by which to judge the results and prospects of managerial actions.

In their conclusions, the committee also highlighted a lack of clear objectives:

The confusion springs from an inherent incompatibility between the concept of a national public service and the economic and commercial realities facing an undertaking enjoined in the Transport Act, 1947 to make both ends meet 'taking one year with another'.

In their view, this was reinforced by the approach of the transport tribunal and the CTCC, with their emphasis on public service:

The concept of public service blurs the concept of a commercial enterprise.

This simple sentence set the course of the rail industry for the future. We are still living with the consequences. On 'unremunerative lines and services', the committee said:

We are aware that the commission is making efforts to cut out uneconomic railway services, including the closure of unremunerative lines, and that during the past two or three years this process has speeded up. The chairmen of some of the consultative committees told us, however, that, in their view, the majority of the cases now coming before them for the withdrawal of uneconomic railway services could have been put forward several years earlier on equally strong grounds and that, from this experience, there must be a similar number of cases not yet prepared. Other evidence put before us indicated that faster progress was necessary. This is a field in which we think that action may have been retarded by a sense of public obligation. We recommend that, with a view to expediting progress, a dated programme of further proposals for closure be prepared.[20]

Dr Beeching saw the picture even more clearly and had prepared a paper for the committee, dated 3 May 1960, as an 'Interpretation of the Terms of Reference of the Special Advisory Group'. Logically, he argued that the first requirement was to decide what functions the railway should be asked to perform. From this, judgements could be formed about the modernisation schemes required. He believed that the main responsibilities of the committee were to advise the Transport Minister on:

The size and pattern of railway system appropriate to the present and foreseeable needs of the country. The foundation of the whole investigation must be an assessment of the inherent merits of rail transport, relative to alternative forms of transport, for various forms of traffic. Answers to questions about the desirability of closing some parts of the present railway system and about the effects of statutory obligations upon railway economics may be expected to follow naturally…

Beeching's efforts to rewrite the Stedeford committee's terms of reference were exactly what the Government wanted to hear. Marples was looking for a process which would lead to massive closures and an individual prepared to be its champion. In Beeching he had both, and it is reasonable to suppose that the Government's extreme reluctance to publish any of the Stedeford committee's findings – either as a report, or as a series of recommendations – was because they did not

The Westerham branch was closed in 1961, although it was a busy commuter shuttle service. The route was required for the London Orbital Motorway (now the M25) and attempts to reopen the line following closure were frustrated by the County Council and the Ministry of Transport. The train was a push-pull operation and ran 22 trips a day, with two peak trains per hour. Southern Region had prepared contingency plans to electrify the branch using 2-car trains in case approval was not given.

want any serious debate on wider issues such as the role of the railway. They just wanted to get on with shrinking the system and to be allowed to implement their rail closures agenda.

The subsequent White Paper of December 1960, *Reorganisation of the Nationalised Transport Undertakings*[21], drew heavily on Stedeford's recommendations. Dispelling any possible doubt about the resolve of the Government to make dramatic changes to the railways, the language of the White Paper was surprisingly direct:

Sweeping changes will be needed. Effort and sacrifice will be required from all. The public will have to be prepared to face changes in the extent and nature of the services provided and, when necessary, in the prices charged for them. [Para 4]

The practical test for the railways, as for other transport, is how far the users are prepared to pay economic prices for the services provided. Broadly, this will in the end settle the size and pattern of the railway system. It is already clear that the system must be made more compact. [Para 7]

An earlier draft (25 November 1960) of the White Paper included the sentence, 'It is clear, however, that there must be a streamlining of the system,' but this was removed from the final version. Old scores were settled as the Government blamed the railwaymen themselves for demanding a reasonable wage:

Those working in these undertakings, if their livelihood is to be assured, will have to play their part in increasing productivity and enabling the labour force to be deployed so as to secure maximum efficiency in operation. When the Government made funds available to implement the Guillebaud Report[22] last spring they made it clear that far-reaching changes would be necessary. [Para 4]

Emasculating the TUCCs

One anticipated problem was that of the TUCCs. At a meeting on 25 November 1960 between the BTC and the department, chaired by David Serpell, the BTC's chief legal adviser complained that the Commission had to pay for the TUCCs and provide them with accommodation: 'In the discussion that followed it was agreed that further consideration would have to be given to the powers and responsibilities of the TUCCs in relation to closures.'

The process of 'streamlining' the closure procedure – in order to get rid of more lines, more quickly – had begun.

As early as February 1961, Serpell recorded a meeting on the future role of the TUCCs and the need to reorganise them to separate the handling of complaints resulting from closures. Interestingly, at that early stage, consideration was also given to assessing the social needs of lines that might in future be subsidised.

On 25 May 1961, Serpell met Spencer Wills from British Electric Traction Ltd[23], the bus holding company, who offered that BET subsidiaries would provide rail replacement services for five years, without subsidy, if the Ministry would give them advance notice of the lines to be closed: 'clearly, something has to be done if uneconomic railway services on branch lines are to be cut out'.

The following month, the future shape of the TUCCs was clearly anticipated by the Commission. In a memorandum to the Ministry, it proposed that the remit of the committees should be limited to service quality and closures – specifically, in the case of the latter, to determining hardship in the event of closure – and suggested that inquiries should be limited to a maximum six months. The Commission had clearly lost patience with the central committee (CTCC) by this stage and proposed its abolition, to be replaced by *ad hoc* meetings of the chairmen of the area committees.

In July 1961, at a meeting between officials, BTC went a stage further and proposed that the railways should not be obliged to provide any estimates of savings from closures as they were irrelevant to the new TUCC remit. It also pressed for a maximum two-year period during which it would be liable for funding replacement bus services.

Even as late as 1962, there was no statutory requirement for closures to be referred to the TUCCs, although there was an expectation that all major closures would be considered by them. In April 1962, Serpell formulated his ideas on the role of the committees. They should:

- Consider proposals for major withdrawal of passenger services, but their remit should not extend to freight services.
- They should not have a general remit on lines proposed for closure but should consider specific issues, such as how far potential savings would be outweighed by other factors, such as negative implications for passengers.
- They should recommend the extent and duration of any replacement bus services 'on the assumption that the State will not be prepared to subsidise individual railway services'. [24]
- The emphasis was on speed. At a meeting with the TUCCs in June 1962, while the Transport Bill was going through the House, the Ministry suggested that they might want to form panels of members to deal with closure cases if the workload was heavy.

The Transport Act of 1962 did indeed limit the remit of the TUCCs to considerations of hardship, but the CTCC was retained and the Ministry agreed to the provision of basic financial information to objectors.

With the emasculation of the TUCCs, ministers were impatient to get on with the closure programme. In a debate a year later, initiated by a question from Lord Stonham[25], Lord Chesham spoke on behalf of the Government:

> But it is, I suggest, another thing that every time the board want to rid themselves of an unremunerative service every user, and a lot of people who have virtually ceased to use it, should have the right to ask how they arrive at their figures.[26]

The policy had swept all before it and had become politically polarised. Empirical evidence was ignored, as was any thought of changing circumstances, or that this huge programme of disinvestment should first consider the longer-term requirements for transport. The policy had to be defended and Lord Chesham did so with his assertion that, 'A large part of the predicament of the railways at the moment is that people have ceased to use them.' In spite of his dismissive comments, 938 million passenger journeys were made by rail in 1963.

Setting up the British Railways Board

The stage was set. The first step was to bring Dr Beeching on board as Chairman of the railways. Marples announced on 15 March 1961 that Sir Brian Robertson would retire as Chairman of the BTC on 1 June that year and that Beeching would become his successor, as well as Chairman-designate of the new British Railways Board. He also announced that Beeching would be paid the same salary as that which he had been earning at ICI: the sum of £24,000 a year (approaching £400,000 in today's money – £10,000 a year more than Robertson was being paid).

The appointment of a leading industrialist with no rail background as Chairman of the BRB was intended to demonstrate a marked change of direction for the railway. Beeching was to bring new commercial disciplines from the private sector, to be applied to a railway organisation that had lost its way under the British Transport Commission.

Cabinet papers from March 1963 describe in great detail how the Government and the railways board colluded in both producing and implementing the extensive programme of closures which became known as the Beeching Report.

Marples had been invited by the Cabinet at its meeting on 14 March to submit proposals for:

(a) a revised draft of the Government statement to be made on 27 March, the day of publication of the railways report;
(b) securing the most effective public presentation of proposals in the report;
(c) ensuring implementation of the board's proposals, when appropriate, as rapidly as possible.

His memorandum for Cabinet on 19 March 1963 described what he planned to do. He was concerned about the consultations which the railways board needed to undertake with the railway trade unions:

> To avoid any suggestion of failure to consult (as occurred in relation to the workshops), Dr Beeching has decided not to give formal notice of any of the passenger closures in Appendix II of his Report until some four weeks after its publication … An interdepartmental working party under Ministry of Transport Chairmanship, is urgently considering the merits of the railways' proposals. Special attention is being given to their implications for

(i)   Government policies and plans (including employment);

(ii) local Government, industry, other forms of transport, &c.

Initial responsibility for work on the various problems has been allocated among departments. Also there will be consultations with the appropriate representative bodies (e.g. local authority associations, bus and road haulage interests, major industrial associations, etc).

However, there appears to have been no reference to passengers in the plans, giving some indication of the determination with which the policy was to be driven through.

Launching the report

The following paragraph in Marples' memorandum was headed 'Machinery for Effecting Closures'. It showed the urgency with which he intended the closure proposals to be implemented:

A lot depends on the speed and efficiency with which [the TUCCs] carry out their responsibilities in regard to passenger closures. The new procedure under Section 56 of the Transport Act, 1962, has therefore been explained to, and discussed with, the Transport Users' Consultative Committee Area chairmen. Special reference was made to their relationship with the Traffic Commissioners (in regard to bus services), and to the practicability of expediting business by dividing the committees into panels. They have also been invited to strengthen their secretariats, where necessary.

Annex I to the memorandum was the latest draft of the Government statement to be issued when the Beeching Report was published. It bore a close resemblance to that made by Marples in the House of Commons on 27 March (see below), but also contained the following sentence: 'The board's lucid analysis and bold proposals fully accord with the Government's expectations.'

Annex II was the 'Proposed Publicity Programme'. This described a comprehensive and remarkably sophisticated programme to sell the Beeching Report to Parliament, railway staff and the general public. (It is reproduced in Appendix A.)

All was now in place for the launch of the report on 27 March 1963. Its publication was accompanied by a statement in the House of Commons[27] by Ernest Marples. His opening words made clear that this was the British Railways Board's report, not the Government's:

The Government are greatly indebted to Dr. Beeching and his board for their comprehensive proposals, which flow from the most massive compilation and systematic analysis of information about our railways ever attempted. We agree that extensive reshaping on the lines now proposed is essential.

The report offers a firm prospect of an efficient and modern railway system handling those traffics technically best suited to rail. Reductions in the present subsidy of about £150 million will release economic resources which can be better used in the national interest elsewhere. The board's aim is, therefore, wholly consistent with our policy of modernisation and redevelopment.

The report is a major contribution to the Government's policy of providing an efficient, economic, and well-balanced transport system for Great Britain as a whole. When the new shape and pattern of the railways are clear we shall have a foundation on which we can create such a system. It is not possible to have effective and efficient co-ordination until we have as a basis a modern 20th century railway system.

In the meantime, steps are being taken by the secretary of state for Scotland and myself to see that any additional demands on our roads will be met. Also, I am meeting representatives of the bus operators on 9th April and both the railways board and myself will consult the road haulage industry.

On passenger services, Marples remarked:

No opposed closure may be carried out without my consent, and I shall take into account all important factors, including social and defence considerations, the pattern of industrial development and possible effects on roads and road traffic.

The report makes it clear that in the remoter areas of the country there will be special problems. This applies not only in Scotland and Wales, but in some parts of England, and to communications with Northern Ireland. But in this country a widespread network of bus services already exists and I shall see that, where necessary, adequate alternative means of transport are available before a railway passenger closure takes place.

Given the intensity and passion engendered by subsequent debates on rail closures, the immediate response by principal Opposition transport spokesman George Strauss[28] was extraordinarily complimentary to Beeching:

I should like to congratulate Dr Beeching on producing a very able report. It is lucid, comprehensive and well-argued, and he has carried out admirably the task entrusted to him by the Government. That task was to see how best the railways could be reshaped to fit modern conditions and, above all and particularly, what steps should be taken to make them remunerative.

Strauss even said that Beeching's recommendations for making the railways more efficient and increasing traffics had Labour's wholehearted support:

On the other hand ... the proposals to curtail the railway services on the drastic scale suggested confirm our very worst fears. In particular ... we are surprised and distressed at the scant attention which Dr Beeching devotes to the consequences – the congestion on the roads, the making of new roads and the general social consequences of the closures, which he dismisses as being practically non-existent.

As the minister will be responsible for authorising these closures ... every proposal for closure which will come before him – and they all will – will be scrutinised and opposed by honourable members, at least on this side of the House, unless they are accompanied by full assurances that adequate and satisfactory alternative services will be provided and that where that does not happen necessary subsidies should be paid to maintain the existing services.

Marples' statement received a mixed reception in the House. The one-term Conservative MP for the railway town of Darlington, Anthony Bourne-Arton[29], called it a 'bold and sensible plan'. However, another Tory MP, Sir John Maitland[30] who represented Horncastle, spoke of 'the fury of resentment' of 'places like Lincolnshire and other scattered areas [which] will feel that in many cases they are dealt with as second-class areas'.

According to Harold Wilson[31], then Leader of the Opposition, 'some of the sycophantic pronouncements which have been made this afternoon do not express the mood of the whole House or of the country about this report. While members on both sides of the House will be very concerned about individual closures – the procedure for closures, safeguards, and so on – what is clear is that the responsibility for forcing Dr Beeching to do this job is uniquely and unequivocally the responsibility of Her Majesty's Government and that the whole of the responsibility for the very grave state of affairs shown in the report goes back to what the Tory Government have been doing ever since 1953, when they started the disintegration of the transport system.'

Marples' reply was clear: 'The responsibility is mine and the Government's, and I have never tried to shirk that responsibility. Dr Beeching was not forced to do it. He has a job to do, but the responsibility ultimately is the Government's.'

The final response to Marples' statement came from Scottish Labour MP Archie Manuel[32]:

These closures of main lines, many branch lines and stations will inevitably turn many people on to the roads. We have already 350,000 casualties a year and about 132 deaths a week. Will not this inevitably increase the toll on the roads, because he will be forcing on to the roads more traffic than there is on them at present?

Marples' own response ran as follows:

I have already said that we should look at the question of the roads and see what traffic is forced upon them, but, frankly, it is in the rural areas that we have most of the difficulties, where the railways will be closed. In these areas there is not the congestion that there is in the urban areas. In the urban areas we are trying to take people off the roads by building such lines as the Victoria-Walthamstow underground line, which will cost over £60 million, and in Glasgow providing the electrified Blue Trains. The main point is that people who want to use the railways will spend the money. If they do not, there is no point in having the railways.

The argument that only rural railways that saw little use would be closed was compelling at the time, but ignored the congestion that would result where additional road traffic joined the main roads approaching the towns or cities of destination (or sometimes the rail access points) of displaced rail passengers. It was also a somewhat disingenuous statement by Marples, given that the closure list included many busy urban routes such as the North London line and Southport-Liverpool, as well as some main lines like the Great Central and the Waverley route. (Indeed, traffic congestion in Edinburgh is now one of the driving forces behind the reopening of the latter.)

When the House of Commons debated the Beeching Report over two days in the following month, Marples began his subsequent speech by making five points related to the report:

The first one is that it is not based on emotional thinking or wishes. It is based on actual research and scientific analysis. I am quite certain that the whole of the House would wish to thank Dr Beeching and his board for a report of great clarity, something which, I think, we have not had in the history of our railways before. All the credit for that is due to them. The Government are examining all the aspects of this and, naturally, consulting the many interests which are concerned.

The second point is that the railways' deficit must be reduced. In 1963, it is expected to be £150 million. The last railway wage increase added £22 million to the total expenditure. In the future, unless we do something, then, about 1970, the deficit will be astronomical. Therefore, we cannot afford to delay the implementation of this plan. The resources which will be so freed could be used better elsewhere.

The third point is that contraction of a part of the railway system is quite inevitable and ought to be done as quickly as possible. A third of it is scarcely used. One third of the route mileage carries 0.8 of 1% of passenger miles. One third of the route mileage carries 1.5% of freight ton miles. A third of the stations produce 1% of the passenger receipts. A third of the stations produce 0.6 of 1% of freight receipts.

A third of the system is not used at all – or hardly at all. One third of it is very good and ought to be developed; a good deal of money should be spent in making it viable and competitive with the roads. The other third of it is doubtful – some of it good, some of it bad – and ought to be looked at after we have disposed of the third which is proposed to be dealt with in the plan. There should be continuous examination of what the railways are contributing both to freight and passenger transport. This is just the first instalment of that.

This is not only a negative report. It has a positive side as well. The Railways Board is trying to exploit the railways' natural technical advantages and to capture those traffics which are suitable to the railways. They have shown that in this report. They have made enormous studies of what is carried by road, the greatest traffic studies made in the history of this country. The effort is to take the freight off the road in certain areas where it is technically suitable to the railways and to put it on the railways.

The fifth point is possibly the most difficult of all to make. It is about manpower. The 1960 White Paper said: If the railways are to regain solvency, and provide a fair livelihood for their workers, efficiency of operation and the most economic use of manpower are crucial.

Marples' speech also contained details of bus replacements for rail services:

> When a passenger railway closes, the problem is to avoid hardship to the passengers who have been using the railway. There should be either the railway or the bus in sparsely populated areas where neither system has been patronised reasonably, but not necessarily both. If it is more economic to use the bus than to use the railway, the bus it should be.
>
> In general, we have had discussions with the bus companies, with the independent bus companies and with the Transport Holding Company, which controls quite a lot of the buses. British Electric Traction has been present, also. They believe that they can do the job. They believe that in some cases the passengers displaced from the railways will go on to the buses and help their cash position. They will need 700 extra buses in all.
>
> The decision to close anything in the case of passengers, whether a station or a railway line, is taken not by the Railways Board, or by Dr Beeching. It rests fairly and squarely on the Government. It is their responsibility. I accept it. I do not want the House to think that we close down anything, either with or without conditions, until we have consulted a large number of other people.
>
> Let me give some examples in particular cases. I can refuse consent or give consent subject to certain conditions, and I will give examples of the variety of methods. First, we can insist upon the railway remaining, as we did in the case of Rhondda and Swansea, when, on merit, the railway should be kept.[33]
>
> We can close a railway and insist upon a bus service because buses may be cheaper. That was done in the case of Ditton Junction and Timperley. Such a bus service cannot be taken off until the Minister of Transport and the Government of the day agree that it can be taken off.
>
> The bus service can be provided either on an economic basis or on a subsidised basis. In the case of Westerham-Dunton Green, the railway was closed and a subsidy of £8,000 a year was given originally by the railways to the bus company to cater for the passengers displaced by the closure of the railway.

Marples also set out the closure procedure:

> If the railways wish to close any station or line concerned with passengers, the procedure is for the railways board to put forward the proposal and advertise it twice. After the second advertisement, six weeks later, the transport users' consultative committee for the area in question can, if it wishes, take evidence and advise me. It advises me on two things: first, the degree of hardship to passengers; and, secondly, what alternative services can, in the committee's opinion, be provided. Then, and then only, when that evidence is given to me as minister, can I make a decision. I have already given examples in which the Railways Board has put proposals and I have turned them down.

He pooh-poohed the suggestion that rail closures would add significantly to road congestion:

> What will be the effect upon the road system of the closure of the third of our railways system? Many judgments have been given. Many honourable members opposite have said that there will be chaos, congestion and road casualties. If the proposed one third of the railway system is closed completely, and everything goes through the procedure laid down by Parliament and the whole of the one third is closed – that is, lines, stations, stopping trains and the lot – what will happen is that the traffic which is diverted to the roads will add 1% to the total road traffic over the country as a whole.
>
> This is less than two months' normal increase in road traffic. (Honourable Members: 'Chaos.') Honourable members opposite can say what they like about it, but less than two months' normal increase cannot be considered as chaos or any of the whole lot of adjectives which have been applied to it.

The Reshaping report

The report itself was a model of clarity and succinctness, as a relatively short 148pp A5 booklet accompanied in a folder by a dozen maps. There was no attempt to hide the dramatic transformation revealed by the maps and the lists of lines and stations for closure. The sheer scale of what was proposed, set out so clearly, formed the basis of much of the opposition that followed. The long list of doomed lines and stations in the appendices and the skeletal maps entrenched the view of an industry in terminal decline. The picture painted by the main text was a much more positive one, however, balancing retrenchment with the need for investment in the principal routes.

Development of the network of long-distance express passenger services was to be matched with huge investment in new wagons to handle coal traffic more efficiently. It was a move toward company trains for primary commodities such as oil, cement and aggregates, while containers carried on liner trains would supplant the costs, delays and damage associated with marshalling yards. The move from aggregating mixed traffics through marshalling yards to 'block' trains carrying a single commodity would save costs and improve transit times and reliability while reducing damage.

The main thrust behind the report was the adoption of a businesslike approach to the railway, focusing the industry on what it could achieve profitably and withdrawing from unprofitable activities like running branch lines, passenger trains calling at local stations on main lines and pick-up goods trains. It also meant that the summer peak demand to holiday resorts could no longer be met, saving the cost of a fleet of coaches used only on ten summer Saturdays a year:

> The thought underlying the whole report is that the railways should be used to meet that of the total transport requirement of the country for which they offer the best available means, and that they should cease to do things for which they are ill suited.[34]

Nevertheless, it was the closures that received the most attention at the time (and subsequently) from the press and the public. More surprisingly, it became the focus of attention for many railway managers, seen as the principal way of achieving the economies required to restore BR to profitability.

The bare statistics set out in the report were, on the face of it, compelling. Of the BR route mileage of 17,830 in 1961, one third carried just 1% of total passenger miles and 1% of freight ton miles. Half the network carried 4% of passenger business and 5% of freight. At the other end of the spectrum, the top 34 stations (less than 1%) accounted for 26% of the passenger receipts.

The cost of the branch lines was just one of many problems to be addressed and not the greatest source of revenue loss. More money was lost by the great urban networks where resource costs were huge, with fare income low by virtue of short distances travelled. Equally, it was here (as it still is now) where the greatest social benefit was delivered by the railways in supporting the economic needs of the cities they served and reducing traffic congestion. Moreover, little information existed on how the costs and revenues were generated or spent on individual lines. Income was built up from daily returns from ticket offices and goods offices and, with mileage-based tariffs, income could be allocated to branch lines. How much would be retained, however, if the branch were no longer there remained (as it does now) a matter of conjecture. Reworking the figures in this way was a manual task which, in the absence of computers, was both labour-intensive and time-consuming.

Costs were only brought together at the regional level and for inter-regional traffic were not matched to the revenue generated. Any allocation to individual lines was fairly arbitrary. The cost of a bridge renewal could be calculated, but most branch lines used second-hand track cascaded from the main lines, and shared resources such as drawing offices, procurement, payroll or training. In some cases, a locomotive and set of coaches were allocated to an individual branch, but in many others they too were a shared resource. The same was true of the wagon fleet.

In short, the railway has always been run as a network, and any attempt to produce a separate balance sheet for an individual line means allocating costs which may or may not actually arise. The real questions are: What costs are reduced by the closure of a branch line? How long does it take to realise such savings? These issues were not addressed in the Beeching Report, or indeed subsequently for many years.

Instead, Beeching used average costs for track maintenance, train operations and staffing, along with an assessment of the renewals of structures and earthworks required to maintain services over the ensuing five years. The latter figure was also potentially misleading, as the maintenance of track and structures was not determined by a preset formula but expertly assessed by experienced engineers used to making accurate judgements about when a structure or length of

Waverley route

Eighteen months before closure of possibly the most significant strategic route listed in the Beeching Report, the 14.45 Edinburgh to Carlisle train arrives at Galashiels in July 1967. The platform loop line for the Peebles and Selkirk branches has already been recovered, as have the carriage sidings that run alongside. The Borders railway project will later put Galashiels on the national network once again, tackling the inaccessibility from which it has suffered over the last 42 years.

track required renewal, given the traffic passing over it. This was done through a process of daily line walks, routine local inspections and annual visits by the district engineer, a regular tour using his special saloon coach and an effective way for him to meet his inspectors and observe things at first hand. Inevitably, if a five-year forecast had to be made, renewals would be included that might, in practice, have been deferred or undertaken more cheaply.

Passenger income was only brought together at the national level. For traffic costing purposes, only revenue originating on the branch was credited to the line – even on those holiday routes where much income was collected in towns and cities around the country, rather than on the branch line itself.

Worse than this, the financial picture presented was just a snapshot at the time of the assessment when most lines were still run with traditional equipment, many with steam engines. No attempt was made to consider the scope for developing new business, even though the experience of introducing diesel railcars had resulted in very significant traffic increases and reductions in costs. Nor was any attempt made to assess the costs of running a basic railway with pay train operation and simplified signalling.

Inexcusably, the analysis was based on a one-week traffic survey taken during the week ending 23 April 1961, highlighted as a major weakness by the report's critics. While this was a reasonably representative period, it was a mistake to base momentous decisions on a single week and to ignore the summer traffic that was such a feature of many routes. As the report itself acknowledged, 'The year 1961 was not a good one from the traffic point of view, because the recession in the steel industry affected the latter part of it.'[35]

Underlying the report was an assumption that passengers were indifferent to mode of transport and would happily transfer to bus, even though all the evidence pointed in the opposite direction. The 'Q&A brief' used by BR staff at the press conference that launched the report summed it up in relation to lines that today form part of the very successful Passenger Transport Executive (PTE) services in the great cities outside London: 'Suburban services in other cities are, by comparison with London, quite lightly used and are hopelessly unremunerative.'

As to the question of whether or not these services should be subsidised: 'If any subsidisation [*sic*] is needed it at least should be kept to the minimum by using the most economical type of service. This nearly always means a bus rather than a train.'

Most people took the view that the Government was proceeding with implementation of the closures proposed by Beeching with indecent haste. However, it was not fast enough for some politicians. A secret memorandum to the Cabinet, dated 14 January 1964, was written not by Ernest Marples but by Viscount Blakenham[36], the chancellor of the duchy of Lancaster who chaired the Rail and Road Committee. It reported that they had looked at 'the extent it was possible for the Government to influence the sequence in which the Railway [*sic*] Board brought forward their proposals in such a way as to minimise controversy and to ensure that due regard was paid to relevant Government policies such as regional development and the management of urban traffic'.

The memo then described the statutory procedure for consideration of the Railways Board's closure proposals, as set out in the 1962 Transport Act:

The extent to which the Minister of Transport can usefully seek to influence the timing of the board's publication of their proposals is limited by the fact that the board have the statutory right to bring forward proposals when they see fit in the light of their statutory duty to make the railways pay and by the practical difficulty of judging how long the consideration of a particular proposal will take. The hearings are arranged to suit the convenience of their [the TUCCs'] members, who serve part-time and are unpaid, and that of the objectors. It is difficult for the Government to interfere too much with the board's discretion – particularly to secure the deferment of proposals – without appearing to withdraw our support for their efforts to make the railways pay; and we cannot seek to influence the

Holiday Trains at Skegness
At the end of the summer that followed the Beeching Report, four 'B1s' head trains taking holidaymakers back to the Midlands from Skegness. (Note how, even at this late date, the station was still lit by gas.) The report identified 6000 coaches (one third of the fleet) that were only used up to a maximum of 18 occasions per year, strongly urging that this situation should end. Within two years, much of the holiday traffic travelled by private car – or had gone abroad – whereas, only 10 years before, most people had holidayed in Britain and got to their resort by train. Even today, chronic overcrowding at holiday times on this busy route remains a problem.

TUCCs' programme of hearings without undermining public confidence in their independence. Any interference with the normal procedure is likely to attract public attention.

Having given the impression that both the Railways Board and the TUCCs possessed independence and discretion, Blakenham's memorandum goes on to demonstrate just how much the Government was interfering with the process. He reported that the board had agreed in the autumn of 1963 'to advance the publication of certain Scottish services so that the following could be published together in November:

'Dumfries-Kircudbright
'Inverness-Wick/Thurso
'Inverness-Kyle of Lochalsh
'Ayr-Stranraer
'Dumfries-Stranraer.'

But it is clear now that the fast-track strategy had collapsed due to the time required by the TUCCs to hear objections, and so the Government gave up the idea:

Since there is no advantage in advancing the publication of controversial proposals if the TUCCs cannot dispose of them, my Committee have concluded that no further requests should be made to the board for publication dates to be advanced.

This consideration points, on the contrary, to deferring publication of some proposals which might otherwise overload the TUCC machinery. Some members of the Committee have thought it was undesirable that either the Railways Board or the TUCCs should spend time on proposals which clearly could not be approved.

Blakenham explained that what his committee had in mind was commuter services, particularly in those areas where, within a few years, industrial or housing developments might increase the demand for rail passenger services. This relatively sensible approach had not found favour with Minister for Transport Marples, as he felt it was undesirable to interfere with the Railways Board's discretion and it might not have been clear as to what the future pattern of travel in those areas was likely to be. He preferred to let the proposals take their course through the statutory procedure, making his decision once they reached him. Marples suggested it might make sense to make immediate savings by discontinuing services, on the condition that the track could be retained and a service 're-introduced if and when development in the area renders it necessary':

The Minister of Transport is prepared, however, to ask for the deferment of a small number of proposals the publication of which may be particularly embarrassing in the light of our policy for regional development or the problem of urban traffic. The committee have selected eight of these:

Liverpool Exchange-Southport Chapel Street
Manchester Victoria-Bury-Bacup
Edinburgh-Hawick-Carlisle
Manchester Victoria-Bury-Accrington-Colne
Wrexham/Chester Northgate-New Brighton
Manchester Piccadilly-Hadfield/Glossup [sic]
Manchester Piccadilly-Romiley-Hayfield/Macclesfield
St Pancras-Barking.

Subject to the Cabinet's concurrence, it is proposed that the Minister should ask the Chairman of the Railways Board to arrange that these should not be published during the next six months, or thereafter until it appears that the relevant TUCC can consider objections soon after the expiration of the statutory period of notice.

Is it unfair to suggest that such postponements may have been linked to the political calendar? In 1964, a general election would be held and it would have been understandable if controversial railway closure proposals were to be kept out of the campaign.

At holiday resorts, 127 stations had been proposed for closure. Regarding these, Blakenham's committee was in no doubt:

Few of them receive large numbers of visitors by rail . . . As more families acquire cars, any loss of visitors which holiday resorts experience as a result of the closing of their stations is likely to be compensated for by the increasing numbers arriving by car,

and the effect of the closures on hotels and employment in these places is expected to be negligible in relation to other normal fluctuations in the number of visitors they receive. We do not think, therefore, that holiday resorts need to be considered as a special case.

The final section of this remarkable memorandum drew attention to what it described as the 'public misunderstanding' of the closure procedure:

The Railways Board's proposals are widely attributed to the Government, and decisions by the Minister of Transport to reject or modify proposals are represented as a victory won by the objectors at the Government's expense. There is also criticism of the fact that the TUCCs are confined to considering the issue of hardship, and there is no public examination of wider questions such as the possibility of running a threatened service more economically. The procedure could not be changed without legislation, however; and the broader questions of management which objectors seek to raise could not usefully be examined by a public enquiry. An independent accountant[37] appointed in August to consider the most appropriate financial information for the Railways Board to supply to the TUCCs endorsed (in a published report) the board's existing practice and commended 'the meticulous care' with which the figures were compiled.

In these circumstances we see no way of improving the present procedure, but it is important that every available occasion should be taken to remove public misunderstanding of its nature.

The report from the Rail and Road Transport Committee was considered at the next meeting of the Cabinet, in January 1964. They endorsed its entire approach: on holiday resorts, they decided that the best course was 'to suggest to the board that they should take the initiative themselves in announcing that proposals which could not be disposed of before the holiday season would not be published until the end of September', as 'uncertainty about the continued availability of a service would be liable to aggravate the losses which it incurred'.

The Cabinet also confirmed that they would not amend legislation covering the closure procedure, but 'invited the chancellor of the Duchy of Lancaster (Lord Blakenham), in consultation with the Minister for Transport (Mr Marples) and the Minister without Portfolio (Mr Deedes[38]) to consider the means by which the public might be more fully informed about the statutory procedures for rail closures'. So not for the first time (and certainly not for the last), ministers came to the conclusion that a policy was deeply unpopular not because it was mistaken, but because the public had failed to grasp it properly.

1 Although, in the case of St Erth to St Ives, the service has not 'passed out of our lives'. Every Monday to Friday, there are 28 trains in each direction on this amazingly busy little branch line which carried 440,000 passengers in 2010.
2 Dr Richard Beeching (1913-85) was ennobled as Baron Beeching in 1965. As a member of the Stedeford committee (1959-61) and Chairman of the British Railways Board (1961-65), he was on secondment from ICI – to which he returned after the Labour Government, elected in 1964, declined to renew his appointment to the BRB.
3 Alfred Ernest Marples (1907-78) was a Conservative politician who served as Postmaster General and Minister of Transport. He was the MP for Wallasey (1945-74) when he was ennobled as Lord Marples. He was also an immensely controversial figure, for reasons explained in this chapter.
4 Robert Mellish (1913-98) Labour MP for Bermondsey 1950-82 (for Rotherhithe 1946-50). Chief whip in Government and opposition 1969-76. Resigned from Parliament, and later the Labour Party in protest over what he saw as a Militant takeover of his constituency party. Joined the SDP, and later sat in the Lords as Baron Mellish on the cross benches.
5 Richard Austen Butler (universally known as 'RAB' – 1902-82) was a Conservative politician who entered the House of Commons in 1929 as MP for Saffron Walden, thanks to the intervention of his wife's family. (She was a Courtauld and he was selected unopposed while they were on their honeymoon.) He was a minister for the entire time that the Conservatives were in Government from 1932 onwards, including spells as Minister of Education, Chancellor of the Exchequer, Leader of the House of Commons, Home Secretary, Deputy Prime Minister and Foreign Secretary. The only great office of state denied him was Prime Minister. In 1965, Harold Wilson offered him the mastership of Trinity College Cambridge, which he accepted, with a life peerage. In his autobiography, Butler recounts how, as Chancellor of the Exchequer, he was kept out of a railway wage dispute by Churchill and Sir Walter Monkton, Minister of Labour. Churchill told Butler in 1954 that he and Monkton had 'settled the rail strike in the early hours of the morning', and that there had been no need to keep him up. 'On whose terms?' asked Butler. 'Theirs of course,' was the reply.
6 HC Deb volume 616, 28 January 1960, cc371-3.
7 HC Deb volume 616, 28 January 1960, cc380-1. The controversy did not end there,

because it later emerged that the purchaser of the shares was not some disinterested third party, but Marples' own wife – a material fact he had failed to share with the House of Commons. He retired from the House at the February 1974 general election and was made a life peer in May of that year. This was not the start of a new parliamentary career, however, as there is no record of his ever having spoken in his four years in the House. Richard Stott, editor of the *Daily Mirror*, takes up the story in his autobiography with an account of Marples' sudden flight to Monaco early in 1975:

'In the early 70s ... he tried to fight off a revaluation of his assets which would undoubtedly cost him dear ... So Marples decided he had to go and hatched a plot to remove £2 million from Britain through his Liechtenstein company ... there was nothing for it but to cut and run, which Marples did just before the tax year of 1975. He left by the Night Ferry with his belongings crammed into tea chests, leaving the floors of his home in Belgravia littered with discarded clothes and possessions ... He claimed he had been asked to pay nearly 30 years' overdue tax ... The Treasury froze his assets in Britain for the next 10 years. By then most of them were safely in Monaco and Liechtenstein.' (Richard Stott, *Dogs and Lampposts*, Metro Publishing, 2002, pp166-171.)

In addition to being wanted in Britain for tax fraud, it was reported that Marples was being sued by tenants of slum properties he owned and by former employees. He never returned to Britain and died in hospital, close to his French château, in July 1978. One of the first pieces of motorway graffiti in Britain was a 'Marples Must Go' slogan painted on an overbridge on the M1, which remained visible for years. It's unlikely that the artist would have expected Marples to take the advice quite as literally as he eventually did.

8   Harold Macmillan (1894-1986) served as Conservative Prime Minister from 1957-63. Formerly the MP for Stockton-on-Tees (1924-29 and 1931-45), which he lost in the 1945 Labour landslide, he was almost immediately elected MP for Bromley at a by-election, which he retained until his retirement in 1964. His early political life was hugely influenced by his experience as a junior officer in the Great War. He served on the Western Front and was wounded three times – at Loos, on the Somme and at Beaumont-Hamel – and never forgot the scenes of horror he witnessed. As an MP in the north-east during the Depression of the 20s and 30s, his political thinking was greatly influenced by the poverty in his constituency. It caused him to become a 'One Nation' Conservative, calling in his book *The Middle Way* (1938) for a centrist political philosophy based on co-operation between the state and the private sector. He was a vocal opponent of Baldwin, Chamberlain and appeasement, serving in Churchill's wartime Government in two junior minister jobs before becoming Minister for the Mediterranean in 1942. After the coalition Government ended in 1945, he served for two months as Air Minister. When the Conservatives returned to power in 1951, Macmillan was successively Housing Minister, Defence Minister, Foreign Secretary and Chancellor of the Exchequer. Macmillan succeeded Eden as Prime Minister after the Suez disaster, turning around Conservative fortunes and winning the 1959 election with his oft-quoted statement, 'You've never had it so good.' His premiership was brought to a close by a combination of the Profumo scandal (and others) and ill health. In 1960, he was elected Chancellor of Oxford University, a position he held until his death in 1986. Macmillan received the Order of Merit in 1976 and eventually accepted a hereditary peerage in 1984, when he became the Earl of Stockton. He had a strong link with the railway, having been one of the last directors of the Great Western before nationalisation in 1948. The obituary of former NUR General Secretary Sidney Greene (*Daily Telegraph*, 28 July 2004) recalled how, 'More than once, pay disputes culminated in peace talks at Downing Street with Harold Macmillan, a former GWR director. "We are all railwaymen together," Macmillan would say, and he enjoyed chatting with Greene, as another GWR man, about the comparative merits of King and Castle class locomotives.' On the advice of Richard Faulkner (co-author of this book), Peter Parker agreed in October 1979 that the BR rule that locomotives should not be named after living people should be waived. The naming of a Class 86 express electric locomotive (86232) *Harold Macmillan* was attended by Macmillan himself, at a ceremony at Euston station.

9   *HC Deb volume 619*, 10 March 1960, cc642-52.

10 Sir Ivan Stedeford (1897-1975) was a British industrialist who became Chairman and managing director of Tube Investments. After service in World War 1 with the Royal Naval Air Service, he returned to Birmingham and established Reeve & Stedeford, a motor dealership specialising in limousines and sports cars. Writing about him in *Conservative Viewpoint* in December 1963, Margaret Thatcher said, 'In 1960, Sir Ivan Stedeford became Chairman of an Advisory Group on British Transport and as a corollary of that group's work, radical reforms on the railways have now become possible.'

11 Sir Frank Kearton (1911-92), industrialist and scientist, was Chairman of Courtaulds from 1962-75 and played a major role in opposing the attempt by ICI to take over the company in 1961-62. He was ennobled as Lord Kearton in 1970.

12 Henry Benson (1909-95) was created Baron Benson in 1981. His mother had been the daughter of Francis Cooper, one of the founders of Coopers & Lybrand. In 1962, on Dr Beeching's recommendation, Benson carried out a study of the railway lines in Northern Ireland, on behalf of the Ulster Transport Authority. He recommended that they all be closed, with the exception of three Belfast commuter lines and the main line to the Republic of Ireland.

13 Sir David Serpell (1911-2008) joined the Ministry of Transport in 1960 as Deputy Secretary responsible for railways and roads. He became its Permanent Secretary in 1968 and retired in 1972, becoming a member of the British Railways Board from 1974-82.

14 *HC Deb volume 621*, 06 April 1960, cc393.

15 John Hay (1919-98), Conservative MP for Henley 1950-74, was remembered thus in the obituary written by Patrick Cosgrave for *The Independent* (6 February 1998): 'When you next use a parking meter, or cannot find a parking space next to one, bless, or curse, according to your inclination, John Hay.
'When you next want to get to a remote destination by rail, and find that the line was probably used by your parents, you will almost certainly curse Hay; for he was the junior minister at the Department of Transport – under the flamboyant Ernest Marples – who, over four years from the Conservative general election victory of 1959, devised and introduced meters, and it was he who implemented the swingeing cuts in the rail network which Lord Beeching recommended to the Government of Harold Macmillan. If you are sympathetic to so-called "green" issues, you may also blame Hay for being the executive minister who put in place the massive road-building programme visualised by Marples.'

16 National Archives MT 73/385.

17 *The Great Railway Conspiracy* by David Henshaw, Leading Edge, 1991.

18 Herbert Morrison (1888-1965) was created Lord Morrison of Lambeth in 1959. The Labour politician had served as Deputy Prime Minister, Home Secretary and Foreign Secretary, as well as Minister of Transport from 1929-31. He also became leader of London County Council in 1935, where his principal achievement was the creation of the London Passenger Transport Board, forerunner of today's Transport for London. Morrison unsuccessfully stood twice for the Labour Party leadership – in 1935, against Clement Attlee, and again in 1955, when Attlee retired. He was the grandfather of former Labour Cabinet minister Peter (later Lord) Mandelson.

19 The fifth Baron Chesham (1916-89) was a member of the Cavendish family and thus a kinsman of the Duke of Devonshire. He served as Joint Parliamentary Secretary to the Ministry of Transport from 1959-64, and was later Chairman of the International Road Federation, executive vice-Chairman of the Royal Automobile Club from 1966-70 and president of the British Road Federation from 1966-72.

20 Recommendation 5, September 1960.

21 Cmnd 1248.

22 *Report of the Railway Pay Committee of Inquiry*, Chairman C. W. Guillebaud, 2 March 1960. It took the view that railway staff were underpaid as compared with workers in other nationalised industries and recommended pay increases of between eight and 18 percent. If implemented, the report's recommendations would have cost around £40m.

23 Sir John Spencer Wills (1904-91), managing director of BET Ltd.

24 National Archives, MT 131.

25 Victor Collins (1903-71 – created Baron Stonham in 1958) was Labour MP for Taunton 1945-50 and for Shoreditch and Finsbury 1954-58. He served as a minister in the Home Office from 1964-70.

26 *HL Deb volume 250*, 20 June 1963, cc1466-85.

27 *Hansard HC Deb volume 674*, 27 March 1963, cc1319-27.

28 George Strauss (1901-93) was the MP for Vauxhall. Formerly a junior transport minister from 1945-47, he later became 'Father of the House' and was made a life peer in 1979.

29 Anthony Temple Bourne-Arton (1913-96) was the MP for Darlington from 1959-64. He took on the name 'Arton' as a condition of his marriage.

30 Sir John Francis Whitaker Maitland (1903-77) was Conservative MP for Horncastle from 1945-66.

31 (James) Harold Wilson (1916-95) was the leader of the Labour Party who won four general elections (1964, 1966, February and October 1974) out of five. MP for Ormskirk 1945-50 and Huyton 1950-83, he was an Oxford don at the age of 21 and, at 31, became the youngest Cabinet minister of the 20th century when he was made president of the Board of Trade in 1947. (He resigned in 1951 over the imposition of National Health Service charges.) Wilson's first thesis as an academic was a study of 19th-century commercial railway policy. Elected Labour leader following the death of Hugh Gaitskell in 1963, he served as Prime Minister from 1964-70 and 1974-76, and was ennobled as Lord Wilson of Rievaulx in 1983.

32 Archibald Clark Manuel (1901-76) was the Labour MP for Central Ayrshire 1950-55 and 1959-70. He was also a former engine driver and member of ASLEF.

33 In fact the rail service from Treherbert to Bridgend would be withdrawn in February 1968, because of the condition of the Rhondda tunnel. The southern section of the line from Bridgend to Maesteg would reopen with a through service from Cardiff in September 1993.

34 *Reshaping Report*, p.57.

35 *Reshaping Report*, p5.

36 John Hugh Hare, the First Viscount Blakenham (1911-82), was the Conservative MP for Woodbridge from 1945-50 and Sudbury and Woodbridge from 1950-63. He was ennobled in November 1963 and was Chairman of the Conservative Party at the time of the Reshaping Report.

37 Sir William Carrington, 1904-75, council member of the Institute of Chartered Accountants in England and Wales, and its president from 1955-56.

38 William Deedes (1913-2007) was the Conservative MP for Ashford 1950-74. A journalist and newspaper editor (of the *Daily Telegraph* for 12 years), later Baron Deedes of Aldington (1986), he was widely believed to be the model for William Boot, the journalist in Evelyn Waugh's novel *Scoop*. Deedes was also the fictionalised recipient of the spoof 'Dear Bill' letters from Denis Thatcher in *Private Eye*.

IV

IMPLEMENTING BEECHING

Major rail closures will be halted.

LABOUR PARTY MANIFESTO, 1964

Q. If you could bring something extinct back to life, what would you
   choose?
A. The railways axed by Beeching. – Julia Donaldson, children's
   laureate/author of *The Gruffalo*, Guardian Weekend, 13 August 2011

**Harold Wilson addressing the anti-Beeching rally
in Central Hall, Westminster, 25 June 1963 .**

The final two years of the 1959 Parliament were a period of political turmoil. Prime Minister Harold Macmillan had resigned after the Profumo scandal and a subsequent prostate cancer scare in October 1963. He was unexpectedly succeeded by a hereditary peer in the House of Lords – the 14th Earl of Home[1] – who was able to take advantage of a change in the law brought about by Tony Benn's[2] campaign to renounce his hereditary peerage in order to continue sitting in the House of Commons. Despite their change of leader, the Conservatives remained far behind in the polls and it looked very likely that Labour would win the general election, after 13 years in opposition.

There was therefore considerable interest in how Labour would react to the Beeching Report. Although some closures had already taken place by October 1964, when the election was called, there was still a lot to play for.

Initially, it appeared that Labour would halt the closure programme. At a huge rally at Central Hall, Westminster on 25 June 1963, a resolution was passed which attacked 'the folly of a policy which attempts to direct the future development of the railways solely on the basis of profit consideration'. According to a report in *The Times* the following day, 'Harold Wilson said the meeting was the national send-off to a great campaign to be organised by the Labour Party and the transport unions.

'The Labour Party said and the transport unions said no major decisions on closures should be made until a comparably ruthless survey of the transport system as a whole had been made. The plan as a whole should be referred for a full study of the national economic circumstances.'[3]

Harold Wilson expressed a similar commitment at a meeting in Liverpool during March 1964:

> We shall halt the main programme of rail closures – allowing, as we have said, individual closures to take place *in one or two clear cases* [authors' emphasis] – pending a national transport survey, relating the railway programme to the needs of national and regional expansion and to the requirements of a national integrated transport policy, covering roads and other forms of transport as well as railways.[4]

Harold Wilson's pledge to Whitby

There were many controversial closure proposals in the Beeching Report, but few attracted the degree of political attention granted to those for the Yorkshire town of Whitby. The town was then served by three railways, since the line along the coast from the north had closed in 1958: one from Middlesbrough to the north-west, one from Malton (on the main York to Scarborough line) to the south-west and one from the south, which ran up the coast from Scarborough.

Beeching had proposed the withdrawal of all three passenger services. Despite furious vocal opposition from in and around Whitby, BR had issued formal closure notices for these lines in February 1964. The North Riding County Council co-ordinated the opposition, helped by local weekly newspaper the *Whitby Gazette*, whose front page carried reports about the closure almost every week in 1964 and into the early part of 1965, sometimes devoting an entire page to the issue.

The Spa Pavilion in Whitby was the venue for two days of public hearings on 8 and 9 July 1964, covering all three proposals. The TUCC had acknowledged by this point that there had been a total of 2,260 objections – apparently a record.

The hearings appeared to go well for the objectors. There was much reference to the unreliability of bus services in winter weather,

to the needs of schoolchildren coming into Whitby and to the effect on the Whitby holiday trade if it lost its rail services. The TUCC reported in August that withdrawal of the Middlesbrough service would 'cause grave hardship not only to the many users but also to those whose business is very largely dependent upon providing for the large numbers of holiday makers who come to the area by train'. Their view on the other two closure proposals was similar, although the degree of hardship was described as 'serious' rather than 'grave'.

Unsurprisingly, the *Whitby Gazette* claimed a great victory and believed that its campaign had saved all three services. Three weeks later, however, jubilation turned to despair when Minister of Transport Marples announced that the Middlesbrough-Whitby line would be reprieved, but closure of the other two would go ahead.

As the general election approached, Peter Hardy[5], Labour candidate for Scarborough and Whitby, produced a letter written by Harold Wilson on 15 September to John Longbottom, Chairman of his prospective constituency's local Labour Party, which said that the two threatened lines to Whitby fell within the manifesto pledge of a moratorium on 'major closures'. The *Whitby Gazette* of 25 September reported the letter thus:

> I confirm that an obviously major decision such as the proposed Scarborough-Malton-Whitby rail closures would be covered by the statement in the Labour Party manifesto which is as follows:
>
> *Labour will draw up a national plan for transport covering the national networks of road, rail and canal communications, properly co-ordinated with air, coastal shipping and port services. The new regional authorities will be asked to draw up transport plans for their own areas. While these are being prepared, major rail closures will be halted.*

Nothing could have been clearer or more unambiguous. Wilson was saying that if Labour won the election, the two threatened lines to Whitby would be reprieved – at least until the regional plans had been prepared and published.

On 16 October 1964, Harold Wilson became Prime Minister for the first time after Labour secured a small overall majority of four seats. The expectation in Whitby – and in other towns facing closure of their railway lines – was that the new Government would move rapidly to rescind their predecessors' decision.

But within three weeks these hopes were to be dashed. The new Minister of Transport, Tom Fraser[6], came to the House of Commons on 4 November and made a statement. It started well enough:

> As the House knows, no passenger closure can take place without my consent. While regional transport plans are being prepared, I shall not consent to any major closure, by which I mean a closure which is likely to conflict with those plans. I shall accordingly consider all closure proposals against the background of future economic and population trends, taking fully into account the possible economic and social consequences, including road congestion.

As the statement went on, it became decreasingly hopeful:

> Honourable members on both sides of the House have asked me to stop closures to which my predecessor gave his consent, or to resume services already withdrawn. I am advised that I have no power under the Transport Act, 1962, to withdraw a consent

already given' or to insist on the restoration of a service already withdrawn. But I have power to vary or add to the conditions attached to those consents, and I shall not hesitate to do this where I think it desirable. [7]

These events were duly reported in the *Whitby Gazette*. On 27 November, defeated former Liberal candidate Richard Rowntree was quoted as saying that Labour had won votes in Whitby because of its promises on the future of the railway, and on 4 December a gloomy piece appeared headed 'Railway Closures Can Proceed'.

On 22 December Sir Alexander Spearman[8], who had been comfortably re-elected as Conservative MP for Scarborough and Whitby, asked the Prime Minister what representations he had received on Government action with regard to the closure of the Whitby rail lines and what replies he had sent. The subsequent exchange was reported in *Hansard* as follows:

> **The Prime Minister (Mr. Harold Wilson)** I have had representations from the Whitby Urban and Rural District Councils, three local associations, and four individuals, asking me to stop or postpone the closure of these services. The position as set out in my right honourable friend the Minister of Transport's statement on 4th November has been explained to them.

> **Sir A. Spearman** May I remind the Prime Minister that on 15th September he wrote to the Chairman of the Scarborough and Whitby Labour Party a personal letter, which was much publicised during the election...stating that these railway closures would be halted pending the new regional authority's report. My constituents expect him to fulfil that pledge.

> **The Prime Minister** Yes, sir, of course, the position was that when this Government took over, the decision had by that time been taken by the then minister. Under the terms of the 1962 Act we could not halt the closure which had already been decided. I do feel that an explanation is called for to those concerned, and I think the honourable gentleman should now inform Scarborough and Whitby and all stations between that he voted for the 1962 Act.

> **Sir A. Spearman** The Prime Minister must have known that when he made that pledge.[9]

> **Hon members** Answer.

The next, rather surreal development occurred exactly one month later, on 22 January 1965. Under the headline 'Rail Letter Callous Hoax', the newspaper reported that the Chairman of the Scarborough and Whitby Constituency Labour Party (the same John Longbottom who had received Harold Wilson's missive in September) was the recipient of a letter written on House of Commons paper, signed on behalf of Tom Fraser by 'Joan Hall', saying that the minister had decided to postpone the closures by five months from 8 March to 8 August (a curious date to choose, as it was in the middle of the summer holiday period). It did not take long to establish that the letter was a fake, and to this day no one has admitted sending it. At that same time, the press and PR department of British Railways' North Eastern Region put out a public notice confirming the closure date.

Wilson's promise to Whitby
A Scarborough to Middlesbrough train drops down the steeply graded chord from Prospect Hill to join the main Malton to Whitby line in September 1964, just a fortnight before Harold Wilson's letter confirmed the lines fell within Labour's moratorium on closures. It has travelled from Scarborough on the high-level line to the right, reversing at Whitby's West Cliff station beyond the signalbox. The telegraph wires, semaphore signals, signalbox and retaining walls in a deep cutting hint at the excellent engineering, but also at the high costs required to support the railways. Only the Esk Valley line remains to link the town to the national network, while steam trains on the successful North York Moors heritage railway which uses most of the former principal route to the town still run into Whitby packed with visitors.

The scene then switched back to the House of Commons and the indefatigable Spearman. Despite his earlier brush-off from the Prime Minister, he made one last effort to save the two lines to Whitby. On 9 February 1965, he introduced a '10-minute rule' bill in the Commons which would have enabled the Minister of Transport 'to rescind his consent to a closure of any station or of passenger rail services on any line':

> The purpose of my proposed Bill is to enable the Government to honour the written pledge made by the Prime Minister to my constituents on 15 September. During the election, and after the former Minister of Transport had consented to the closure of the Whitby-Scarborough and Whitby-Malton lines, the Prime Minister wrote to the Chairman of the Scarborough and Whitby

The peace of a Sunday morning in the Cotswolds is shattered, as explosive charges tear apart the viaduct at Dowdeswell on the Kingham-Cheltenham route in 1967. The toil of the navvies and the capital allocated by the prudent Great Western directors for the line's opening in 1881 are laid waste. Dramatic disinvestment of this kind rendered many routes valueless in the 1960s, justified on the savings in maintenance of the structures.

Labour Party. That letter pledged that a Labour Government would halt these particular closures while the new regional authorities prepared transport plans for their areas. That letter was published in the local paper, the *Whitby Gazette*, on 25 September, and I have with me a copy if anyone wants me to read it.

Now the Prime Minister states that the Government do not have the power to do this. His actual words to the House on 22 December were as follows: 'Under the terms of the 1962 Act we could not halt the closure which had already been decided.' It may be said that anyone expecting or hoping to become Prime Minister should not make a pledge unless he had, or intended to take, the power to enable him to carry it out. I am not, however, saying that the Prime Minister has broken this particular pledge – he has not broken it yet; but time is short. These lines are due to close on 8 March.

Last month, the Prime Minister's secretary wrote, on his instructions, to my constituents, a letter which was published in the local paper on 21 January. I want to quote one sentence from it: 'This decision, made by the former Minister of Transport in his concluding days of office, is a matter of great regret to us, for we would have wished, but for the 1962 Act, to stop these closures pending a broad review of transport problems which we are undertaking.' I suggest to the Prime Minister that there is a simple way out: he can accept my proposed Bill, which would enable him to do what he says he wants to do.

I hope that the Government will welcome the Bill. Indeed, I am quite sure that some honourable members opposite will do so. One of them, in fact, has asked to have his name on the Bill [Labour MP Ernest Popplewell[10]]. I ask the Government to welcome it. I ask them to provide time to see it through all its stages. Then, the Prime Minister can fulfil the pledge which he gave on 15 September so clearly, so precisely and so unconditionally.

I realise that except for those of us who are directly concerned, the Whitby railways are a comparatively small matter, but for a Prime Minister to make a positive pledge and fail to fulfil it is not a small matter for any of us who believe in democratic Government.[11]

Spearman's Bill stood no chance of making progress unless the Government were prepared to take it over and fast-track it through all its stages in both Houses of Parliament.

Fraser's intransigence

Cabinet records discovered in the National Archives reveal that the Government did consider adopting the Spearman Bill. In a paper considered at a Cabinet meeting in March 1965, Fraser stated that he was being pressed by backbenchers to do three things:

(a) to halt all passenger closures,
(b) to halt all freight closures,
(in both cases at least until Lord Hinton's study[12] is completed)
(c) to accept in some form Sir Alexander Spearman's Bill which would give me power to rescind consents already given to passenger closures.

This pressure, I am convinced, is based largely on a misunderstanding of our policy and the place of railways in a modern co-ordinated transport system. I recommend that it should be resisted.

Fraser's paper stated:

Opposition to passenger closures has always existed. It stems in part from local people (whether or not they use the trains) and from their Members, in the area of each particular closure proposal as it comes up; in part it comes from the railway employees affected. Even the modifications and restrictions which I announced have not significantly diminished it, but it has recently intensified because of two misconceptions over our own principles – the fact that closures are still going in spite of our 'pledge' (everyone regards his own line as 'major')
[*Note the use of inverted commas around the word 'pledge' – a lot of*

people voted Labour in October 1964 expecting the Beeching closures to be halted.]

my 'failure' to prevent closures agreed by my predecessor from taking place or to take powers to rescind closures which he gave.

The attitude of those directly affected is natural and understandable; but that is not to say that it is in the national interest. Moreover I think it is easy to exaggerate the support for these views in the country. I believe that informed opinion accepts the case for modernising our railway system and pruning little-used lines.

The closure programme is not just an end in itself, though we must not forget the very large financial advantages which it could bring; these were estimated in the board's 1963 Report at up to £40 million per annum … The programme is even more important as an integral part of the reshaping of our railways. The present system is largely the result of unplanned, competitive private enterprise growth in Victorian times, and it needs drastic pruning and replanning for the needs of the second half of this century.

Fraser goes on to claim that he was 'already holding up "major closures" in accordance with our election pledge', citing his refusal of consent to the closure of the Manchester-Bury electric line and the Glasgow-Edinburgh via Shotts service. 'I am insisting that the East Lincolnshire services, particularly to the holiday resorts, should be maintained for the time being.' The conclusions in his paper were unambiguous:

> Our present policy is sound. We lean over backwards to protect the individual from hardship and to avoid prejudicing future regional planning or the study on transport co-ordination. The Railways Board deal generously with their staff who are affected by offering other jobs (with transfer grants) or adequate redundancy compensation. I see our present rail policy as an integral part of the Government's plans for modernising the economy. Redeployment of labour is vital to our economic growth.
> I recommend we stand firm.

The minutes of the subsequent Cabinet discussion of 11 March 1965 (marked 'SECRET' and also available in the National Archives) show that other ministers supported Fraser's approach. It was suggested that a small number of closure 'proposals should be brought forward in the near future for rejection'. However, the Railways Board had 'preferred to withdraw one case of this kind rather than allow it to be rejected,' believed to have been the Liverpool-Southport line – now an essential element in the electrified Merseyrail system. With astonishing cynicism, the Cabinet minutes assert that 'proposals of this kind, when submitted, should provide the minister with an opportunity to demonstrate the Government's readiness to reject closures which were incompatible with regional transport plans'.

Barbara Castle comments on this Cabinet discussion in her diaries[13], describing it as 'protracted':

> Apparently he [Fraser] is under tremendous pressure from our people to stop them all and he asked for permission to stick by a previous announcement to halt only the major ones. Frank Cousins[14] had some strong things to say about the need to make a reality of our integrated transport policy. Finally, at Harold's

suggestion, it was agreed that closures should in future be referred to the Regional Councils for study and recommendation.

These Cabinet records demonstrate beyond all doubt that closure of the two lines to Whitby – and a number of others at the same time – went ahead because Labour ministers had decided to go back on their election manifesto commitment 'to halt major closures'. One fundamental principle of our democracy is that no Parliament may bind its successors, and it is always open to a new Government to change a law through Parliament if it wishes to do so. In the case of the lines to Whitby, it would probably not have been necessary for the law to be changed, or for Spearman's Bill to be passed, in order to save them – Fraser could easily have used the powers granted him by the 1962 Transport Act to vary conditions attached to the closure decision, such as placing a much more onerous obligation on bus companies to provide alternative services. The decision not to intervene was followed by the implementation of many other Beeching-inspired closures, as the following table illustrates – showing how many miles of railway were closed on a year-by-year basis:

Table C: Route miles closed by year and by administration

Year	Route miles closed	Route miles closed to passengers	Stations and goods depots closed	Minister of Transport
1956	40	29	100	Watkinson **C**
1957	64	50	50	Watkinson **C**
1958	118	168	130	Watkinson **C**
1959	289	391	192	Watkinson **C**
1960	137	198	178	Marples **C**
1961	170	168	123	Marples **C**
1962	437	782	297	Marples **C**
1963	501	284	399	Marples **C**
Beeching Reshaping Report				
1964	1005	961	398	Marples/Fraser **C/L**
1965	1067	786	355	Fraser/Castle **L**
1966	1127	719	264	Castle **L**
1967	562	183	110	Castle **L**
1968	748	411	137	Castle/Marsh **L**
1969	405	96	84	Marsh/Mulley
1970	310	280	86	Mulley/Peyton **L/C**

Source: BTC and BRB Annual Reports and Accounts.

Notes: 1) *Where route miles closed to passengers exceed total route miles closed in any one year, the balance remained open for freight/parcels. Where they are less, the 'route miles closed' figure includes freight-only lines.*
2) *No separate figures for passenger stations are shown in the annual reports during the period shown. The figures are complicated by frequent 'adjustments' which make year-on-year comparisons difficult.*

Regional resistance

The pace of preparing and implementing closure cases was relentless as the momentum of the programme increased. Many working railwaymen were strongly opposed to the changes being forced on the industry. Some managers, however, saw it as inevitable if the railway was to survive. Dick Hardy, then district running and maintenance engineer at Stratford, summed up the feeling of inevitability:

> Many of us knew what to expect, some were frightened by those long, long lists of stations and lines and some saw it as an intolerable betrayal by a man who cared nothing for the great railway industry.

Most of us shrugged and got on with the job for we knew, although things would never be the same again, that Beeching was right.[15]

While regional General Managers were committed to the process, not all agreed with every closure they were asked to implement. Detailed evaluation of the Yatton-Clevedon branch line showed that the losses were smaller and the contributory revenue greater than the figures produced by the BRB team. The board nevertheless pressed for closure, which took place in 1966.

As early as that same year, with the appointment of Gerry Fiennes as General Manager of the Eastern Region, a serious attempt was made to reduce or eliminate the losses on secondary routes by running them as a 'basic railway'. This involved:

· Pay train operation, with simplified (and lower) fares issued by the guard with intermediate station staff withdrawn.
· Intensive use of DMUs.
· Reducing track and signalling to the minimum required to operate the service, including singling double-track sections.

This approach was used on the King's Lynn-Hunstanton and Ipswich-Lowestoft lines. The former was still closed in 1969, despite the investment made in track rationalisation and automation of level crossings. Today, Hunstanton bitterly regrets the loss of its railway and its development is hampered by chronic congestion on the A149. The East Suffolk line, however, survived and prospered (see Chapter 6). The pay train approach was extended to many other local services over the next few years. A similar approach was adopted by David McKenna[16] on the Southern Region who thought the Ashford-Hastings and Alton-Winchester lines were worth retaining.

Electrified lines

Electrification was no guarantee of immunity from closure. As early as 1951, the Commission took the view that it was not worthwhile to renew the electrical supply system for trains running to Holcombe Brook in Lancashire. While reinvestment was taking place in the Manchester-Bury line (now part of Manchester Metrolink), Bury-Holcombe Brook reverted to steam operation for the last year of its life, before closing to passengers on 4 May 1952. Other electrified lines that closed included:

Nunhead-Crystal Palace High Level	1954
Acton Town-South Acton(London Transport)	1959
Haywards Heath-Horsted Keynes[17]	1963
Southport-Crossens	1964
Lancaster Green Ayre-Morecambe Promenade	1966
Manchester Piccadilly-Sheffield Victoria[18]	1970
Elmers End-Selsdon/Sanderstead	1983
Broad Street-Dalston Junction	1986
Epping-Ongar (LT)	1994
Aldwych-Holborn (LT)	1994
Watford High Street-Croxley Green[19]	1996

The social effects of Beeching

It was a major failure of the time not to make any assessment of the social or economic value of the railway to the communities it served –17 years would pass before there was an intellectually respectable study. When it came, however, it would be worth waiting for.

Carried out by Mayer Hillman and Anne Whalley on behalf of the Policy Studies Institute and paid for by the British Railways Board, The

Social Consequences of Rail Closures sought to find out what happens to a community when it loses its rail services. After considering 47 lines closed in the 10 years from 1968 to 1978, the authors chose 10 that they felt 'were broadly representative of the different characteristics of rural lines':

    Haltwhistle-Alston
    Maiden Newton-Bridport
    Paignton-Kingswear
    Alton-Winchester
    Exeter-Okehampton
    Keswick-Carlisle
    Cambridge-St Ives
    Bangor-Caernarfon
    Dundee-Newport-on-Tay
    Edinburgh-Hawick-Carlisle.

The study concentrated on former rail users living along one part of each closed line; sample sizes ranged from 250-450 and yielded 79-99 successful interviews in the case of each line. The findings showed, unsurprisingly, that there had 'been most curtailment among those who made most use of the line':

The impact has been socially regressive, for it is the older people, those without cars and those in blue-collar households who have cut back most on their activity and thus who are the hardest hit. Women have been harder hit than men.

The principal explanation for the substantial changes in former patterns of activity recorded in the survey can be attributed to the partial failure of the new or augmented bus services to provide an adequate alternative to the withdrawn rail services. The inadequacy of these services is most obviously revealed in the fact that less than half of the former rail users transferred to these bus services at all after closure, and those that did so did not transfer all their journeys, but stopped making some of them. Perhaps still more revealing, whilst car owners found the train as acceptable as the car for some of their journeys, they clearly did not feel the same way about the bus.

The conclusions go on to describe why people prefer trains to buses: rail has the advantage when it comes to carrying prams, pushchairs or bulky goods; other factors include 'problems of travel sickness, the absence of shelters or waiting rooms at stops, and by no means least, the lack of toilets needed by some people on longer journeys'.

'The only possible conclusion that can be drawn, therefore … is that, necessary as the buses are for people without cars, they cannot serve as adequate substitutes for rail.'

Given such conclusive findings, it is astonishing that both the Department of Transport and the British Railways Board continued to go down the bus substitution route throughout the 1980s, almost up to the privatisation of the railways (as will be demonstrated in Chapter 14). There is also an immense irony in the fact that one of the routes studied by Hillman and Whalley was Cambridge-St Ives, which has recently been converted into a busway (not without controversy – also see Chapter 14).

Closed lines today

Having witnessed a number of closures at first hand from the 1950s to the 1970s, the authors recall the sense of disappointment and sadness as each line succumbed. This was coupled with a feeling of inevitability

about this juggernaut of a process which, it appeared, no argument, however cogent, could counter.

Most lines were seen off in style, to the accompaniment of exploding detonators, a wreath on the smokebox door of the locomotive or, in some cases, a brass band or a coffin with pallbearers. Come the following Monday, however, the awful truth would dawn on the staff that had worked on the lines and the passengers that had used them: they were cut off and somehow life would never be the same again.

The fears were well enunciated by the Squire in the classic Ealing comedy *The Titfield Thunderbolt*, when he addresses the public inquiry into the light railway order which would allow the villagers to run the line themselves, and it seemed that the inspector was about to turn them down:

'Don't you realise you are condemning our village to death? Open it up to buses and lorries, and what is it going to be like in five years' time? Our lanes will be concrete roads, our houses will have numbers instead of names, there will be traffic lights and zebra crossings, and that will be twice as dangerous.'

And for many with fond memories of a gentler way of life, that is exactly what happened.

The huge disinvestment in rail facilities, particularly in the period from the 1950s to the 1970s, should have opened up opportunities to use valuable sites and transport corridors, but in practice these opportunities were missed. There was certainly pressure to use rail routes as roads (see Chapter 14), but in general the closed lines were not in areas where new roads were required. Many valuable city centre sites might have adapted stations or used new construction to create iconic buildings as part of the urban environment. At the very least, local or central Government might have taken the time to consider how best use could be made of the unique opportunities offered by line closures on such a massive scale.

In fact this did not happen, and it was left to BR, through its property subsidiary, to obtain the best price possible through disposal of land. The only consistent Government objectives for BR were to maximise the value of non-operational property. It turned into a fire sale, with relatively low prices obtained and little imagination shown in finding uses for old railway lines and station sites.

There are exceptions, of course. The St Enoch shopping centre in Glasgow is of high quality, even if not as impressive as the former Glasgow & South Western Railway station. G-Mex is an imaginative use of the Midland Railway's Central station in Manchester and the British Library has provided a facility of international importance on the site of the Midland's Somers Town goods depot at St Pancras. Bristol's Old Station has been carefully preserved and some imaginative conversions have been made, such as Southport Lord Street and Nottingham Victoria (shopping centres), Green Park station in Bath (Sainsbury superstore), Richmond in Yorkshire (community arts centre and artisan food market) and Morecambe Promenade (Tourist Information office, pub/restaurant and community space). Many smaller station sites have become housing developments, or else the station buildings themselves have been retained and lived in.

In some cases, use has been made of surplus space at stations to provide a good bus/rail interchange, as at Hull and Bradford, while some lines have found alternative transport uses as roads, as at Bournemouth West, part of the former Great Western branch between Martock and Yeovil, or even the little Westerham branch, buried beneath the M25 between junctions 5 and 6.

In 1977, a charity called Cyclebag, with the support of local authorities, was able to create the Bristol to Bath Cyclepath – a 17-mile section of the former Midland Railway route between the two cities that had been closed six years before. Part of this cycle/pedestrian route is shared with the Avon Valley heritage railway. The initiative was very successful and the concept was widely adopted, leading to formation of the National Cycle Network, formally launched in 1995. Promoted by Sustrans, this now covers 12,000 miles of route across the country, a third of which was built on former railway formations, or along canal towpaths, with money from the National Lottery Fund and local authorities. This is a very creative use of former branch lines and keeps the routes intact as transport corridors for the benefit of future generations. Extensions are still being made and expensive challenges overcome, such as the 'Two Tunnels' project in Bath. This £1.9 million project provides a new route south from the city using Devonshire and Combe Down tunnels and Tucking Mill viaduct on the former Somerset & Dorset line to meet the National Cycle Network at Midford.

(Chapter 16 tells of the reopening of a number of closed lines as heritage railways and Chapter 14 of the attempts to convert lines into roads.)

Unusual uses for closed railways include a rifle range in a tunnel in Bristol (on the line to Hotwells, closed in 1921), while other tunnels are used for growing mushrooms. St Boniface Down tunnel on the Isle of Wight carries Ventnor's water supply, while the old Woodhead tunnel through the Pennines carries cables for the National Grid. On part of the formation of the former Oxford-Cambridge line, near Old North Road in Cambridgeshire, sit the tracks carrying the Mullard radio telescopes belonging to Cambridge University. The station building at Pocklington serves as a school sports hall. A few stations have even been converted to boutique hotels, such as Petworth in West Sussex, while others are pubs or restaurants.

Some railway bridges have been retained and used to carry road traffic. Most striking of these is the bridge that carried the Ballachulish branch of the Caledonian Railway across Loch Etive and today forms part of the A828. In Lancaster, the former Midland Railway bridge across the River Lune at Green Ayre now carries the A683, while in Lincolnshire the A17 crosses the River Nene on the former M&GN swing bridge, with its control room atop the girders still looking like a well-kept railway signalbox.

Disappointingly, many other station sites have just ended up as car parks, as at Blackpool Central and South but also at smaller towns such as Devizes, Hunstanton or St Andrews. Others have been the subject of low-grade development, usually as warehousing or industrial units, or as supermarkets. Many have ended us as council depots, as at Rhayader in Powys, or as builders' merchants yards like Watton in Norfolk. Many remained open as coal yards for domestic fuel for many years after closure, until demand fell as people switched to electric, gas or oil-fired central heating in their homes.

Many other lines were sold in piecemeal plots, breaking the continuity of the routes and generally leaving the liabilities (such as tunnels and viaducts) to BR. BRB Residuary has some 4,000 structures in what is known as its 'burdensome estate', a phrase which sadly emphasises the lack of vision of earlier Governments which failed to put the routes to better use. It costs the taxpayer £7.5 million[20] a year to maintain these structures in a safe condition and is part of a continuing legacy of costs never foreseen by politicians and civil servants, who rushed to close down so much of the network half a century ago.

1   Alexander Frederick Douglas-Home (1903-95) was known as Baron Home of the Hirsel KT, PC, the Earl of Home from 1951-63 and Sir Alec Douglas-Home from 1963-74. He served as Conservative MP for Lanark from 1931-45 and from 1950-51, after which he had to step down on succeeding his father as the 14th Earl. In 1935, Prime Minister Neville Chamberlain had appointed Home his parliamentary private secretary, whereupon he accompanied Chamberlain to Munich to meet Hitler in 1938. From 1955-63, he was successively Commonwealth Secretary, Leader of the House of Lords and Foreign Secretary. He unexpectedly became Prime Minister on 18 October 1963, on the resignation of Macmillan – the last peer ever to obtain that office. After five days he renounced his peerage; two weeks later he was elected MP for Kinross and West Perthshire in a by-election. After the Conservatives' defeat in October 1964, Home became Leader of the Opposition, eventually resigning in July 1965. He made a comeback in 1970, when Edward Heath won the election and Home once again became Foreign Secretary, serving until 1974. He later returned to the Lords with a life peerage. Home was the only Prime Minister to have played first class cricket – for Oxford University (where he took a Third, saying later, 'I'm afraid I spent rather too much time at the wicket'), Middlesex and the MCC.

2   Anthony Neil Wedgwood Benn (born 1925) held a series of Labour ministerial offices in the 1964-70 and 1974-79 Wilson and Callaghan Governments. MP for Bristol South East 1950-60, he was disqualified as a member of the House of Commons by succeeding to his father's peerage as the second Viscount Stansgate. Benn subsequently campaigned for the law to be changed so that peers could renounce their titles; his campaign's success in 1963 returned him to the Commons after a by-election, following his successor Malcolm St Clair's honoured promise to stand down if the peerage law were changed. Benn's Bristol South East seat was abolished in boundary changes in 1983; having been beaten in a selection contest for the safe Bristol South, he stood for the neighbouring seat of Bristol East and lost to the Conservatives. He returned to the Commons after a by-election in Chesterfield in 1984, and later retired in 2001, 'leaving parliament in order to spend more time on politics', as he put it. Following Labour's defeat in 1979, Benn had been the de facto leader of the party's left wing; he came within less than 1% of defeating Denis Healey for the deputy leadership in 1981. Causes he espoused included withdrawal from the EEC and abolition of the House of Lords and the monarchy. In 1987, he stood for the leadership but was defeated by a substantial margin. Benn has written eight volumes of diaries, undertaken numerous one-man stage shows and become a popular figure with middle-class audiences, despite having been the principal cause of Labour's unelectability in the 1980s. Although he gave him a number of significant high-profile jobs in Government, Harold Wilson memorably said of him, 'Tony immatures with age.'

3   The Times, 26 June 1963, p9.

4   'The Railways and the Election' by Ian Waller, Modern Railways, October 1964, p233.

5   Peter Hardy (1931-2003) was the Labour MP for Rother Valley from 1970-83 and Wentworth from 1983-97. (He also unsuccessfully contested Scarborough and Whitby in 1964 and Sheffield Hallam in 1970.) Ennobled as Lord Hardy of Wath in

1997, the former schoolteacher was passionate and knowledgeable about wildlife and conservation. He was also the parliamentary private secretary to Tony Crosland from 1974-77.

6   Tom Fraser (1911-88) was Labour MP for Hamilton and Minister of Transport from 1964-65. He left Parliament in 1967 to become Chairman of the North of Scotland Hydro-Electric Board. Ironically, the service from Hamilton to Coalburn closed during his period as Transport Minister, although Hamilton remained linked to Glasgow by the Blue Trains.

7   HC Deb, volume 701, 4 November 1964, cc195-203.

8   Alexander Cadwallader Mainwaring Spearman (1901-82) was the Conservative MP for Scarborough and Whitby 1941-66. He served briefly as a parliamentary private secretary from 1951-52 and was knighted in 1956.

9   HC Deb volume 704, 22 December 1964, cc1045-6.

10 Ernest Popplewell (1899-1977) – Labour MP for Newcastle upon Tyne West 1945-66, Government whip from 1947-51 and ennobled as Lord Popplewell in 1966 – was a former railway signalman.

11 HC Deb volume 706, 09 February 1965, cc210-1.

12 Lord Hinton of Bankside joined the Ministry of Transport as a special adviser on transport planning. Announcing his appointment, Fraser told the House of Commons, 'The task Lord Hinton will undertake is, broadly speaking, to inquire into the means whereby and the extent to which the transport of goods and passengers in Great Britain can best be co-ordinated and developed in the national interest.' HC Deb volume 706, 08 February 1965, c30.

13 The Castle Diaries, Weidenfeld & Nicolson 1984, p19.

14 Frank Cousins (1904-86) was general secretary of the Transport and General Workers' Union 1956-69, Minister of Technology in Harold Wilson's first Government (1964-66) and MP for Nuneaton (1965-66). He found the House of Commons and ministerial office uncongenial, finally returning to his old trade union job at the TGWU.

15 Beeching, Champion of the Railway? by R. H. N. Hardy, Ian Allan Publishing, 1989.

16 David McKenna (1911-2003) was General Manager of BR's Southern Region from 1963-68, and then for a further 10 years a member of the British Railways Board. He was the son of the Liberal MP Reginald McKenna who, between 1908 and 1916, was successively First Lord of the Admiralty, Home Secretary and Chancellor of the Exchequer under Asquith.

17 The line from Haywards Heath (Copyhold Junction) to Ardingly was retained for aggregates traffic, but the third rail was removed.

18 The local service from Manchester Piccadilly to Hadfield and Glossop remains electrified. The remainder of the route to Sheffield remained open for freight, but was closed completely in 1981 (see Chapter 5).

19 Currently to be largely reinstated as part of a new link connecting the Metropolitan Line's Croxley and Watford branch to Watford Junction.

20 BRB Residuary Annual Report, 31 March 2011.

V

THE TRUNK ROUTES REPORT

*'The overall demand for rail transport over the trunk routes
could show an appreciable increase in the next 20 years.'*

THE DEVELOPMENT OF THE MAJOR RAILWAY TRUNK ROUTES (FEBRUARY 1965) – CONCLUSIONS, P45

'Surplus capacity' at Seaton Junction
Looking east in 1968, the daily Brighton-Plymouth express races through Seaton Junction while a steam
locomotive positions milk tank wagons from London in the up sidings. The connection to the Seaton branch
can be seen on the right. Only a single track runs through the site today.

The first Beeching Report made the greatest impact, with the media concentrating on branch line closures. The second, on trunk routes, followed two years later (in 1965) and was a more modest presentation – although it had more significant consequences.

The latter report set out to eliminate the duplication of trunk routes resulting from the competition of an earlier age. Inevitably, it was treated by the press as a blueprint for further closures. Although in retrospect a remarkable document, it hobbled the railway in terms of the capacity needed to meet further growth from the 1990s onwards, even more than the first report. Today, the urgent need for additional infrastructure is evidenced by the Government's proposals for a high speed network, replicating in modern form the capacity that was destroyed following the second report in 1965.

In the context of the day it was, as with the Reshaping Report, a competent analysis of traffic flows of the time and of the need to reshape the network to reduce its cost. It looked ahead 20 years, to 1984, and did indeed forecast a doubling of long haul (over 100 miles) freight and intercity passenger traffic over this period. It did not, however, consider the need for diversionary routes to accommodate incidents or pre-planned engineering work, and was predicated on the basis of substantial investment in chosen routes – an assumption persistently challenged by the civil servants (as we shall see in Chapter 7).

Clearing the way for InterCity

It has to be acknowledged that the withdrawal of main line stopping trains and the closure of small goods yards at wayside stations on main lines paved the way for the development of InterCity services, from 1966 onwards. Even with the goods refuge sidings and passenger loops that then existed, and with diesel traction rather than steam, it simply would not have been possible to find paths for the speed and frequency of service that would form the basis of the InterCity network in the 1980s and 1990s – let alone today.

On the Great Western main line beyond Didcot (where the four tracks gave way to two), for example, intermediate stations and goods yards to Swindon were cleared away, as were stations between Peterborough and Grantham or Berwick and Dunbar on the East Coast main line. On the Southern Region, where most intermediate stations remained, speeds of the fast services were noticeably slower and remain so today, except in Kent (where HS1 has reduced journey times to Ashford and beyond considerably). One current example, Welwyn North on the East Coast Main Line, illustrates the problem of an intermediate station at a two-track bottleneck on an otherwise four-track high-speed intercity railway.

The pattern of service in the 1950s had been of relatively infrequent steam expresses, with variable timings, but with one or two headline

named trains a day running on very fast schedules, such as the *Elizabethan* and the *Bristolian*. This was replaced with regular-interval (usually hourly) diesel or electrically hauled intercity trains with consistent stopping patterns and timings, from the 1970s onwards.

Surplus capacity grant

Capacity was further degraded by dequadrification (reducing four running lines to two) and the removal of running loops, with additional funding provided by Government for 'track rationalisation' under a provision in the Transport Act of 1968. A total of £15 million was to be made available to BR in 1969, tapering away to nothing by 1974. The elimination of such a level of excess track capacity was once again only possible because of the withdrawal of local passenger services, particularly the closure of local goods yards and the end of many local trip workings. Beyond that, the grant was certainly helpful in terms of removing a lot of ironwork once required for the steam railway, now superfluous to a network run by diesel units. However, the reduction in running line capacity has proved to be a real constraint for today's much busier railway.

The press assumed that lines not listed in the report as 'for development' were slated for closure. Some indeed did close, such as the Great Central, the Waverley route, the Woodhead route (despite being one of those selected for development in the Trunk Routes Report), the Southern route to Plymouth and the Caledonian route from Stanley Junction to Kinnaber Junction. In other cases, the lines remained open but were substantially downgraded and partly singled.

The approach was well summarised by Gerry Fiennes, then General Manager of the Western Region, when speaking about the Salisbury-Exeter line: 'The price of survival was assent to the closure of the small stations, and to the pruning of the railway to single line, simplified signalling and at stations to bare essentials of buildings and staff.'[1]

In other cases, such as Settle-Carlisle and Newport-Shrewsbury-Crewe, routes did not keep pace with changing technology. Even today, some still have long headways and even some semaphore signalling.

Trunk route closures

The late 1960s saw the closure of a number of strategic routes, many of which have subsequently been reopened in whole or in part, or where reopening has been considered to meet the capacity required by today's railway. The principal examples follow below listed by closure date.

Subsequently reopened:
- Pontefract-Wakefield, 2 January 1967.
- Erewash Valley (Trent-Chesterfield), 2 January 1967.
- Kettering-Nottingham via Corby, 1 May 1967. (Kettering-Corby reopened to passengers; Manton Junction-Oakham retained for Peterborough-Leicester-Birmingham service).
- Birmingham Moor Street-Snow Hill, 4 March 1968. (Snow Hill station and route to Wolverhampton closed 6 March 1972.)

Quart in a pint pot
Photographed from the cab of the 'Cornish Riviera' in April 1970, two Southern region 2-Bil units are squeezed into platform 4a at Reading with the site of Reading (Southern) station in the background, then in use as a car park. The four-platform station had been closed five years previously, but 4a was inadequate to handle both the Waterloo and Redhill services and a second platform (4b) was added in 1975 which also served the Reading-Gatwick Airport service, introduced in 1980. Today a third platform has been added to handle growing demand.

- Chippenham-Trowbridge, 6 May 1968.
- Stirling-Dunfermline via Alloa, 7 October 1968.
- Romsey-Eastleigh, 5 May 1969.

Reopening examined (in the context of Government, rail industry or local authority studies):

- Great Central/Aylesbury/Ashendon Junction-Rugby, Woodford Halse-Banbury and Nottingham-Sheffield, 5 September 1966. Rugby-Nottingham, 5 May 1969.
- Harrogate-Ripon-Northallerton, 6 March 1967.
- Oxford-Cambridge, 1 January 1968.
- Exeter-Plymouth (Okehampton-Bere Alston), 6 May 1968.
- Midland Main Line to Manchester (Matlock-Chinley), 1 July 1968. Chinley-Manchester (Central), 5 May 1969.
- Waverley route, Edinburgh-Carlisle, 6 January 1969. (Work is now under way on reopening Newcraighall-Tweedbank as the Borders Railway project.)
- Uckfield-Lewes, 24 February 1969.

Closed, without reopening or review:
- Perth-Aberdeen (Stanley Junction-Kinnaber Junction), 4 September 1967.
- Cheltenham Spa-Stratford-on-Avon, 25 March 1968. (Partly reopened as Gloucestershire & Warwickshire heritage railway.)

In other cases, major investment in the remaining routes has been necessary to replicate the capacity lost during this period. For example, a third platform has been added at Bristol Parkway and a fourth is planned to provide for traffic growth and the capacity lost when the Bristol-Yate via Mangotsfield line was shut in 1969. Huge investment has gone into the West Coast Main Line and more is planned for the East Coast Main Line to provide more capacity for freight that might have been routed via the Great Central or the Midland route to Manchester.

Perhaps the most damaging period in terms of cutting the capability of the network was in 1970, with no fewer than six strategic routes losing their passenger services on the same day (5 January of that year):

1. Woodhead route (Manchester-Sheffield electrified service), including Sheffield Victoria station. The route closed to freight in July 1981.
2. Burton Salmon-Castleford-Normanton.
3. Cowdenbeath-Perth via Kinross.
4. Calder Valley Line, Mirfield-Brighouse-Sowerby Bridge.
5. Rose Hill, Marple-Macclesfield.
6. The former Midland Railway Birmingham-Bristol line between Yate and Bristol via Mangotsfield was due to close on the same day, but services were withdrawn from 27 December 1969 because of a landslip.

The Peterborough-Boston-Grimsby route closed on 5 October that year, after the summer season, although Boston-Firsby remained for the Skegness service (from Grantham) and the section between Ludborough and North Thoresby is now the Lincolnshire Wolds heritage railway.

From small acorns …
One of the quietest spots in rural Essex on Easter Monday 1971 was Cressing station on the Braintree branch. The signalbox, the level crossing gates pushed by hand, the telegraph wires and the post for the oil lamp all suggest a leisurely rural existence on this byway from the junction at Witham, served by two-car diesel units. Who would have foreseen that, 40 years later, the line would be electrified and carrying 12-car trains to Liverpool Street?

Putting back the track

In almost every case, the Trunk Routes Report was even more damaging to today's railway than the first Beeching Report, creating bottlenecks which have either been opened up again at significant cost or await funding to replace capacity lost in the 1960s and 1970s. Examples include:

Reconstruction of Birmingham Snow Hill in 1987 and the reopening of Moor Street bay platforms in 2010, as it became apparent that New Street had inadequate capacity to handle the demands placed on it.

Reading (Southern), with its four platforms, was closed in 1965 and its trains transferred to a single new platform, 4a at Reading General. An office block was built on the site of the old station. Subsequently, a second platform had to be added to handle the number of trains running and construction of a third platform has now been undertaken, to handle growing demand from the Wokingham direction.

A partial redoubling scheme costing £70 million for the Cotswold line (Oxford-Worcester) was completed in 2011.

Redoubling the line between Swindon and Kemble is among plans for delivery during the current control period (up to 2014).

Additional capacity has been progressively restored between Salisbury and Exeter, starting with a down loop between Templecombe and Yeovil Junction added at the outset to the original minimalist proposal, followed by a second platform at Yeovil Junction, Tisbury loop and the extended loop at Axminster. The latter allows an hourly service to be provided throughout and a half-hourly service as far west as Yeovil Junction.

Some additional loops and reinstatement of double track on the Highland main line (Perth to Inverness) took place as early as the 1970s, as a result of increased demand on the line with the development of North Sea oil. Capacity has subsequently been increased on the Glasgow & South Western route from Kilmarnock to Dumfries and Carlisle for trains of imported coal through Clydeport.

---

1 *I Tried to Run a Railway* by G. F. Fiennes, Ian Allan Publishing, 1967.

VI

ESTABLISHING THE SOCIAL RAILWAY 1968-74

'Round the table the others were in favour of the £300,000 subsidy, because three seats were in danger in central Wales.'

THE DIARIES OF A CABINET MINISTER BY RICHARD CROSSMAN[1]

Saved by the politics
The Central Wales line, built to give the L&NWR access to Swansea and West Wales, was saved on more than one occasion by the fact that its long, straggling route served seven constituencies, some of them marginal. Today, it is a rural lifeline and the limited train service is full, thanks to active support by the Heart of Wales Line forum. Seen in June 1960, the 6.15am from Swansea Victoria has just crossed Knucklas viaduct in Radnorshire, before crossing into Shropshire on its way to Shrewsbury.

The strong public reaction to the 1963 Beeching Report, and the Trunk Routes Report two years later, had a political effect, as did pressure from constituency MPs and pressure groups. It was accompanied by reaction from railway staff, many of whom were not persuaded of the value of some proposed closures. Indeed, detailed examination of some of the routes showed that it would be financially more prudent to retain them, either because of the value of their contributory revenue or because the savings achievable were insignificant.

It also led to the creation of the remarkably entitled Society for the Reinvigoration of Unremunerative Branch Lines in the United Kingdom (known more succinctly today as Railfuture). The National Council on Inland Transport played an important role in the debate too, while a few local campaigning groups formed to support individual lines. At that time, however, consumers did not assert their rights as they would today, and at national level there was no railway lobby group to command similar political attention to the Road Haulage Association.

Revolving doors

As we have seen, the Labour Government of 1964-70 found it difficult to develop a distinct policy towards the railway. The election commitment to halt the programme of closures was effectively abandoned following Tom Fraser's disgraceful paper to the Cabinet in March 1965, but nothing coherent was put in its place. The pursuit of 'integrated transport policy' remained the party's priority, but what it meant depended on which sectional interest was being promoted. To the rail trade unions it was halting railway closures, encouraging the transfer of freight from road to rail and promoting local bus services (but not in place of trains). The Transport and General Workers Union, on the other hand, was happy to be part of the road lobby, encouraging motorway building, the unrestricted growth of road haulage, the encouragement of long-distance coach travel, and the expansion of private car ownership and usage.

One symptom of political indecision is a frequent change of minister – something which has occurred throughout the entire post-Beeching period (see Appendix G). From the general election of 1964 up until 2012, the Minister of Transport's average tenure of office has been only 17 months. Fraser lasted little over a year as Transport Minister and was succeeded, on 23 December 1965, by Barbara Castle. She served until 6 April 1968, to be followed by Richard Marsh[2], until 6 October 1969, and then Fred Mulley[3] to 19 June 1970.

John Morris[4], who was brought in as a parliamentary secretary with a brief that concentrated on the railways, says in his autobiography[5] that Fraser was 'a delightful man, whom I suspect would have made an ideal secretary of state for Scotland ... He had no interest in transport and after more than a year had failed to deliver a policy ... He had, I believe, been put in the wrong job, and the department could have been more helpful.'

Morris also says that Castle viewed the permanent secretary, Sir Thomas Padmore[6], 'with distaste. He and the department had let down Tom Fraser ... It seemed, and I may be wrong, that Sir Thomas's absences in Liverpool playing his violin were not unwelcome.'[7]

There were almost as many changes of chairmen at the British Railways Board as there were changes of minister at the Department of Transport. It was no surprise that the 1964 Labour Government wanted to be rid of Dr Beeching and his contract was not renewed in June 1965. He was succeeded by Stanley Raymond[8], described by Anne Perkins, Castle's biographer, as 'an industry man, an edgy character, a Barnardo boy who had worked his way to the top first in the army and then in

public transport. During a brief period in the trade union movement he had made powerful friends now in the Labour Cabinet: both Jim Callaghan[9] and Ray Gunter[10] at the Ministry of Labour were old allies.'[11]

Raymond and Castle did not get on, and his temper was not improved by reading in the press that he was going to be fired. At the heart of Government policy at this time was the search for the 'profitable railway', and Castle was being endlessly briefed by officials that Raymond was not going to be able to reform the management of the board sufficiently to deliver it.

He did, however, succeed in one respect. Castle reports in her diaries that, on 16 February 1966, Raymond and the board officials 'demonstrated to John Morris and me the existing closure policy and how they thought it should be modified. Raymond had organised it very well. Seventeen thousand miles of track had been reduced to 15,000 and under Beeching was due to go down to 8,000. He wanted to stick at 11,000 though this would mean a further 2,500 miles of passenger closures. I was impressed and I think even my cynical officials were, too.'[12]

Castle goes on to describe how, at a subsequent meeting that afternoon, she persuaded Raymond to agree to a 'joint study under a joint steering committee to identify the "social cost" elements and give BR realistic financial targets,' chaired by the 35-year-old parliamentary secretary, John Morris. The actual analysis would be done by consultants together with economists from the ministry. '"The whole purpose of the exercise is to make an honest woman of you," I told him. Touchy as always, he was a bit suspicious at first but finally agreed on the understanding that the exercise would be undertaken in the context of a political decision that we intended to maintain a certain network and to find a new financial basis.'[13]

Raymond had walked into a trap, and by agreeing to the joint review effectively signed his own death warrant. Seventeen months later, in July 1967, the independent experts on the steering group told Castle that Raymond was incapable of delivering the change in management culture and practice that the railway needed. As Morris recalls in his autobiography:

> We came to the conclusion that things were not good at British Rail. They seemed to be sucking in an enormous amount of good Treasury money, with very little to show for it. Their only efficiency strategy was to follow Beeching and continue to cut down the railway system. This caused immense public unpopularity, although the public in turn were not particularly keen to avail themselves of the railways.[14]

Castle's political adviser Christopher Foster[15] noted privately:

> The main outcome of the review was that the loss-making social services should be subsidised explicitly but that even if the Government subsidised all the so-called social services, the railways would still make a loss. [BR] was less efficient in its use of people and assets than other railways. Its administrative overheads were exceptionally high. It was a mammoth management task to turn it round ... The inquiry had shown up the painful inadequacy and lack of management skill and initiative of most of the BR top team.[16]

Morris's recollection is similar:

> After a year we reported to Parliament that the main problem of the railways was not their length but their breadth. A great

deal of fat could be trimmed by reducing the number of parallel lines. This capacity was undoubtedly excessive and far from fully used. We proposed slimming the railways as opposed to cutting off their ends. We also proposed relieving British Rail of many of its historical burdens such as pensions, museums and so on. We hoped these reforms would bring financial responsibility.[17]

Castle then set about getting rid of Raymond; both her own diaries and Perkins' biography of her demonstrate that this was done with a remarkable degree of brutality. 'I must force him to resign,' wrote Castle. 'I suggested we must draw the attention of eminent journalists to the fact the report is a scathing indictment of BR management ... I hope that the comments in the press will bring a reaction from Raymond that will give me my chance.'[18]

However, following the appearance of the press articles which Castle herself had intentionally inspired, she seems to have had a fit of conscience. 'Having thought a great deal about this I have come to the conclusion it would be altogether too cruel – as well as too risky – just to sack him outright. In any case I have no power to do so: I would have to blackmail him into resigning.'[19]

In classic *Yes Minister* fashion, she decided that the way to remove Raymond from the railways was to invent a new body for him to chair instead. He was offered the chairmanship of the then non-existent Freight Integration Council, being called out of a meeting with the trade unions for that very purpose. According to Perkins[20], Raymond 'was deeply wounded, and understandably furious. He "stalked out, cold with anger," Barbara wrote, "and almost spat at me." Foster recalled: "It had been an appalling experience for her. She was white and shaking. His rage had been volcanic. All his pent-up insecurity as a Barnardo boy had poured out."'[21]

Castle had already decided whom she wanted to replace Raymond – a businessman supporter of the Labour Party (at that time) called Peter Parker[22], who had been recommended to her by Jock Campbell[23] and had served on the board of Booker McConnell, the company which Campbell chaired.

However, Ministry of Transport officials were not keen on Parker, emphasising that he had never run anything the size of British Railways and pressing on Castle the need to look at other candidates. '... There seemed to be an absolute conspiracy in certain quarters to blacklist Parker and to encourage others to do so. I personally think that the independent members of the Joint Steering Group, having pressurized me into getting rid of Raymond, are now trying to dictate his successor and are turning a little nasty in the process. It really is absurd that, having rejected Parker as not having enough managerial experience, they should be so keen to put in [Henry] Johnson who, they admit, is not over blessed with grey matter. What is behind their anti-Parker obsession? Jock Campbell says it is straight political: these people hate Socialist businessmen. He may be right. Certainly it smells and their attitude only toughens me."[24]

Toughened she may have been, but Castle was not able to nominate the BR Chairmanship in the way that she wanted. She succeeded in seeing off the other candidates officials had made her consider. John Morris was sent to Montreal to interview Douglas Macmillan, Chairman of Canadian National Railways[25], but he came back with the bad news that Macmillan was not interested[26]. A second candidate was Alf Robens[27], whose suit was promoted by Harold Wilson, as was that of John Morris himself who said: 'Barbara rightly blocked it on the grounds I lacked business experience.'[28]

Eventually, she was able to offer Parker the Chairmanship but he turned it down, saying that the nationalised industry Chairman's rate of pay (then £12,500 a year) would have represented a pay cut of 12.5% on what he was earning in private industry.

The job was subsequently offered to Henry Johnson, who made it clear to Castle when she interviewed him on 8 November 1967 for the intended position of Parker's deputy that his lifelong ambition was to be the head of British Railways.[29] He accepted it on the going-rate salary (and would likely have done it for nothing, so keen was he to have the job). Parker would eventually become Chairman ten years later, on his own terms.

The 1968 Transport Act

While many people felt dismayed and let down by the programme of rail closures which carried on despite the change of Government, the issue did not appear to influence voting behaviour. Writing in his memoirs, Willie Whitelaw[30], himself the grandson of a railway director (see Chapter 10) and MP for Penrith and the Borders, noted that the antipathy of voters to railway closures was not reflected at the ballot box. He was particularly angry at the cavalier way in which closure of the Silloth branch had been approached:

> Ernest Marples, then Minister of Transport, referred scornfully to the absurd number of petitions against closure compared with the small number of inhabitants of the area. This, in any event, was a weak approach, because Silloth reasonably prided itself as a holiday resort dependent on the railway, and many of the petitions against closure therefore came from holidaymakers.
>
> Certainly, I lost some support in the areas concerned ... However, despite these difficulties and despite the fact that I have been consistently blamed for the closure of these railways ever since, I won my seat with a good majority in the constituency. It did not seem to be reduced much more than the party average over the country as a whole.[31]

The swing noted by Whitelaw meant that, having first won with a tiny majority in 1964, Harold Wilson was able to call a second election within 18 months, winning in March 1966 with a majority of almost 100 seats.

In July of that year, the Government published a White Paper[32] which sought to deal with transport policy in conjunction with the location of industry and employment opportunity, housing and land use. It also stressed the role of public transport in solving urban traffic problems.

The White Paper was followed by a major transport bill in 1968, covering almost every aspect of inland transport. It dealt with issues as diverse as the creation of the National Freight Corporation and the new Freightliner Company as a subsidiary of the NFC, with British Rail owning 49 percent. This combined the freight services of British Railways with the state-owned Transport Holding Company (THC): '*The flexibility and door-to-door facility of road haulage will be combined with the speed and economy of rail over long distance.*'[33]

Also in the bill was a new licensing system for road haulage, restrictions on lorry drivers' hours and the creation of the National Bus Company as a holding company with a large number of local subsidiaries – 93 percent of passenger stage services were then either publicly or municipally owned – and the establishment of the Scottish Transport Group, taking over the Scottish Bus Group, the THC's shares in MacBrayne's shipping services and the Caledonian Steam Packet Company.

Passenger railways also featured prominently in the bill. The most significant counterbalance to threatened closures was the establishment of Government grants to finance 'loss-making' services, amounting to more than £50 million a year, guaranteed for three years. According to a Labour Party publication at the time[34], 'The railway network will consist of about 11,000 miles; this will include many lines which cannot hope to pay their way, but which must be retained because of their value to the community. Grants will be fixed for three years on the estimated loss of a service and paid each month. B.R. will then be given an inducement to cut actual losses.'

The piece concluded, somewhat optimistically, 'the railways, as a result of these new policies, should break even in 1969 and from then on operate economically and efficiently. They will not be burdened and demoralised by those parts of the deficit that are due to factors outside their control. The result will be efficient commercial operation of a nationwide network after taking account of the railways' social obligations.'

There was therefore political pressure to find a formula which would allow some of the more contentious routes to be retained, while it was also becoming clear that the closures were not going to narrow the gap between income and costs on the nominally profitable surviving core network.

The solution for most lines lay in the Cooper Brothers accountancy formula which, from 1968 onwards, enabled revenue and costs to be attributed to services, together with details of passenger numbers, so that both subsidy and value for money could be assessed for routes throughout Britain. This in turn provided intellectual justification for the political imperative of bringing the closure programme to an end.

For the Whitehall mandarins, the formula was seen as valuable in terms of highlighting the cost of routes they believed might ultimately be closed. Indeed, the subsidies allocated were for periods of one or three years, demonstrating the stopgap nature of this policy.

By November 1968, Richard Marsh (who had succeeded Barbara Castle as Minister of Transport on 6 April) was able to publish a lengthy written answer in *Hansard*, setting out the precise arrangements for the payment of the grants:

Loss-making passenger services (grants)

I have considered applications by the British Railways Board for grants under Section 39 of the Transport Act, 1968 in respect of a large number of such services. I have given very considerable weight to social questions and to the needs of regional development and have consulted, as appropriate, the Regional Economic Planning Councils, the Scottish Economic Planning Council, the Welsh Council and the Area Transport Users Consultative Committees.

I have now decided to pay grant as from 1st January for the following 135 services in addition to all those London commuter services for which the board has applied for grant and which are not mentioned elsewhere in this statement.

[The statement then listed the services which are shown in Appendix D.]

Barbara Castle
The new minister takes over at the Department of Transport in 1965.

I have also decided to grant-aid two services which, it seems to me, could be re-routed. These are as follows:—

Edinburgh-Perth

I am satisfied of the need for a railway passenger service between these two points, but consider that the service, which at present runs via Kinross, would give better value for money if it were diverted via Stirling. British Railways agree that this would be feasible, and I understand that they intend shortly to publish a closure proposal for the section of route between Cowdenbeath and Hilton Junction including Kinross Station.

London-High Wycombe-Aylesbury

I am satisfied that this service should be grant-aided but consider that it would represent better value for money if it were diverted from its present London terminus of Marylebone to Paddington, where passengers would have a wider choice of interchange facilities. This diversion would entail the closure of the section of route between Neasden Junction and Northolt Junction including four stations – Wembley Hill, Sudbury and Harrow Road, Sudbury Hill (Harrow) and Northolt Park.

I shall not, of course, be able to take a final decision as to the future of these two services until all the statutory closure procedures have been completed; in the meantime they will continue to run in their present form.

British Railways are also applying for grant in respect of the following 56 services and although examination of these applications is not yet complete I expect to be able to grant-aid them.

[The statement then listed the services, which are shown at the end of Appendix D.]

Early in 1969 I intend to announce in respect of each service the length of the period for which I shall undertake to pay grant, and the amount of the grant itself. I am not yet able to do this because certain adjustments have yet to be made before the figures can be finalised. Initially the proportion of short term grants appears likely to be fairly high partly because it has not been possible for me to examine all the services thoroughly, partly because of the impending structural changes in arrangements for passenger transport in the West Midlands, Merseyside, South East Lancashire/North East Cheshire and Tyneside, and partly because of proposed changes in the organisation of public transport in London.

I have reached the tentative conclusion that the following 10 services should not be grant-aided. These services, and the approximate amount of grant which would be required annually if they were to continue in the long term, are as follows:—

- *Bridgend-Treherbert (£150,000).*
- *Bangor-Caernarfon (£60,000).*
- *Newport-Gloucester (local trains only)(£100,000)*
- *Colchester-Sudbury (Suffolk) (£90,000).*
- *High Wycombe-Bourne End (£60,000).*
- *Colne-Skipton (£110,000).*
- *Kidderminster-Hartlebury-Bewdley (£55,000).*

total will be in respect of services in or to Development Areas. British Railways have been under extremely heavy pressure in preparing these grant applications, and in some cases I have not been able to consider the services in sufficient detail to take long term decisions. I intend to review these as soon as possible and may decide that some which I am proposing to grant-aid at the present level of service should be grant-aided at a lower level. In other cases I may reach the provisional view that the service does not, after all, represent value for money and may convey this view to British Railways. In these circumstances, they would be free to publish a closure proposal, which would enable the hardship involved in withdrawal of the service, and the feasibility of provision of alternative services, to be examined in greater detail.[35]

This was an immensely significant announcement. A very large number of the services listed had been proposed for closure in the Beeching Report (and were to appear again on future lists of possible closures, as we shall see in subsequent chapters on the 1970s and 1980s). But, for the moment, it looked as though more than 200 'uneconomic' services would be safe, and even some lines which appeared certain to close – such as Colchester-Sudbury and Northolt Junction-Marylebone, for the misguided attempts to turn this into a busway) – are still very much with us.

According to a report in *The Sun* newspaper[36] on 16 November 1968:

Apart from closure schemes already in the pipeline, only a negligible 123 miles of the 13,000-mile railway network are now threatened with closure. The £62 million grant, which will be paid from next year, will replace the present open-ended subsidy which the railways receive from the Exchequer. Now the railways know what aid they are to get and what services it is paid for. The new scheme marks the end of the era of Dr Beeching and his ruthless rail closure programme.

Passenger transport executives

Amidst the gloom of the post-Beeching era, there was one other bright spot as far as securing rail services was concerned, for which Barbara Castle deserves full credit. Shortly after the Transport Act of 1968, five Passenger Transport Authorities and Passenger Transport Executives were created to plan and fund the local rail services required within their own areas. These were:

- West Midlands on 1 October 1969 (later expanded to include Coventry)
- SELNEC (South East Lancashire North East Cheshire) on 1 November 1969 (later Greater Manchester)
- Merseyside on 1 December 1969
- Tyneside on 1 January 1970 (later Tyne and Wear, including Sunderland)
- Greater Glasgow on 1 June 1973 (later Strathclyde).

Initially, the PTAs were made up of representatives of local authorities in each area; this role was taken over by the metropolitan

- Cambridge-St Ives (£120,000).
- Exeter-Okehampton (£150,000).
- Kirkham-Fleetwood (£120,000). In all the above cases the Railways Board will be free to publish proposals for the withdrawal of the service, and I understand that, in order to qualify for a transitional grant under Section 39 (4) of the Transport Act, 1968, they intend to publish these proposals in the very near future. In all these cases I shall not be able to take a final decision until all the statutory procedures involved in closures have been followed. Meanwhile, of course, the services will continue to run as at present. I have also decided that I cannot give grant for the following two services, consisting only of local trains between the two terminal points:—
- Doncaster-Retford (£15,000).
- Newport-Hereford (£75,000). In both these cases, the routes and stations concerned are served by other trains, so that British Railways are free to withdraw the trains which they had put forward for grant without the necessity for any statutory procedures. All services which are the subject of unresolved closure proposals on 1st January, 1969 will be grant-aided for the time being under the transitional powers contained in Section 39 (4) of the Act. These will include the following three services in respect of which I understand British Railways intend to publish closure proposals before the end of the year:—
- Bolton-Bury-Rochdale.
- Skipton-Carlisle (stopping trains only).
- Romford-Upminster.

Total expenditure on all these grants is likely to be at an annual rate of £62 million initially. Over one third of this counties created by local Government reorganisation in 1974, also including South Yorkshire and West Yorkshire which had their own PTEs. The PTAs were abolished in 1974, but later reinstated in 1986 after abolition of the metropolitan counties.

Despite this bewildering series of local government reorganisations, the creation of the PTEs led to the development of thriving urban rail networks outside London including many lines listed in the Beeching Report for closure. Examples include:

- Glasgow-East Kilbride (Strathclyde)
- Newcastle-Hexham locals (Nexus, Tyne and Wear)
- Leeds City and Bradford Forster Square-Keighley and Skipton local trains (now electrified as part of the West Yorkshire Metro network)
- Manchester Victoria-Bury Bolton Street (now part of Manchester Metrolink)
- Liverpool Exchange-Southport Chapel Street (Merseyrail Electrics)
- Doncaster-Leeds Central locals (South Yorkshire, now electrified)
- Walsall-Rugeley Trent Valley (West Midlands Centro).

It also ultimately included a programme of expansion which allowed the urban networks of today to become substantially larger than would have been the case if they had continued to be managed by the BRB under the remit set by Government.

In some areas, particularly South Yorkshire, there was a slow start as councillors were wedded to the principle of cheap (and even for a time, free) bus travel, and this meant that rail fares were kept very low. Despite increased levels of ridership, the return from the fare box was initially insufficient to justify much new investment in railways. This eventually changed, as we shall see.

In London no PTE was established and the number of lines under threat was limited. Nevertheless, some non-radial routes had closed during the 1960s, including West Drayton-Uxbridge in 1962 and Palace Gates-Stratford in 1963. It was also a period in which local opposition to further retrenchment took root, with the formation of user or action groups such as the North London Line Committee. Most of these were seen as a troublesome irritant by the BRB and civil servants, but a number marshalled their arguments carefully and, with the support of many working railwaymen, made the case successfully for development rather than regression.

Additions to the list

A number of routes were not included for closure in the Beeching Report, but were nevertheless put forward for closure after his departure from BRB. Some of these were explained by Richard Marsh in his statement to the House, setting out the justification for payment of grant to a large part of the network. They included:

- **Edinburgh-Perth via Kinross:** this busy 25-mile double-track route from Cowdenbeath-Hilton Junction carried 11 passenger trains a day between Edinburgh and Perth, three of which continued to Inverness. It was actually listed in the second Beeching Report as a route for development, but was brought forward for closure in the Marsh statement of November 1968 (see above) on the grounds that an alternative route already existed from Edinburgh-Perth via Stirling, although it was 21 miles longer. This left Dunfermline and Cowdenbeath on the local line to Edinburgh,

but with no rail link to the north, and removed the shortest rail route between Edinburgh, Perth and Inverness, along with Kinross station which was the railhead for an extensive area. Nevertheless, the TUCC found no evidence of hardship and the Scottish Economic Planning Council agreed not to oppose closure. The Minister of Transport gave his consent quickly on 10 October 1969 and the line closed on 'Black Monday', 5 January 1970.

- **Okehampton-Yeoford Junction (and Exeter):** the stub end remaining after the lines to Bude, Padstow and Plymouth had been closed. The line itself was retained to serve the railway-owned quarry at Meldon which provided much of the ballast for Southern Region track renewals, but it illustrated the truism that if all the branches are pruned, the trunk too will wither and die. The line suffered from the location of the station at Okehampton, a long walk at some 500ft above the town. With expansion of the A30 into a dual carriageway, Exeter became a more attractive railhead than Okehampton with its enforced change of trains. The line was sold, along with Meldon Quarry in 1986, and is now operated by Dartmoor Railway, part of British American Railways. Limited summer services run, including a Sunday service from Exeter, but the line has now been offered for sale.

- **King's Lynn-Wymondham (and Norwich):** following closure of the Wells next the Sea-Dereham branch in 1964 and the King's Lynn-Dereham line in 1968, the remaining route from Dereham to Wymondham, where trains joined the main line to Norwich itself, became unsustainable and closed in 1969. There was evidence that the feeder bus service from Wells to Dereham was too slow and, as it also involved changing, was little used, with people driving or taking the bus direct from Wells and Fakenham to Norwich. None of the route from King's Lynn-Wymondham had been included in the Beeching Report.

- **Oxford-Cambridge:** this was more surprising, given the

Local support
It may have the longest name in Britain, but Llanfair PG was still closed in 1966. Four years later, following the fire on the nearby Britannia Bridge over the Menai Strait, it was reopened temporarily, and with local authority support this became permanent in 1973. The station is shown in 1978.

development of Milton Keynes and the value of a route linking the Great Western, West Coast, East Coast and Cambridge main lines without travelling via London. In the event, it proved difficult to provide replacement buses and local services were preserved over the middle section of the line between Bletchley and Bedford, while freight traffic was retained over the route between Oxford and Goldington power station at Bedford, with Chiltern line diesel units at one time using part of the route to access Bletchley depot each night for maintenance. Only the eastern end of the line between Goldington and Cambridge was closed completely. Subsequently, a local passenger service between Oxford and Bicester Town has been restored and there are plans to reopen the whole route between Oxford and Milton Keynes/Bedford as well as for a Marylebone-Oxford service via a new spur at Bicester. The decision to close the line was taken by Barbara Castle – one of the authors of this book remembers challenging her about it at an Oxford University Labour Club meeting on 28 May 1965 (not long before she became Transport Minister). Her response was testy and rude: 'You can't possibly expect me to comment on something so trivial,' was the gist of it.

- **Blackpool Central:** the direct line from Kirkham & Wesham-Blackpool South and Central brought passengers to a major terminus right under Blackpool Tower. The line was not listed for closure in the 1963 Reshaping Report, but early in the following year its closure was announced. This took place on 1 November 1964, after the illuminations. Even on the last day, Central station saw 55 departures. Part of the line is now the link road between the M55 and the town, but the only use of the station site and its approaches is as a car park – a scandalous example of disinvestment and wasted opportunity.

The ones that got away

The move towards systematic support for the 'social railway', as it became known under Parker, meant that many of those lines that survived the dark days of 1964-67 would continue under the general direction issued by Fred Mulley after the Railways Act of 1974, to provide services 'broadly comparable' with those operating on 31 December 1973. (See Chapter 8). Some of these survivors were not so much branch lines as strategic secondary routes, like the Kyle line and Fort William-Mallaig, and had originally been targeted by the British Transport Commission (although the Branch Line Committee declined to take the proposals forward until completion of the branch line assessments).[37] The 1968 Act facilitated their survival, the 1974 Act ensured their continuation and most remain thriving today. It is significant that of the 192 services listed by Marsh as approved or considered for grant in 1968, only nine were subsequently withdrawn and one of them is today limited to a 'parliamentary' service (see Chapter 18).

The more striking examples are listed below:

- **The Kyle of Lochalsh line** was built by the Highland Railway as its Dingwall-Skye route, with which the North British Railway competed by building its later route to Mallaig from Fort William. Closure had not been possible due to the inadequacies of the road network. To overcome this, a new road was built along the southeast side of Loch Carron. This was completed, but the Minister of Transport told BR not to proceed with closure in 1974, by which time prospects were starting to look different due to

exploration of the North Sea oil field. A siding was laid at Strathcarron to handle construction traffic for the oil rigs, and the tourist potential of the line started to be developed. By the end of the decade, it had become clear that closure of long-distance rural routes in Scotland was off the agenda.

- **Central Wales line** trains (now the Heart of Wales line) run from Shrewsbury to Swansea. The route runs for 100 miles through seven parliamentary constituencies, three of which were marginal in the 1970s, and this made closure a difficult proposition for any Transport Minister. It is now the archetypal 'basic railway' with a limited train service, basic signalling and long single-line sections. Nevertheless, it remains an important link for the communities it serves and brings many tourists who would otherwise miss out the quiet towns and villages of Shropshire, Powys and Carmarthenshire. In *The Diaries of a Cabinet Minister*, Richard Crossman writes the following entry for 31 July 1969:

The final item was the proposal to close down at long last the Central Wales Railway line which has in winter only 100 people travelling on its 90 miles, 200 in summer and only six regular passengers. This is a parody of a railway and there is an overwhelming case for permanent closure next January, because otherwise we will have to pay a £300,000 subsidy. Dick Marsh moved this proposal and the Chancellor supported him. I barged in and said, 'Look, if you are going to start playing politics with this, you mustn't do it,' but they did. Roy [Jenkins][38] half-heartedly stood out, I stood out with Dick Marsh, and round the table the others were in favour of the £300,000 subsidy, because three seats were in danger in central Wales.[39]

John Morris refers to that same Cabinet discussion in his autobiography:

When George Thomas[40] became the Welsh secretary, after my time at transport, he apparently opposed the closure of the line in Cabinet, on the grounds that it went through five [sic – it's curious how the number changes, depending on who is recalling these events – Ed.] marginal constituencies: such were the pressures we were under. The line is still running.[41]

Indeed it is, with four trains a day in each direction six days a week – and there are even two on Sundays, a service which did not exist in 1969. It is actively supported by the Heart of Wales Line Forum, a dynamic community rail partnership that has done much to promote the line and the attractive part of the country that it serves, marketed via special events and on-train entertainment.

While BR would have had no choice but to implement a closure decision if one had been taken, their staff deserve great credit for promoting the line once closure had been refused.

Writing to the authors, Alan Marshall[42], then a PR assistant in the Western Region public relations department at Paddington, recalls:

The word that came back to us was that the Cabinet had reprieved the line but that we were to reduce the deficit by half. How was this to be done (bearing in mind operating costs were pretty low – DMUs, single track much of the way, etc)? I suggested a major PR campaign to drum up business.

I spent many happy days in mid-Wales, based in Llandrindod Wells where the campaign to keep the line open was centred on the unlikely venue of The Automobile Palace, then the BMC dealership for mid-Wales but with the walls and windows festooned with old bicycles (originally

opened as a cycle store in 1898, it is now home to the National Cycle Collection). The dealership would always furnish me with a car for my stay (usually a not-very-reliable Morris 1100) so I was able to visit supporters of the line, especially hoteliers and places to visit. I would always stay, free of charge, in one of the town's hotels, The Park, sadly now gone, whose owner had previously run an engineering business in Wolverhampton and strongly supported the need to retain the railway to connect with the West Midlands.

From these visits I was able to plan a series of trips for travel writers from national and regional media to promote the train services, the local attractions and where to stay (many of the hotels, principally in the Llandrindod and Rhayader areas, agreed to offer discounts for rail travellers). In addition, with the help of Leslie Bettis, the Western Region's Fares Officer who initiated market instead of mileage-based pricing, which was eventually adopted by all of BR, we introduced a round-trip ticket, valid from Paddington to Euston via Swansea and Shrewsbury, or vice versa. I believe the ticket is still available today.

We were also able to operate some occasional special loco-hauled trains for local residents from the Central Wales line to destinations such as Birmingham, Cardiff and London.

We achieved massive editorial coverage, with the result that revenue increased substantially (and the deficit reduced commensurately) – it was a classic case of effective public relations – and, of course, in due course, the line was subjected to further cost saving measures, such as no signalman key token signalling.

I recall that when the Welsh Assembly Government introduced free train travel for bus pass holders two or three years ago, Central Wales Line trains were so popular that the scheme had to be either rescinded or scaled back as fare-paying passengers complained of overcrowding.[43]

- **The East Suffolk** was a secondary main line that carried expresses from Liverpool Street to Lowestoft and Great Yarmouth (South Town) including the crack 'East Anglian'. The northern end of the line, from Yarmouth to Beccles closed in 1959, and the Norfolk &

Suffolk Joint line from Yarmouth South Town to Lowestoft Central in 1970. The branch line to Aldeburgh was discontinued in 1964, Tivetshall in 1953 and Framlingham in 1952, while the independent Southwold Railway from Halesworth was closed as early as 1929. Bealings station was closed in 1956 and Melton in 1955, although the latter was reopened in 1984. In 1967 the introduction of pay train working and high utilisation of diesel multiple-units (DMUs) had started to turn the line round, even though the service was reduced to a DMU shuttle between Ipswich and Lowestoft with a single through train to and from London each day. Singling and level-crossing automation secured its survival in 1984, and it has subsequently grown to the point where more capacity is required with an additional crossing loop just completed at Beccles. Through services to London were reinstated by Anglia Railways, but have subsequently been withdrawn.

- **The branch lines to Sudbury and Braintree** are all that is left of an extensive rural railway network in north Essex, Suffolk and Cambridgeshire. There were a number of services which connected these places with Cambridge, Bishops Stortford and Bury St Edmunds, which had all gone by the end of the 1960s. Following its inclusion in the Beeching Report closure list, the line from Cambridge to Marks Tey was included in a closure proposal published by BR in April 1965, but the line south of Sudbury was reprieved as alternative bus services were deemed inadequate and because of the potential growth of housing in the town. The service is now flourishing, with an hourly train in each direction between Sudbury and Marks Tey for almost the entire day, supported by a community rail partnership.

- **The Braintree** branch is an even more remarkable story. This too was proposed for closure by Beeching, but, following persistent lobbying by local Conservative MP Tony Newton[44] (later Lord Newton of Braintree), the branch was included in the Anglian electrification programme completed in 1986. It now has an hourly through train service to and from London Liverpool Street with capacity for 12-car trains.

- **Ashford-Hastings** had long been on the Southern's allocated list of lines for closure, losing its branch line from Appledore to Lydd and New Romney in 1967. General manager David McKenna believed it worth retaining the through route, but matters came to a head in the mid-1970s when the long-deferred track renewals resulted in extended journey times due to speed restrictions. The line also had no fewer than nine level crossings, all manually operated and very expensive to run, particularly as most resident crossing keepers had long since retired and relief signalmen (on higher pay rates) had to fill the gaps. At Rye, the signalbox was on the station platform, while the road crossings at either end of the station required separate gateboxes – common enough in the early days of railways (the line was opened in 1851), but as expensive an arrangement as could be devised. The decision was taken to single the line from Appledore to Ore to limit the full cost of track renewals, but this in turn required modernisation of the level crossings, few of which met the latest safety requirements but where 'grandfather rights' allowed them to remain until any change to track or signalling was made, which would require them to be brought up to date. Co-author Chris Austin was the planning officer responsible for this project in 1978, when the threat of closure was removed. Now the line is run as a through service with new rolling stock from Ashford International to Brighton. Demand has increased and the time is approaching when some of the double line will require restoration to allow the hourly service to be expanded.

Passing the parcel to local authorities

Saddled with a system that supported lines under the 1968 Act, civil servants tried a different approach to stem what they saw as an unjustifiable outflow of funds. If ministers could not be persuaded to approve closure of these lines, then perhaps local councillors would do it for them.

In August 1973, a working party was set up to study the devolution of unremunerative railway passenger services. The proposition was that responsibility for specifying and funding local rail passenger services would be devolved to local authorities, presented as decentralising power and allowing local people to exercise democratic choice.

The real purpose, however, is made very clear in a memorandum dated 21 August 1973 from Mr D. Holmes of the Department of the Environment to colleagues in the department:

> We all accept that we must try to find a way of producing a package which puts effective financial responsibilities on the local authorities, and thereby produces an incentive for them to close railway services which the department has been unable to get rid of.[45]

But here, too, the department was not prepared to pay for the consequences of its actions. Transport supplementary grant would have covered only around three-quarters of the cost of running the railway, leaving the rest to be picked up by the ratepayer in England. In Scotland and Wales powers were 'devolved' to the secretaries of state rather than local authorities, with both making it clear that further closures in their areas were not politically acceptable.

Nothing immediate came of Holmes' memorandum in 1973, but it would resurface at the Sunningdale conference four years later when, once again, the network came under threat of extensive reduction (see Chapter 9).

1   Richard Crossman (1907-74) was a Labour politician, academic, journalist, World War 2 propagandist and MP for Coventry East from 1945-74. Passed over as a minister in the 1945 Government, allegedly for being too pro-Zionist, Crossman was a prominent member of the Labour Party's left wing who held a series of Cabinet positions in the 1964-70 administrations. He also edited *New Statesman* magazine from 1970-72 and authored the three-volume *Diaries of a Cabinet Minister*.

2   Richard Marsh (1928-2011) was Labour MP for Greenwich from 1959-71. He succeeded Barbara Castle as Minister for Transport in 1968, serving until 1970, and was then appointed by the Conservative Government as Chairman of British Rail in 1971, serving until 1976. Ennobled as Lord Marsh in 1981, he sat on the cross benches in the House of Lords. In his *Guardian* obituary on 2 August 2011, Julia Langdon wrote: 'His early posts in Government after the 1964 election were as a junior minister at the Ministry of Labour for one year and then at Technology for another. He then became Minister of Power for two years, closing 100 pits during that time, until in 1968 Wilson promoted him to succeed Barbara Castle as the Minister of Transport, with a seat in the Cabinet. He celebrated his new job, he admitted privately, by driving at 90mph on the M4. His appointment was not a success, not least with Castle, who regarded him as a dilettante, not really interested in pursuing his policies and proposed legislation. She pleaded with Wilson to sack him on one occasion, claiming that he was "cynical, superficial and lazy", and the Prime Minister did indeed subsequently sack him after just a year in the post.'

3   Fred Mulley (1918-95) served as Minister of State for Transport for the last six months of the 1966 Labour Government and again from March 1974 to March 1975. He was MP for Sheffield Park 1950-83, also serving as Minister of Aviation and Minister for Disarmament in the 1966 Government, and after 1975 as Secretary of State for Education and, later, Defence. He had been a prisoner of war in France from 1940, using his time in the PoW camp to study voraciously, enabling him to go to Christ Church Oxford after the war where he got a first class honours degree after two years' study. For many years Mulley was a member of Labour's National Executive Committee. He was ennobled as Lord Mulley in 1985. In a fair and sympathetic obituary published in *The Independent* on 16 March 1995, Tam Dalyell wrote: 'it would be a travesty of justice if Mulley were to be remembered for that cruel picture of him dozing off during a royal visit to the Forces. Seeing him voting at four in the morning the night before, I can easily understand why the exigencies of a slim majority which became non-existent brought that lapse about.'

4   John Morris (born 1931) was the Labour politician who served as Parliamentary Secretary Responsible for Railways from 1966-68, when Barbara Castle was Minister of Transport. He served continuously on the Labour front bench from 1964-99, in a variety of senior positions including Secretary of State for Wales and Attorney General. Morris was MP for Aberavon from 1959-2001, when he was ennobled as Lord Morris of Aberavon. He was a Cambridge-educated QC who became a Recorder, Lord Lieutenant of Dyfed and Chancellor of the University of Glamorgan. He was knighted in 1999 and became a Knight of the Garter in 2003.

5   *Fifty Years in Politics and the Law* by Lord Morris of Aberavon, University of Wales Press 2011, p67.

6   Sir Thomas Padmore (1909-96) was a lifelong civil servant who started in the Inland Revenue and moved to the Treasury in 1934, where he was second secretary from 1952-62. He then became permanent secretary to the Ministry of Transport from 1962 until his early retirement in 1968. Padmore was Chairman of the Rehearsal Orchestra from 1961-71 and the Handel Opera Society from 1963-86, and used to rehearse his violin playing in the office at lunchtime. His relationship with Barbara Castle was 'glacial' and she says in her autobiography that a condition of her taking the Transport Minister's job was that Padmore was got rid of; she claimed that he hated the department and was bored with transport (*The Castle Diaries 1964-70*, p492). It was, however, Castle's successor Richard Marsh who succeeded in getting him to retire. Padmore had been awarded the KCB in 1953 and the GCB in 1965.

7   *Fifty Years in Politics and the Law*, p69.

8   Stanley Raymond (1913-88) was a former Barnardo boy who became the second

Chairman of the British Railways Board from 1965-67, appointed to replace Beeching and fired by Barbara Castle. As a consolation prize, he became Chairman of the Gaming Board for Great Britain (1968-77) and Chairman of the Horserace Betting Levy Board (1972-74).

9   Leonard James Callaghan (1912-2005) was the Labour politician who rose to become Prime Minister from 1976-79, after being a Royal Navy chief petty officer, an Inland Revenue tax officer, a trade union official, Cardiff MP (1945-87), Chancellor of the Exchequer, Home Secretary and Foreign Secretary. He was also a Junior Transport Minister in the Attlee Government and Opposition Spokesman on Transport 1951-53. He was ennobled as Lord Callaghan of Cardiff in 1987.

10 Ray Gunter (1909-77) was a Labour politician and railway trade unionist. He became a booking clerk with the Great Western Railway in South Wales on leaving school aged 14, and was later elected MP for Essex South East in 1945 and Doncaster in 1950, losing the latter seat in 1951. Gunter became treasurer and then president of the Transport Salaried Staffs' Association, returning to Parliament as MP for Southwark in 1959. He served on the National Executive Committee of the Labour Party from 1955-66, where he was a hard-line opponent of the party's left wing. Wilson appointed him Minister of Labour in 1964 (a job Gunter famously described as 'a bed of nails'), but moved him to Minister of Power in 1968 to make way for Barbara Castle, whom he loathed. Gunter stayed just two months in that job and resigned in a huff 'to return to the people from whence he came'. He was a passionate pro-European who resigned the Labour whip and his seat in Parliament over the party's then opposition to the Common Market in 1972 and the abandonment of its working-class roots.

11 *Red Queen* by Anne Perkins, Macmillan 2003, pp221-222.

12 *The Castle Diaries 1964-70*, Weidenfeld & Nicolson 1984, p108.

13 Ibid.

14 *Fifty Years in Politics and the Law*, p69.

15 Christopher Foster (born 1930) has worked in the capacities of transport economist, academic and temporary civil servant. He was political adviser to Barbara Castle, Richard Marsh, Tony Crosland and Peter Shore, and advised ministers on the poll tax and rail privatisation. Foster has been Director General of Economic Planning at the Ministry of Transport, 1966-70, Head of Unit for Research in Urban Economics at the London School of Economics, 1970-76, Professor of Urban Studies and Economics at the LSE, 1976-78, associated with Coopers & Lybrand almost continuously from 1978-94, and a member of the board of Railtrack, 1994–2000. He is widely regarded as the principal author of the *Socialist Commentary* report on transport policy (see Chapter 8) and is currently Chairman of the Better Government Initiative. Foster has been involved with the RAC since 1994, as successively Non-Executive Director, Vice Chairman and Vice President.

16 Christopher Foster – private paper quoted in *Red Queen* by Anne Perkins, p222.

17 *Fifty Years in Politics and the Law*, p70.

18 *The Castle Diaries 1964-70*, p292.

19 Ibid p295.

20 *Red Queen: The Authorised Biography of Barbara Castle* by Anne Perkins, Macmillan 2003, p223.

21 Christopher Foster's private papers, quoted in *Red Queen* p223.

22 Peter Parker (1924-2002) was the Chairman of the British Railways Board 1976-83, knighted in 1978. He was described by Prue Leith as a 'prodigiously energetic polymath who pioneered modern management methods at British Rail. Interested in education, the arts, sport, politics, to all of which he brought knowledge, enthusiasm, charm and prodigious energy, he could have been a soldier, a politician or an actor.' (*The Guardian* 30 April 2002.) He was also a Labour parliamentary candidate in 1951 and later became a member of the Social Democratic Party (SDP). First Great Western Trains named class 43 HST power car number 43127 *Sir Peter Parker 1924-2002 – Cotswold Line 150*. See Chapter 13 for a longer appraisal of his career.

23 Jock Campbell (1912-94) was ennobled as Lord Campbell of Eskan in 1966. He was the Chairman of Booker McConnell Ltd from 1952-66 (and its President from 1967–79) and the former Chairman of Statesman and Nation Publishing Company (owners of *New Statesman* magazine). For 34 years he was also Chairman of the Commonwealth Sugar Exporters' Association.

24 *The Castle Diaries 1964-70*, p318.

25 According to *The Castle Diaries 1964-70* (p312), Douglas Macmillan had 'enormously impressed' Christopher Foster, because he had 'succeeded in cutting the operational deficit of CNR considerably'.

26 *Fifty Years in Politics and the Law*, p75.

27 Alf Robens (1910-99) was a trade union official who became Labour MP for Wansbeck, Northumberland in 1945. He was also a Government minister from 1947-51 and Chairman of the National Coal Board 1961-71; ennobled as Lord Robens of Woldingham in 1961.

28 *Fifty Years in Politics and the Law*, p75.

29 *The Castle Diaries 1964-70*, p319.

30 William Whitelaw (1918-99) was the Conservative MP for Penrith and the Borders from 1955-83. He served in the Heath Government of 1970-74, successively as Leader of the House of Commons, Secretary of State for Northern Ireland and Secretary of State for Employment. He was Deputy Prime Minister from 1979-88, combining the job with that of Home Secretary, and Leader of the House of Lords from 1983, where he sat as the First Viscount Whitelaw. Margaret Thatcher once memorably said of him, 'Every prime minister needs a Willie.' Whitelaw also had a distinguished World War 2 record and had been awarded the Military Cross.

31 *The Whitelaw Memoirs*, pp 61-2, Headline, 1989.

32 *Transport Policy*, Cmnd 3057, July 1966.

33 *Transport of Freight* White Paper, Cmnd 3470.

34 *Talking Points*, issue six, May 1968, pp4-5. The article was written by Richard Faulkner, who was working at party headquarters at that time.

35 *HC Deb volume 773, 15 November 1968 cc172-80W*.

36 *The Sun* was very different in 1968, compared with its present-day incarnation. It was started in 1964 as a popular broadsheet to replace the *Daily Herald* by IPC (International Press Corporation), who sold it to Rupert Murdoch in 1969.

37 Letter of 29 September 1952 from the railway executive to the BTC, from the National Archives.

38 Roy Jenkins (1920-2003), the politician/author/European Commission president/Oxford University chancellor, held a succession of senior ministerial offices in the 1960s, including Home Secretary and Chancellor of the Exchequer. The son of a miners' union official who was MP for Pontypool from 1935-46, Jenkins was Labour MP for Southwark Central from 1948-50 and Birmingham Stechford from 1950-77, leaving Parliament to take up the presidency of the European Commission. He returned to Britain in 1981 and was one of the four founders of the Social Democratic Party. Jenkins was elected SDP MP for Glasgow Hillhead at a by-election in 1982 and was briefly the leader of the party, making way for David Owen in 1983. He was defeated at the 1997 election and ennobled as Lord Jenkins of Hillhead, leading the Liberal Democrats (the new party formed by merger of the Liberal Party and most of the SDP) in the House of Lords until 1997. In 1987 he was elected chancellor of Oxford University, a position he held until his death in 2003. Jenkins is principally remembered for the social reform legislation passed during his time at the Home Office in the 1960s: these included final abolition of the death penalty and reform of penal policy and laws relating to divorce, homosexuality and abortion – all measures in support of what he called the 'civilised society'.

39 *The Diaries of a Cabinet Minister Volume Three* by Richard Crossman, Hamish Hamilton 1977, pp 603-4.

40 Thomas George Thomas (1909-97) represented Cardiff Central 1945-50 and Cardiff West 1950-83 as a Labour MP. He held a succession of ministerial appointments from 1964-70, including Secretary of State for Wales, presiding over the investiture of Prince Charles as Prince of Wales at Caernarfon Castle in 1969. Elected Speaker of the House of Commons in 1976, he served until 1983 when he was given a hereditary peerage as Viscount Tonypandy. In his obituary, published in *The Independent* on 23 September 1997, Lord Ardwick (John Beaven) wrote: 'George Thomas was the archetypal middle-of-the-road Welsh MP of his generation, formed by the fortifying curriculum of the valley, the pit, the chapel, the temperance movement, the Co-op, the trade union and the Labour Party.'

41 *Fifty Years in Politics and the Law*, p70.

42 Alan Marshall (born 1945) was chief reporter for the *Reading Evening Post* 1965-67, before joining the BR Western Region public relations team, later becoming regional press officer. He later worked as PRO to South Yorkshire Passenger Transport Executive from 1974-79; information services officer in BRB's public affairs directorate, 1979-83; BRB chief press officer 1984-85; public affairs manager, BR London Midland Region 1985-91; BRB group public relations manager 1991-97, and is now editorial director of Railnews, which continued publication of the rail industry's national newspaper after BR's privatisation.

43 Email to the authors from Alan Marshall, 3 June 2012.

44 Tony Newton (1937-2012) was the Conservative MP for Braintree from 1974-97. He also served as Secretary of State for Social Security and Leader of the House of Commons, joining the House of Lords as Lord Newton of Braintree in 1997. Newton worked closely (and privately) with BRB's advisers from 1977-9, who helped him draw attention to the potential political and social damage if the Labour Government's proposals for huge commuter fare increases became reality. With Peter Parker's encouragement, they worked together to demonstrate that there were numerous constituencies in the South East where the number of commuters exceeded the incumbent MP's majority. Newton put this information to excellent use, concentrating ministers' minds on the short-sighted and electorally damaging proposals in their White Paper.

45 National Archives MT 124/1667.

VII

THE 'BLUE PAPER', 1972

'I remember a seminar on public accountability at which a department of transport under-secretary said the DofT was accountable to the Road Haulage Association.'

RETIRED SENIOR CIVIL SERVANT IN CORRESPONDENCE WITH THE AUTHORS

In search of a profitable 'core'
A Darton to Wigan coal train passes Penistone in May 1974. Passenger trains had been withdrawn four years
previously, and in 1981, with coal mines closing, the freight had gone too, leaving just a single line at this point
conveying the Huddersfield–Sheffield Penistone line service.

From Stedeford onwards, policymakers believed that there was a profitable 'core' within the existing (unprofitable) network. While the relationship between the components of the network was not understood and the concept of cross subsidy neither appreciated nor condoned, Beeching's report was designed to build on the core and to develop new profitable services such as Liner Trains.

Peyton's pragmatism

In his autobiography, *Off the Rails*, Richard (later Lord) Marsh recalls how he tried to convince ministers and officials that the 'Holy Grail' of the profitable railway was largely mythical. He had been appointed Chairman of British Rail in 1970 by John Peyton[1], soon after the change of Government in the election of that year. As Marsh told Peyton:

> We set up a high-powered exercise to produce a number of theoretical railway systems of different sizes and shapes on computers to see if anywhere among them there was a profitable railway. It emerged very early on that none of them, of any size or shape, and some were very small, were theoretically viable, or if they were likely to be at some point in the future, the cost of getting to that size was so astronomical that nobody would be able to impose it.
>
> We held a meeting on a Saturday morning and asked John Peyton to come with his civil servants, gave them a complete rundown of the different shapes and sizes of railway network, and demonstrated that all of them required financial support on a very large scale.
>
> If they were to lose as little money as possible, then massive increases in investment had to be authorised. The apparently profitable parts of the railway were the inter-city services, but we could not charge high fares if we did not provide reasonably comfortable conditions. Peyton was very impressed by this argument. His civil servants, some of whose mothers must have been frightened by diesel locomotives when they were pregnant, were less enthusiastic.

Marsh then describes how he played what he admits was 'a slightly underhand political trick'. He had asked for an overlay of the railway map to be produced on transparent paper, which 'illustrated the Conservative and Labour party seats as blue and pink areas'. He replaced the existing map with one showing a much smaller British Rail network with the political map superimposed on it. This showed Peyton that 'all the closed lines were in rural areas and, by sheer coincidence, happened to be Conservative seats. He said something to the effect, "Well I don't know why you didn't show me that at the beginning, and why we wasted all that time this morning."'[2]

Notwithstanding this unpromising start, officials continued to press ministers to search for the profitable core railway and, in July 1972, Peyton initiated studies into the 'Financial effects of the radical contraction of the railway service network'. Work was started by the Department of Transport with input from BRHQ. By this stage the railwaymen understood a lot more about the nature of railway economics and were sceptical about the value of yet another study by civil servants.

The *Sunday Times* leak

Early indication of a possible outcome came on 8 October 1972, when the *Sunday Times* led its front page with a story across four columns headed 'Cut trains by half, says secret report'. This was supported by an article which took over the whole of page seven: 'Shunting off

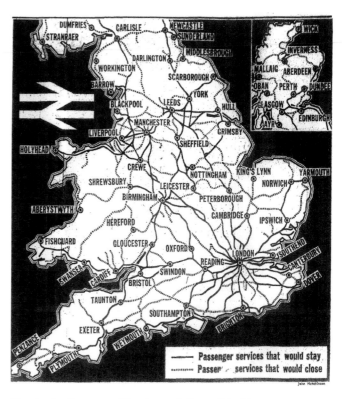

Map showing the proposed line closures in the confidential 1972 'Rail Policy Review'. *Sunday Times*

250,000 passengers and 180,000 tons of freight a day'. There were pictures of Peyton and Marsh, and of the iconic Forth rail bridge ('Will it become redundant?'). Even more sensational was a map showing 'Where rail experts say passenger services will end if official planners get their way'. There would be no railways west of Plymouth, nothing in Scotland north and west of Perth and Aberdeen, only a single line to Great Yarmouth in East Anglia, with no services north of Cambridge, the whole of Wales would lose its railways apart from main lines to Holyhead and Fishguard, the direct Great Western line from Reading to Taunton would close, as would the Southern main line from Woking to Exeter ... and much more of the same:

> Many services regarded as 'main lines' would have to go if the department was to achieve its target of lopping the rail network from its present 11,600 miles to a mere 6,700 miles ... The officials believe the railways should be skinned to the bare bones – the main revenue-earning lines.

The newspaper claimed it had been given a copy of a confidential 61-page report entitled 'Rail Policy Review', which in subsequent newspaper reports became known as the 'Blue Paper'. As Marsh recounts in his autobiography:

> One Friday afternoon I received a telephone call from the *Sunday Times*, saying that they had evidence that the Government was planning a major and rapid reduction in the size of the railway system ... The chief leader writer and one of his colleagues came to see me, bearing a document. I looked at it and laughed. 'I am sorry to spoil a good story,' I said, 'but there are another dozen copies of that document in the cupboard there. It is one of a number of hypothetical studies of different sized railways that we have produced and certainly does not represent Government policy.' ...

I went to the Department on the Monday and said that this was absolutely monstrous. The story was not only untrue, it was clearly highly damaging in terms of commercial confidence and staff morale. All the copies of the document were numbered. I had checked that every copy allocated to British Rail was still *in situ* and I asked the Ministry to kindly check on theirs. We were able to trace the actual document which had been taken from the Department of Environment and, at my suggestion, the police were called in.[3]

Secretary of State for the Environment Peter Walker[4], who was Peyton's boss, ordered a leak inquiry. As generally happens on occasions like this, however, no culprits were found. Marsh describes how he was visited by two policemen who told him that they were in no doubt the document had been stolen and it was therefore a breach of the Official Secrets Act. They planned to put all the evidence before the Director of Public Prosecutions but, said one of the officers, 'I shall be very much surprised if any action is taken against anyone.' As Marsh comments, 'In the event he was proved right. Everyone knew the circumstances and absolutely nothing was done about it.'

Notwithstanding the BR Chairman's claim that the leak had come from the Department of Environment, suspicion naturally fell on British Rail and a report in *The Times* on the following day (9 October), which said that 'British Rail is fighting a powerful rearguard action against any future cut,' did little to dispel the assumption that – unlike at the time of the Beeching Report and earlier – BR was resisting reductions in the size of the network.

The 'profitable core'

Additional corroboration came in the form of an unreported briefing by Marsh to Alastair Hetherington[5], editor of *The Guardian*, on 17 November 1972. In a lengthy note which his private papers (deposited at the London School of Economics) indicate that he dictated two days later ('John Cole[6] also present'), Hetherington says this:

1. Railway Finance

They [British Rail] had come to the conclusion that the railways could never be self-supporting in their present form. After two years of operating under the 1968 Act in which they had made a profit, by last June they had realised that they were going back into a deficit situation. There were a number of reasons for this. These had been studied. So had the experience of other railway systems. In fact it turned out that the British system was one of those least in deficit. Others such as the Deutsche Bundesbahn and the French SNCF were losing sums of the order of £400,000,000 to £500,000,000 each year. Comparatively British Railways was doing very well. Nevertheless the financial basis would have to be changed again. If they simply went on as now then within five years they would once more have accumulated debts which the Government would have to write off as it had done in 1968.

A number of studies had been carried out. They had begun earlier this year. It was one of these that the *Sunday Times* report had consisted of. They had intended to do five but in practice had done four (I think he said). They had looked at chopping off various bits of the system and at the resulting economies, costs, and profits. *They had in fact found that with the smallest network the loss was highest* [our emphasis]. There were two principal reasons for this. One was the level of inescapable fixed costs and the other was what he called the 'cascade' effect.

On the inescapable costs there was track maintenance, signalling, staffing, and so on. On the cascade effect you might think that by cutting off this little bit of line (he drew a short thumb mark on the table cloth beside a very long mainline thumb mark) that you were going to save money. On a strict reckoning of that line's costs alone perhaps you would. But it was a feeder line and you couldn't really tell how much you were going to lose in traffic that started on that line and then went through onto the main line. The feeder lines generated a lot of traffic. The *Sunday Times* document showed one level at which they would have cut the services pretty heavily. Even this however didn't bring you to an appreciably better financial position.

On replacement costs he said that the total capital expenditure by British Railways on the rail system was running at about £100,000,000 a year. Of this about £20,000,000 was on new work such as electrification and the remainder was on replacement. Compared with the sums being spent on the road programme it was tiny. The amount of new work going on was really not great.

He suggested that in calculating any future basis there should be a much wider approach to the study. You had to undertake some kind of social costing. You had to consider for example what the effect would be in heavier road traffic, more accidents, the need for more vehicles and so on if you were to close a number of lines and divert passengers or freight onto the roads. You also had to consider the pollution and environmental effects. He mentioned that in one part of a study they had done the position of some lines around Leeds had been considered. It had been determined that if these lines were to be closed only between 1.5 and 2% would be added to the road traffic in the area and this could easily be absorbed. On the other hand this was also based on the assumption that the Leeds road programme with a capital expenditure there of £78,000,000 (but presumably not all in one year) was going ahead. This showed something of the disparity in the financial factors that were involved.

On the present basis – and with the need to cover replacement costs – there was no possibility of generating enough capital from within the system to do all that they needed. If you put charges too high both for freight and for passengers then you would price yourself out of the market. He also mentioned again the old point that one shouldn't regard road taxation as all available for road construction. The money raised through various forms of taxation on road transport was part of the money raised for Government purposes as a whole.

He also said incidentally that the railways' chief competitor was something you might call British Road Transport Ltd which had as the equivalent of its Managing Director the Permanent Secretary in the Ministry. That enterprise was operated directly from and through the Ministry which had a vested interest in it. The British Railways Board was in a rather less favoured situation.

2. Other points

Marsh says that when the *Sunday Times* published its report it knew it was not a fair picture. John Whale[7] and one other person had previously presented the document to him. After looking at it, he told them that he had a dozen copies in his cupboard

and it was only one of a number of studies. Nevertheless, they went ahead with publication in a misleading form and did not publish the statement he had issued some days later. The only papers which actually published it were *The Guardian* (*circa* the bottom of page 19) and the *Financial Times* (somewhere around the bottom of page 23).

He admitted nevertheless that the *Sunday Times* publication had in the end been beneficial. It had produced a substantial public reaction – an 'emotional' reaction he called it. It had produced a lot of letters to ministers and this had had an effect on them. It had concentrated their minds wonderfully and made them realise that unlike the Beeching period there was no political benefit in being seen to cut further on railways.

A further angle on the *Sunday Times* story can be found in another of Hetherington's papers. He reports on a private dinner he had with Gordon Campbell[8], Secretary of State for Scotland, on 6 December 1972. According to Hetherington, Campbell told him 'he was not

Back to nature
Affectionately known as the 'Cardi Bach', the Whitland-Cardigan branch lost its passenger service in 1962 and its goods trains the following year. Boncath was one of the larger stations on the branch, with a passing loop, goods shed and sidings. The former station building and up platform are seen slowly returning to nature in 1971: the trackbed is becoming choked with vegetation, while slates slip from the roof and plaster peels from the walls. The scene of so many greetings and departures has become an eyesore, its original purpose, once a source of local pride, lost in the encroaching undergrowth.

currently engaged in any discussion of reorganisation of the railway system in Scotland. He had seen the *Sunday Times* piece and knew that this was only one of a number of studies on the economic consequences of different levels of railway operation. He did not believe however that there was any serious possibility of the Government agreeing to reduce the railway network on anything approaching such a drastic scale as that outlined in the *Sunday Times* document.

'He recalled that somewhere about 1966 or 1967 Mrs Castle had achieved great headlines by "saving" the railway system in Scotland. There had been a lot of puzzlement over this. In preceding months he himself had regularly received replies from Mrs Castle and from Willie Ross[9] saying that there would be no threat to the Inverness and other Highland lines. Since he had regularly reported these back to his constituents (they were mostly written replies) he had them all there to quote. In other words Mrs Castle's "saving" of the Scottish railways was really quite unreal. He was prepared to say now as much as was necessary that there was no threat to the main highland lines.'

Marsh's view that senior officials in the Department displayed a blatantly pro-road bias (he was quoted by Jeremy Bugler in the *New Statesman* of 24 September 1976: 'Some civil servants are so anti-railways that I can only assume that something nasty happened to their mothers in a steam train') was widely shared. It was felt to be the prevailing culture at the time. As a former very senior civil servant in another Government department has told the authors:

> There was an extraordinary anti-railway and pro-road culture at the DofT at that time, and later. I remember a seminar on public accountability at which a DofT under-secretary said the DofT was accountable to the Road Haulage Association.

In the same *New Statesman* piece, Bugler also said:

> The DoE, from the first, employed vastly more officials on roads than it did on public transport – last year [1975] there were some 1,700 working on highway planning, with some 70 on railways and public transport. The manning reflected the DoE's task-in-hand: highway building.

When it came to railways, the Department had it in mind to move to a core network of between 3-5,000 route miles, but did not see the need to invest in modernising that core network to make it fit for purpose. Consistently, they questioned the need for track renewals with continuous welded rail, or resignalling, despite the amount of mechanical signalling remaining on the main line network. They even cavilled at the continuing programme to replace telegraph wires with cables.

The authors recall that the scheme for cabling the Berks & Hants line (the main line to the West of England) only went ahead after BR had furnished the Department with evidence that telegraph poles were so rotten they snapped when linemen placed a ladder against them to effect repairs. Nor did they want to fund the short-term losses from withdrawal of services where revenue exceeded operating costs, but did not cover the cost of renewals. Finally, they did not understand the process of cost escapement and the time taken to eliminate liabilities.

Their conclusion suggested a network of 5,450 route miles, of which 3,105 were for commercial passenger and freight services, with 2,345 for grant-aided services in London and the South East and the PTE areas. There were to be no provincial grant-aided services outside those areas. Significantly, however, the report concluded that, 'No viable railway or group of services has been identified.'

The BR planners pressed for future work in this area to be done as part of the corporate planning process, rather than as one-off hypothecated exercises – but it was not to be, and the Department sought a further review in October 1974.

1   John Peyton (1919-2006) was the Conservative MP for Yeovil for 32 years and Secretary of State for Transport from 1970-74, becoming Lord Peyton of Yeovil in 1983. Ten years later, he forced and won a vote on an amendment to the Railways Bill, which would have enabled BR to bid for franchises. Had this become law, it would have changed the nature of privatisation, but it was reversed when the Bill returned to the Commons for consideration of amendments from the House of Lords.

2   *Off the Rails: An Autobiography* by Richard Marsh, Weidenfeld & Nicolson, 1978, p167.

3   *Off the Rails* p170.

4   Peter Walker (1932-2010) was the Conservative MP for Worcester from 1961-92 and Secretary of State for the Environment 1970-72. He also served as Minister of Housing and Local Government and Secretary of State for Trade and industry in the 1970-74 Heath Government. After the Conservatives returned to office in 1979, Walker was successively Minister of Agriculture, Secretary of State for Energy (during the miners' strike) and Secretary of State for Wales, leaving office in 1990. He was a 'one nation' Conservative, a prominent Young Conservative and a businessman who had been a partner in Slater Walker and Chairman of Kleinwort Benson. He was ennobled as Lord Walker of Worcester in 1992; Walker's son, Robin, would be elected MP for Worcester in May 2010.

5   Hector Alastair Hetherington (1919–99) was editor of the *Manchester Guardian*, later *The Guardian*, from 1956–75. He won Journalist of the Year at the 1970 National Press Awards. The notes are reproduced by kind permission of the London School of Economics: LSE/Hetherington/20/39 for note 1, and LSE/Hetherington/20/35 for note 2.

6   John Cole (born 1927) was then deputy editor of *The Guardian* and later became political editor of the BBC.

7   John Whale (1931-2008) was a journalist and editor, at various times the political reporter and Washington correspondent with ITN, a long-time writer with the *Sunday Times*, head of religious programming at the BBC and editor of Anglican weekly the *Church Times*.

8   Gordon Campbell (1921-2005) was the Conservative MP for Moray and Nairn from 1959-74, who served as Secretary of State for Scotland from 1970-74. Ennobled as Lord Campbell of Croy in 1974, he was a war hero who commanded 320 Field Battery in 15 Scottish Division; wounded and disabled in 1945, he won the MC and Bar.

9   William Ross (1911-88) was Labour MP for Kilmarnock, 1946-79, and Secretary of State for Scotland, 1964-70 and 1974-76. He entered the House of Lords in 1979 as Lord Ross of Marnock. A former schoolteacher, he was also Lord High Commissioner of the General Assembly of the Church of Scotland, 1978-80.

VIII

THE NO RAIL CUTS CAMPAIGN

Thou shalt not kill, but needst not strive officiously to keep alive

ARTHUR HUGH CLOUGH, 'THE LAST DECALOGUE'

Death by a thousand cuts

At Morecambe, salami slicing saw the town's Euston Road (L&NW) station close in 1958, although it continued to handle the heavy summer holiday traffic until 1963. Beyond the buffer stops the Midland line from Wennington and the electrified section from Lancaster Green Ayre closed in 1966. The Torrisholme curve which allowed boat trains to run direct to Heysham went at the same time. In 1975, the branch from Morecambe to Heysham closed but was reopened for a daily ferry connection to Douglas, Isle of Man, in 1987. Promenade station on the seafront, closed in 1994 and was replaced by the current station, seen here in 2010 with a train to Lancaster in the bay platform. The platform for the Heysham train is on the left, as is the run-round loop for the periodic nuclear flask train to and from Heysham power station. The line now benefits from the support of a community rail partnership, while the town has had a boost from restoration of the wonderful art deco Midland Hotel of 1933 opposite Promenade station, now the town's tourist information centre.

HOLDING THE LINE

As we have seen, the potentially devastating new round of closures envisaged in the Blue Paper had awoken the British Railways Board to its duty to protect the railway from its enemies. From a position of supporting and implementing the closure programme initiated by the Beeching Report – rather more enthusiastically than most objective observers might have expected or wished – the board now sought common cause with those who wished to fight for the railway.

Transport 2000

While there were already a number of organisations committed to supporting the railway, there was initially no single body which brought together users, environmentalists, amenity groups, academics, the railway supply industry and trade unions. Such an organisation came into being early in 1973, largely as the result of an initiative taken by the Assistant General Secretary of the National Union of Railwaymen, Sidney Weighell.[1] Entitled Transport 2000, it was officially launched on 6 February 1973 at a press conference in the Russell Hotel, London.

T2000's opening press statement announced it had been formed because 'these groups feel that Britain is in the grip of a transport crisis: too many vehicles in the wrong places, the threat of widespread rail closures, [and] concern over environmental damage done by heavy lorries.'

(T2000 continues its crucial role today as the Campaign for Better Transport. Its president is Michael Palin[2], the polymath actor/writer/broadcaster/traveller and British national treasure, initially recruited in 1986 as Chairman by co-author Richard Faulkner on Leeds station. Both were waiting for a heavily delayed London-bound train when Palin said, 'Someone ought to do something about the state of public transport in Britain.' Faulkner saw his chance.)

For many years, initially at the behest of Sir Peter Parker, T2000 received significant funding from the British Railways Board as well as core contributions from the railway unions. Its first high-profile outing was in 1975, as part of the rail unions' 'No Rail Cuts – Keep Public Transport' campaign. In his autobiography, *On the Rails*, Weighell describes how his initial high expectations for the new Labour Government of 1974 – based on the explicit manifesto

Reopening Railways:
the case for growing the rail network and how it can be achieved

www.bettertransport.org.uk

commitment to move as much traffic as possible from road to rail and make the country less dependent on the private car – were rapidly disappointed after the rail unions' pay crisis in July 1975: 'I realised that the Government was getting ready to do an about-face in its support for public transport and the railways in particular.'

He goes on to describe how, in the autumn of 1975, he had been told the Government were demanding cuts in the spending programme: 'The board told us privately that the financial restrictions being placed on the industry's investment would have a grave impact on the future of the network.'[3]

Edward Heath's[4] Government had lost office in the 'Who governs Britain?' election of February 1974, but before that John Peyton had announced in the House of Commons that there would be 'no closures of substance' before 1975.

It was widely assumed that Peyton's commitment to maintaining the size of the network would be adhered to by the new minority Labour Government, with supporters of the railway reassured by the party's manifestos for the February and October 1974 general elections. In the former case, the Labour manifesto declared:

The energy crisis has further profound implications for the way we conduct our whole transport system. If we are to conserve precious fuel we must do two things: one, move as much traffic as possible from road to rail; and two, develop public transport to make us less dependent on the private car. This will involve large scale investment in railways, tubes and buses and a fares policy which puts the needs of the travelling public first.[5]

Railways Act 1974

The 1974 Act was a very brief piece of legislation, considering the sums of money involved and the strategic implications for both the railway and the country itself. It was an enabling Act which allowed the establishment of the freight and InterCity businesses as 'commercial', while the 'social' railway (commuter and local passengers services) was supported by an annual block grant to BR. This was based on the concept of 'public service obligation' (PSO) within European legislation (directive 1191/69), and replaced the grants for individual lines under the 1968 Act. Peyton's statement to the House the year before the bill showed a significant and welcome change in Government policy:

The board's studies showed no prospect in the foreseeable future of a railway network of anything like the present size being viable ... In the Government's view, the right course is to maintain a railway network of roughly the present size, and to improve it.[6]

The Treasury had, of course, wanted to prescribe a limit for the grant, but this was resisted.[7] For the mandarins, the objective of the bill was to exercise greater policy control over BR, on the basis that it would continue to need substantial public support. The bill therefore asserted the requirement for the board to take account of ministerial direction, provide information and seek approval for substantial capital expenditure.

The grants were intended to cover the gap between the costs of operating the passenger network and incoming revenue. In practice,

Campaigning 40 Years On
Transport 2000 became the Campaign for Better Transport in 2007, but remains a vibrant campaigning group. As this report from July 2012 shows, their work has shifted from closures to reopening lines and much more.
(Photo courtesy CBT)

the mandarins used it as a device to bear down on costs and the grant settlement was always less than that proposed by BRB, based on its budgeted costs and income each year.

While providing a welcome device to fund what was seen as the 'unremunerative' part of the network, it was an annual settlement and therefore final agreement was sometimes reached well into the financial year to which it applied. This hampered the board's ability to plan in advance and made inefficient use of resources but, nevertheless, it was a start.

The policy was reinforced in the manifesto for the second general election of 1974, which would return Harold Wilson's Government in October with a narrow majority:

> *The energy crisis has underlined our objectives to move as much traffic as possible from road to rail and to water; and to develop public transport to make us less dependent on the private car. Labour's Railway Act 1974 provides for a general subsidy to passenger services and grants for the provision of new private sidings and other freight facilities. Many proposed rail closures have been stopped.*[8]

To begin with, the new Labour Government seemed to be acting in accordance with the commitments of its manifestos. Although permission had been given to close three routes – Inverness-Kyle of Lochalsh, Hastings-Ashford and Bletchley-Bedford – the new transport minister, Fred Mulley (who had returned to the same job he had in 1970) told BR not to proceed with them. Three other proposals were rejected – the Cambrian Coast line from Machynlleth to Pwllheli, Wimbledon-West Croydon and Stockport-Stalybridge. All still operate today with greatly enhanced levels of service, except Stockport-Stalybridge which is kept open with the minimum legal number of trains (see Chapter 18). The Wimbledon-West Croydon branch is now part of the Croydon Tramlink run by Transport for London and also serves New Addington, Beckenham Junction and Elmers End. Passenger numbers have grown to a staggering 27 million a year.[9]

Approval was given to a small number of minor closures between 1975 and 1977:

- Maiden Newton-Bridport (May 1975)
- Morecambe-Heysham (October 1975)
- The fire-damaged East Brixton station (January 1976)
- Alston-Haltwhistle (May 1976)
- Mauchline Junction-Newton Junction and Dubbs Junction-Byrehill Junction, Ayrshire (June 1977)
- Filey Holiday Camp (September 1977).[10]

At this time, British Rail was still working with the Department of the Environment to promote a significant number of closures – 24 to be precise. According to Terry Gourvish, these included Glasgow-Oban, Glasgow-Fort William, Barking-Kentish Town, Manningtree-Harwich, Bournemouth-Weymouth, Rugby-Stafford local services, Ipswich-Felixstowe and Shrewsbury-Aberystwyth.[11] All these proposals were abandoned following introduction of the new public service obligation payments and the effects of the Railways Act 1974, and all services continue to operate today – once again, with many more trains carrying far more passengers than in 1974.

Gourvish also tells us that, later in 1974, 'a more considered list of 82 services was drawn up "just in case" the political climate changed.' These were services where BR alleged the operating ratio (operating costs : revenue) was 200 or worse and the average number of passengers per train 20 or fewer. Getting rid of 38 of these 82 lines would close 939 miles of the network and, it was claimed, 'reduce the PSO by about £3.2 million'.[12]

There were yet more joint studies of closures in 1975, carried out by BR and the DoE with the suggestion of three potential tranches: the first of 900 miles, the second of 1,300 and the third of 2,400.[13] Richard Marsh helpfully suggested to the new Minister, John Gilbert, that he publicly identify a group of services 'with a limited future'. There were 44 on this list, which included all the usual suspects plus Fort William-Mallaig, Lincoln-Skegness, Hull-Scarborough, York-Harrogate, Romford-Upminster, and Kentish Town-Moorgate.[14] Unsurprisingly, perhaps, the offer was not taken up.

The 'regressive railway'

The fact that ministers were unprepared to discuss openly the possibility of rail closures did not lessen their enthusiasm for reducing the size – and the cost, so they believed – of the railway. Rail supporters found they had a new challenge to overcome – a Secretary of State with an ideological dislike of rail subsidies. This was Tony Crosland[15], of whom it was said he had formed his impressions of railway travel in the first-class compartments of trains from London to his constituency in Grimsby. Looking around, he saw people as middle class as himself not only benefiting from subsidies paid to the railway but also quite capable of paying much higher fares. His view, and that of his civil servants, was that rail travel was largely the preserve of the businessman and the London commuter – both of whom he saw as relatively well-off. Subsidies for rail travel were therefore regressive, using the taxes of the less well-off to subsidise those who could readily afford to pay. It therefore justified a policy of less public money in terms of revenue support and capital investment.

While this classic Whitehall view of the railway was clearly wrong, it has remained in the consciousness of opinion formers ever since and is still trotted out whenever rail fares are discussed. However, it was never true of the railway as a whole and was particularly irrelevant to local and regional lines under threat which served poorer communities and those with limited access to alternative public transport.

Peter Parker, then seen as a possible future BR Chairman, met Crosland at this time and found it depressing that his paper implied a reduced railway:

> What he believed came through in a remark in his early briefing: 'Peter, I see a future for BR as a smaller, sensible little railway.' Instinctively, I could not agree; surely we could test the market by having a really determined policy to sell the services of railways.[16]

The prejudices of the Crosland paper were reinforced by a study carried out by a little-read but remarkably influential monthly publication called *Socialist Commentary*. In April 1975 it published a 64-page report from a transport policy study group chaired by Les Huckfield[17], a Labour MP sponsored by the Transport and General Workers Union – though a more significant figure was its Deputy Chairman and Director of Research, Christopher Foster.

In the chapter on railway policy, the report questions whether subsidies for the passenger railway are in the community's interest, '*since resources used to support an unprofitable railway system must inevitably be diverted from other, perhaps more economically and socially worthwhile, uses within the economy.*' Warming to this theme, it goes on:

Subsidisation of the railways might be justified either because the subsidies lead to an improvement in income distribution, or because provision of railway services confers certain social benefits which the railways cannot recover from the prices they charge. Rail subsidies cannot be justified on income distribution grounds, since rail passenger services tend to be consumed by the better-off members of society. Thus in 1972, the top income-earning 20% of households accounted for 51% of personal expenditure on rail travel, while the bottom 20% of households with the lowest incomes accounted for only 5% of such expenditure.

Unsurprisingly the report went on to question the value of railway investment, the opportunities for transferring freight from road to rail, and the levels of subsidy for rural and cross-country passenger services.

Against this background and despite clear election manifesto commitments, it was evident that by 1975 the Labour Government posed a threat to the size of the railway network at least as great as the Conservatives – or perhaps worse, in light of the unequivocal commitment by John Peyton to maintaining it at around the 1974 level and the worsening national economic situation.

The campaign

Despite their somewhat passive acquiescence toward the Beeching closures, the rail unions were not prepared to let it happen again. Having created Transport 2000 three years previously, they realised they had the means to mount a coherent popular campaign against rail closures and in support of investment. They hired a seasoned PR campaigner, William Camp[18], and his colleague Richard Faulkner (co-author of this book), who between them mounted a high-profile campaign entitled 'Keep Public Transport – No Rail Cuts'.

The credibility of the message was greatly enhanced when it became clear the British Railways Board itself was the source and inspiration of the briefing material – Faulkner remembers going into Board HQ at 222 Marylebone Road and interviewing Michael Harbinson, the Chief Rail Planning Officer. Harbinson was asked what the network was likely to look like in 1981 if there was no increase in levels of investment, and whether he had a map of the system which illustrated that. 'We have maps depicting every possible size of network,' he said, and produced one based on the frozen investment level of £281 million a year.

That map formed the basis of a leaflet produced for mass distribution. The language was uncompromising:

The railways are in danger.
Do you want them to shrink to the point where only a skeleton service is left?

*If the future of the railways matters to you, now is the time to speak up. Look carefully at the map inside – **this** is the threat which once again is rearing its ugly head. If the Government's planners and economists have their way, **this** is what could eventually happen.*

Britain's railways – an essential part of the entire public transport system – are due to be led to the slaughter. Or, more accurately, to death by a thousand cuts.

Specifically, what is going on now is a major review of the future of the railways. In secret, conducted under strict orders from the Treasury. Apart from this bare fact, rail users are in the dark. The game is being played by civil servants. Behind closed doors. And with all the cards marked.

*The idea is to announce the result early in 1976. **So unless you act now, it could be too late.***

It has all happened before. As recently as 1972 the same old hatchet-men were sharpening their knives. But their plans were exposed. There was a massive public outcry. The Government did a U-turn. The role of the railways was reasserted and guaranteed – as it has to be – by Government financial support.

Now that support – needed by railways in all other major countries – is going to be axed. Yes, another U-turn. By a Government supposed to be keen on public transport.

*The attack on the railways will be two-pronged. **Slash their investment programme. Clobber their financial support.***

Without enough investment crucial modernisation schemes would be fatally delayed or abandoned altogether. Improvements in the quality of our rail services, such as replacement of worn-out rolling stock and electrification – essential in an up-to-date system – will be impossible. Your trains will be slower and less reliable. Without improvements the railways will become less and less able to attract more customers. The successful trends of recent years will be reversed. When that happens, the planners will point to the railways' falling popularity and happily 'cut them down to size' (look at the map again).

We are not talking about minor investment cuts. Because of the economic crisis some reductions are unavoidable, particularly for 1976. What the planners are studying now are the years 1977-1981 and after. And their declared intention is to axe investment for each of those years to well below the levels set by the last Government – after much careful thought – at the end of 1973.

*Investment cuts will be bad enough. The second prong of the assault on the railways will be even worse. Financial support by the Government for passenger services is going to be **permanently** restricted, and will not even allow adequately for rising prices. Support for freight services will be **totally** removed.*

*So the railways will have no option but to jack up their charges, which have **already gone up enough to drive away customers in ever-increasing numbers.***

When nobody can afford rail travel, the planners will no doubt claim they have proved their point.

*We know that various alternative schemes for slashing services and increasing fares are now being considered by the Rail Board. They have no option. **They are being forced to prepare in advance for the big shrink.***

*So it is up to you, the customers, those who rely on the railways, who have seen them making a real effort to improve services. **Offering advantages no sane society would ever ignore.** On environmental grounds, on energy saving, safety, noise, comfort, convenience, speed – name it, the railways have it.*

***If the railways matter to you, now is the time to act.** If you belong to an organisation, show your fellow-members this leaflet, and make them protest as a body to the Minister for Transport. Write to him individually (by tearing off the strip below), write to your MP, local councillors, national and local newspapers. If you want more information, write to us: The No Rail Cuts Campaign, Greater London House, Hampstead Road, London NW1.*

This time the planners are in deadly earnest. A hell of a row will be needed to make them change their minds.

At the foot of the leaflet was a slip addressed to Dr John Gilbert MP[19], with the words:

> *Dear Dr Gilbert,*
> *I sincerely hope that as Minister for Transport you will stand up for the future of the railways and strongly oppose any policy which commits them to a shrinking role in our public transport system. We need the railways more than ever before.*

One and a half million copies of this leaflet were produced and distributed through a wide variety of outlets, including trade union branches, environmental bodies, local authorities, trade councils, Labour Party branches and, most important of all, at railway stations up and down the country. A parliamentary answer on 4 February 1976 elicited the information that the Government had '*received over 20,000 representations about the future of the network. The majority of these have been in the form of tear-off slips bearing identical wording.*'

The campaign was launched at a packed press conference at the Great Northern Hotel on 11 December 1975. The platform was occupied by Sidney Weighell, Ray Buckton[20], General Secretary of drivers' union ASLEF, Tom Jenkins[21], Acting General Secretary of the white-collar TSSA, three MPs – Labour's Tom Bradley[22], the Liberals' Stephen Ross[23], the Conservatives' John Cockroft[24] – and Dr Leonard Taitz[25], Chairman of Transport 2000. Weighell's principal message was that by cutting investment levels, from the £360 million a year BR was seeking to £238 million, there would inevitably be a reduction in the network by two-thirds and cuts in railway manpower from 260,000 to fewer than 100,000. These facts were taken from documents passing between BRB and the Department of the Environment which, according to Weighell, 'could be authenticated in Downing Street'.

The Times, in common with other newspapers, reprinted the map shown in the No Rail Cuts leaflet and repeated the unions' claim that 'the rail network will be reduced to the present Inter-City and London commuter services during the next six years. They say there would be no Scottish services north of Edinburgh and Glasgow, and none west of Plymouth. Wales would retain only the Swansea and Holyhead lines, and East Anglia only the Norwich line.

'Towns losing their existing service would include Middlesbrough, Harrogate, Huddersfield, Lincoln, Newmarket, Weymouth, Worcester, Shrewsbury, Stratford-on-Avon, Fishguard, Blackpool, Barrow, Aberdeen and Inverness.'

This press conference and launch set the scene for the next big event in the campaign – a rally of Parliament on the following Tuesday, 16 December, consisting of a mass meeting in Central Hall Westminster running from noon to 5:00pm and a lobby of Parliament. *The Guardian* reported that '2,600 rail workers filled every seat in the hall', and there was a robust exchange between Sid Weighell and Tony Crosland (though not face to face – Weighell says in his book that he never met Crosland the entire time he was Secretary of State for the Environment and their only encounter was years later at the British embassy in Beijing, when Crosland was Foreign Secretary).

That morning, Crosland had published a written parliamentary answer:

> *Stories which have appeared in the Press in recent days about massive cuts to the rail network are a load of codswallop. I cannot tell whether they emanate from British Rail, or the railway unions, or both, or neither. Whatever the source, these irresponsible comments*

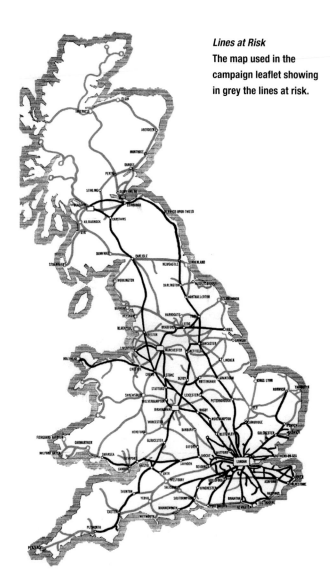

Lines at Risk
The map used in the campaign leaflet showing in grey the lines at risk.

appear calculated to cause alarm and despondency. I advise the travelling public to treat them with incredulity. When decisions come to be made on the Transport Policy Review they will be taken by Ministers and Ministers alone, after full consultation with management, unions and other interests in the transport industry.[26]

That really got Weighell going. He called Crosland 'a bloody liar' and claimed he didn't know what was going on in his own department, as quoted in *The Guardian*:

> It was riddled with people who planned for roads, prayed for roads, and had a vested interest in roads. As for the Minister of Transport, 'We change him as often as I change my shirt.' This Government is on the point of betraying every policy undertaken in the transport field by the Labour Party since the turn of the century.

Weighell also said that the NUR expected the 10 Labour MPs sponsored by the union to withdraw their support from the Government if it went ahead with plans for large cuts in the network. Not unexpectedly, this caused a row, with Weighell accused of a breach of parliamentary privilege. He never quite apologised and justified his comments in his book thus:

… feelings were running high and I was absolutely determined to make sure that Ministers took serious note of what we were saying and changed their minds. There was no good reason why my union should go on pouring money into the Labour Party and giving faithful support to the Government, if they refused to listen to us.[27]

The media backed the campaign against the Government. In an editorial in the *Sunday Times* on 21 September, the paper opined:

Codswallop … struck a welcome note in the leaden technology of written parliamentary answers; but as a response to insistent rumours of rail cuts, it was not enough. Mr Crosland's reticence about railways is a long-standing puzzle. Here is a man and an issue which might have been destined for each other. Mr Crosland has made his political reputation by providing arguments for the survival into the late 20th century of a phenomenon which had its origins in the industrial clangour of the 19th century – British socialism. The railways are a notable parallel. Like socialism they have improved the lives of a great many people; like socialism, they now face the complaint that they have passed the summit of their usefulness and entered on the long gradient into the valley of the shadow. They are a natural Crosland client.

During the winter of 1975/76, there was some doubt as to whether the Government would publish a definitive statement of transport policy as a White Paper, or whether it would produce a green consultative document. (When it finally appeared, in April 1976, it was as a consultative document – but with an orange cover.)

Crosland himself described the April 1975 *Socialist Commentary* paper as 'an essential input' into the review of transport policy in an unpublished paper in February 1976 (deposited at the London School of Economics), echoing the *Socialist Commentary* theme:

We must concentrate our efforts and financial support on providing public transport for the diminishing but substantial number of people who cannot afford or lack access to, a car. We must ensure that transport spending is directed towards the less well-off and not (as so often at present) to the better-off.

At the same time we have to set our policies against tight constraints on expenditure. We have (rightly) given our highest priority in social spending to housing, to pensions, and to cash grants for the worst off. Transport spending will have to take a back seat, and the result is that *all* transport users must expect to pay more.

This policy of requiring more from the fare box and less from the taxpayer has remained consistent from that day to this, whichever party has been in power. Crosland then listed a number of conditions which had to be met if the Government's transport policy were to be carried out. The third of these was most relevant as far as this book is concerned: 'The decline in some services on the railways – inevitable unless BR achieves unparalleled gains in efficiency – must be matched by a greater concentration of public support on the lower cost public transport mode, the bus.'

One month previously – on 21 January 1976 – there had been a high-level meeting in the Department of the Environment attended by Crosland, Minister of State John Gilbert, Parliamentary Secretary Ken Marks[28], First Permanent Secretary Sir Ian Bancroft[29], Second Permanent Secretary Sir Idwal Pugh[30] and a number of officials including David Lipsey[31], Crosland's political adviser. The confidential note of that meeting (discovered in the papers at the LSE) included these comments on rail policy:

On subsidies, both the *Socialist Commentary* report and Pryke[32] had argued that a residual subsidy was essential. The Secretary of State said that in view of the income distribution arguments against rail subsidies it was important to articulate a clearer case for some residual subsidy, e.g. on anti-congestion grounds.

The proposed policy would bear particularly harshly on the poorer long-distance commuter who may have moved to his present home because of relatively cheap housing and subsidised rail fares. The policy had implications for planning and housing in London and the South East.

There were very difficult political problems to be faced in respect of services in the 'remainder' category, where line closures would be necessary. To the extent that costs could be reduced by manpower economies, the need for closures would be less; but the feeling was that recent estimates by Pryke of possible manpower savings were over-optimistic.

The disagreement with British Rail entailed a major presentational problem for the Government. The Marsh line was that the Government should state what sort of rail service they wanted and BR would say how much it would cost. The Government's line was to say what the financial objectives would be for each main sector of the railways and how much subsidy and investment would be available; and to leave BR to manage the system within those financial constraints, involving adjustments in frequency of services, cost reductions through manpower economies and closure proposals.

Getting rid of Marsh

This last paragraph was perhaps the most interesting of all, as it demonstrated how exasperated the Government had become with Marsh and the BR board. Marsh clearly had no wish to do ministers' dirty work for them – if there were to be a smaller network and extensive closures, he intended that they – not BR – should take both responsibility and blame for them.

In his autobiography[33], Marsh describes his growing disillusionment with the Labour Government, recounting at some length how he received a letter delivered by Governmental car:

The envelope was stapled to a large card with dramatic diagonal red stripes all round it, marked 'Urgent, Ministerial Enquiry, by Hand only at all stages.' Thinking that it must at least be a declaration of war, I opened it and discovered that Ministers wanted me to carry out an enquiry into the financial effects of British Rail's recent decision to refuse to carry stray and lost racing pigeons.[34]

Having published the original letter from Transport Minister John Gilbert and his own ironic reply, Marsh comments, 'By this time I had already decided to leave BR, but the last exchange of correspondence removed any lingering doubts I might have had about the wisdom of the decision.'

His temper was not improved six months later, in March 1976, when he read a story in the *Sunday Express* headed, 'Marsh coming off the rails', saying that he was to be replaced as Chairman of BR. He went 'in great secrecy' to see Tony Crosland the next morning, who refused to confirm or deny the truth of the report. As he left he found a *Daily Mail* photographer 'clicking away as fast as he could'.

Marsh resigned as BR Chairman in September 1976 and was succeeded by Peter Parker, whose style in dealing with the Government was very different – as we shall see.

Had Sidney Weighell and his rail union colleagues had the chance to read some of the papers leading up to publication of the transport policy consultative document later in 1976, they would certainly have felt the fears they expressed in the No Rail Cuts campaign were far from being 'codswallop'. The Government was clearly determined to reduce the size of the network. Indeed, in a private memorandum David Lipsey suggested that the words on closures in the paper be toned down. He described an early draft of paragraph 71 as 'too strong on closures: say "or even in a few cases closures". *Closures are our political Achilles' heel* [our emphasis].'[35]

One refreshingly practical observation was made in another note on the consultation paper, this time by Ann Carlton[36] who was also a political adviser at the Department. Commenting on a paragraph on replacing rail services with buses, she says:

> I find this suggestion rather amusing. At one point there was a train service from Sandling Junction to Hythe. This was replaced by a bus service when the line was closed. No doubt at the time suitable assurances were given but alas Kent County Council have now decided to alter their subsidies and the bus service has been reduced – to my chagrin. I am sure that in many areas the suggestion that bus services would replace rail services would meet with a very cynical response since people already had experience of this sort of thing before and would believe that the buses would soon be replaced by nothing.[37]

Confirmation of how hostile Crosland and his closest advisers were to the railway is contained in Lipsey's autobiography[38]:

> The villain of the piece was the railways. They were heavily subsidised and, partly in consequence, run with staggering inefficiency and insouciance towards their customers. Nevertheless the middle classes and business classes used them intensively to commute from their suburban fastnesses or to travel longer distances not quite requiring an aeroplane. The middle classes were onto a good thing.

For those without access to cars, the public transport solution 'did not comprise railways. It comprised the humble bus.' Thus were Crosland and Lipsey attracted by *Socialist Commentary*'s ideas for promoting bus travel. 'I have never understood why one, converting railway lines into cheaper, more flexible bus routes, has never taken hold,' writes Lipsey – those who read the subsequent chapters of this book will easily understand why.

The Orange Paper

By a strange twist of fate, while it had clearly been written by Crosland and reflected all the prejudices displayed previously, the transport policy document was presented at an April 1976 press conference by a new Secretary of State for the Environment, Peter Shore.[39] Lipsey tells us that Crosland 'made a desperate and despairing effort to persude Mr Shore to allow the old Secretary of State to return to DoE to launch the Green [*sic*] Paper. Naturally and rightly, Mr Shore declined. The Green Paper survived but alas the policy fared less well. Mr Shore took a more conventional attitude to the virtues of trains.'[40]

The No Rail Cuts - Keep Public Transport leaflet

The consultation paper was about as bad for the railways as it could have been. Weighell described it as 'one of the most blatantly biased Government presentations I had ever laid eyes on. If it had been produced by one of the road lobby pressure groups I would have recognised the prejudice and accepted it as such, but this document was supposed to represent the balanced view of the Government.'[41]

In its response to the Government's consultation document, the party at large said unequivocally that, as far as the railways were concerned, 'Labour Party policy is quite contrary to the suggestions contained in the Government's paper.'[42]

Much of the *Socialist Commentary* dogma had found its way into the orange paper, including statements such as 'higher subsidies could be paid only at the expense of other vital programmes and would not be socially justified'.[43] Commuters from London's outer suburbs were to be given five years to adjust to fare increases which would wipe out subsidies – supposedly 'long enough to enable people to make any adjustments in their way of life with the minimum of inconvenience'.

It also repeated the assertion that rail subsidies were regressive and better spent on supporting bus services, and that the railway should concentrate only on what it did best: bulk freight haulage, fast inter-city passenger services and dense commuter flows. Having decried rail as the preserve of the upper middle classes, it suggested that BR should maximise its revenue over the whole range of passenger and freight services. This would have neatly made the 'only the rich travel by train' canard a self-fulfilling prophecy, for as the fares went up only the well-off would be able to afford them.

The British Railways Board's response, *An Opportunity for Change*[44], was remarkably outspoken in its criticism of the Crosland Orange Paper and demonstrated the independence of mind of its authors (it was mainly drafted by John Prideaux[45]) and also reflected the uneasy relationship between Marsh as Chairman and the Government. The analysis pulled no punches. 'The board finds little evidence of a systematic approach to the complex problems involved,' was its overall judgement, explaining that 'this response deals at some length with aspects of the document which, in the board's view, lack substance or are just plainly wrong'.

In his introduction, Marsh set out the view that the railway would never produce a conventional commercial return on capital. Most importantly, the document stressed the importance of branch line contributory revenue which, if lost, would weaken the trunk services:

The net effect is that there is only a limited number of cases when closure can lead to an overall improvement in the board's finances. This was one of the lessons of the Beeching era.

Bus substitution

Notwithstanding this robust statement, the board went on to promote the concept of bus substitution on a significant scale. *An Opportunity for Change* identified some 10 per cent of passenger train miles that could be withdrawn and replaced by guaranteed bus services designed to maintain contributory revenue. They would be aided by existing local authority grants and integrated with current road services. Longer-distance rail services which produce reasonable contributory revenue would be replaced by higher standard buses, which would act as feeder links to the InterCity rail system rather than being part of the bus network. These would be financially supported by the Department of the Environment through the PSO grant and would be integrated into the railway timetable with through ticketing.

The proposition put forward by the board might also work in reverse, however. The corollary would be the withdrawal of long-distance coaches where a good InterCity rail service existed. 'It will be in the best national interest for BR's Inter-City services to fulfil the dominant role in longer-distance trunk services and for NBC bus services to fulfil the dominant role in cross-country and rural services.'[46]

Superficially, it appeared that there was some symmetry between the BRB view of bus substitution and the Government's. On 'loss-making rural services', the Crosland Orange Paper suggested:

There is a possible 'trade-off' in certain areas by way of substituting an assured and cheaper bus service in place of a much more expensive local train service ... Previous attempts to provide bus alternatives have often not succeeded because patronage has declined ... It would be necessary to give some assurance that ... rather than simply follow the route of the railway the aim would be to provide a better public transport service better adapted to the needs of the community and with less cost to public subsidy before closure was allowed.

This was a depressing throwback to part of the debate which followed the Beeching closures after 1963. Almost without exception, the bus services which were put on as replacements for rail failed because they halved overnight the former patronage of the train.

From the 1920s onwards, railway companies had listed the alternative road services available when they withdrew from branch lines. Indeed, many ministerial approvals of the Beeching closures required that replacement bus services be provided to relieve hardship. However, most were under contract to the railway for a limited period and within three years many had disappeared. This was for a variety of reasons, the most common of which was that the buses were far slower, and could not carry luggage, bicycles, prams and pushchairs.

This *laissez-faire* approach by the Department – which thereafter left it to bus companies and local authorities to decide whether or not to provide services in the area formerly served by the railway – had an effect on public confidence. Replacement bus services were seen as a short-term expedient by Government to justify the withdrawal of rail services.

British Rail's ingenious suggestion that long-distance coach services should be withdrawn to remove competition with InterCity's operations received no encouragement at all in the Department and nothing more was heard of this idea. Indeed, as we shall see in the next chapter, officials wanted to scale back the InterCity rail network – the complete opposite of what BR had proposed in *An Opportunity for Change*.

Today, there is huge resistance to buses replacing rail services disrupted by engineering works at weekends. As a consequence, train operators now do their best to continue running through services, via a roundabout route if necessary rather than disrupting a journey with a bus ride.[47]

The Railways Board's response deeply dismayed the No Rail Cuts coalition, which felt that BR was effectively doing the Department's dirty work for them. They had hoped BR would stand shoulder to shoulder with them to defend the rural services, but instead here were the board admitting that they had already started talks with the National Bus Company to go down the substitution route.

The NUR produced a new leaflet, entitled 'Rail Cuts – A Warning'. This contained a list of 200 services which were believed to be candidates for closure and bus substitution. Recipients were encouraged to write to Peter Shore, the Environment Secretary.

There had been significant lobbying through 1976-77 by the unions, which included the unusual course of organising private lunches and dinners (behind Tony Crosland's back) with very senior members of the Government believed to be sympathetic to the railways. Separate dinners were held in private rooms at Westminster restaurants with Roy Jenkins, Michael Foot[48] and Tony Benn, at which the shortcomings of the Crosland approach to the railways were frankly discussed. Perhaps surprisingly, given their mass of detail, there is no reference to the dinner that Benn attended in his diaries.

1   Sidney Weighell (1922-2002) was, variously, a railwayman, professional footballer and trade union general secretary. He joined the LNER in 1938, following his father, grandfather and brother to the railway. Initially a fireman, he became an engine driver in 1943 before leaving the railway to play for Sunderland FC in 1945, but returned in 1947. He became a full-time NUR official in 1954. For a fuller appraisal of his career, see Chapter 11.

2   Michael Palin (born 1943) is an actor, writer and traveller; he has also been President of the Royal Geographical Society since 2009.

3   *On the Rails* by Sidney Weighell with Robert Taylor, Orbis Publishing, 1983, p55 *et seq.*

4   Sir Edward Heath (1916-2005) was the Conservative politician who served as Prime Minister from 1970-74. His principal achievement was to negotiate Britain's entry into the European Economic Community (EEC – or Common Market) in 1972. Elected MP for Bexley in 1950 (the constituency later renamed as Old Bexley and Sidcup), he served continuously in the House of Commons until 2001 – his final parliament as 'Father of the House'. Heath was a minister throughout the period of Conservative Government from 1951-64, serving as Chief Whip at the time of the Suez invasion of 1956. He was elected leader of the party in 1965, a position he held until he was overthrown by Margaret Thatcher in 1975 – an 'act of treachery' for

which he never forgave her. Heath was a Kent grammar school boy who went to Balliol College Oxford and became president of the Oxford Union. He was a talented musician – an organ scholar at his college – and a highly accomplished yachtsman. The political mistake which cost him the leadership of the party, and denied him office for the remainder of his life, was to call a general election in February 1974 on a 'Who governs Britain?' platform. Expecting the electorate to back his stand against the National Union of Mineworkers, Heath received an unwelcome response from voters which translated as, 'We're not really sure, but not *you*, matey.' At this point a minority Labour Government led by Harold Wilson took office. Heath declined the chance to become Britain's ambassador to the United States in 1979 and also turned down a place in the House of Lords. For most of his career *Private Eye* magazine referred to him as 'Grocer Heath', or just 'the Grocer' – a reference to his piloting the abolition of retail price maintenance when President of the Board of Trade in 1964.

5   'Let us work together – Labour's way out of the crisis' – from *The Energy Crisis*, in the 1974 Labour Party manifesto.

6   *HC Deb*, 28 November 1973, columns 397-9.

7   DoT memoranda in the National Archive, MT 125/272 volume two.

8   *Britain Will Win With Labour.*

9   *Tramlink User Guide*, January 2010, published by Transport for London.

10 *British Rail 1974-97* by Terry Gourvish, Oxford University Press, 2002, p62.

11 Ibid, pp535-6.

12 Ibid, p62.

13 DoE papers at the National Archives, AN 121/342.

14 Ibid, p536.

15 The Rt. Hon. Anthony Crosland (1918-77) was a Labour politician who served as Secretary of State for the Environment from March 1974-April 1976 and then as Foreign Secretary for the last 10 months of his life. He was also MP for South Gloucestershire from 1950-55 and Grimsby from 1959-77, and a minister throughout the 1964-70 Labour Government – most controversially as Secretary of State for Education. In the biography of her husband, Susan Crosland wrote that he had told her, 'If it's the last thing I do, I'm going to destroy every fucking grammar school in England. And Wales and Northern Ireland' (*Tony Crosland* by Susan Crosland, Cape, 1982, p148). In 1956, during his spell out of Parliament, Crosland had published *The Future of Socialism*, a seminal work which set the agenda for the Labour Party's debate on revisionism.

16 *For Starters* by Peter Parker, Jonathan Cape, 1989, p185.

17 Leslie Huckfield (born 1942) was the Labour MP for Nuneaton from 1967-83 (succeeding Frank Cousins *qv*) and MEP for Merseyside East from 1984-89. He was also the Junior Industry Minister from 1976-79 and latterly represented ASLEF in the House of Commons.

18 William Camp (1926-2002) was a writer/political and corporate adviser. In his obituary (*The Guardian*, 29 January 2002) Ian Gilmour described him as 'an entertaining novelist, whom another novelist, Simon Raven, once called "that memorable troubadour of sexual disaster". He was also a biographer, a political activist and an enthusiastic supporter of charities. His principal occupation was as an adviser on corporate public relations, which he defined not as organised lying – that he thought "too strong" – but as "arranging the truth so that people will like you".' In his history *British Rail 1974-97*, Terry Gourvish described him as 'an accomplished "spin-doctor" 20 years ahead of his time'. Gilmour also wrote: 'His best later work was for the railways. From 1976 to 1977, he was hired by the trade unions to campaign – successfully – against the Labour Government's efforts to drastically reduce the rail network. He was then taken on by the new BR Chairman, Peter Parker, a contemporary from Oxford. Under Camp's guidance, the railways adopted an aggressive, largely successful stance during the debates of the 1980s over the role and scale of their operations.' See also Chapter 9.

19 John Gilbert (born 1927) was Labour's Minister of State for Transport from June 1975-September 1976, during which time he introduced the bill to make the wearing of seat belts compulsory. He was the MP for Dudley 1970-97, and also served as Financial Secretary to the Treasury and Minister of State for Defence in the Wilson and Callaghan Governments. Ennobled as Lord Gilbert in 1997, he went on to serve as Defence Minister.

20 Ray Buckton (1922-1995) was the General Secretary of ASLEF, the train drivers' union, from 1970-87, and President of the TUC 1983-4. Terry Pattinson's obituary of him in *The Independent* (9 May 1995) commented: '"I can't hold my members back any longer" was Ray Buckton's favourite and ominous quote during spells of industrial strife on the railways; and it would provide an appropriate epitaph for the man all commuters loved to hate. Once dubbed "The Most Unpopular Man in Britain" in a newspaper poll, railway passengers probably detested him more than they loathed politicians.' Buckton was a former engine cleaner, fireman and driver who often worked on the York-Scarborough line. Sidney Weighell commented in his autobiography, *On the Rails*: 'Over the years I had many battles with ASLEF, but personally I had nothing against Ray Buckton. I have always had the impression that he was very much controlled by his Executive. He never came to meetings without his ASLEF President at his shoulder, seemingly acting as a minder.'

21 Tom Jenkins CBE (1922-2012) was General Secretary of the Transport Salaried Staffs' Association 1977-82. Elder brother of Clive Jenkins, who was for 20 years General Secretary of the Association of Scientific, Technical and Managerial Staffs, he joined the Great Western Railway in South Wales and the Railway Clerks' Association (the TSSA's predecessor) in 1937, rising up through the ranks.

22 Tom Bradley (1926-2002) was a Labour politician and trade union leader. He was also MP for Leicester East 1962-83 and a member of the Labour Party's national executive committee 1965-82 (also its Chairman in 1976). Bradley chaired the party's transport sub-committee, some of whose deliberations (and Bradley's role in them) are described in Chapter 15. He served as Treasurer in the Transport Salaried Staffs' Association from 1961-64, its President from 1964-77 and Acting General Secretary from 1976-77, having joined the union in 1942. His political career was on the right of the Labour Party and he served as parliamentary private secretary to Roy Jenkins (*qv*) 1964-70. Bradley was passionately pro-EEC, left Labour to join the SDP in 1981 but subsequently came third in his Leicester East constituency at the 1983 election. Disappointed by politics, Bradley threw himself into non-league football, becoming Chairman of Kettering Town FC.

23 Stephen Ross (1926-93) was a Liberal Party politician and estate agent. MP for the Isle of Wight from 1974-87, he was the leader of Isle of Wight County Council from 1973-74 and 1981-83, and was ennobled as Lord Ross of Newport in 1987.

24 John Cockroft (born 1934) has been a Conservative politician, journalist and businessman, serving as MP for Nantwich from 1974-79. He has written for the *Financial Times*, the *Daily Telegraph* and the *Sunday Telegraph*.

25 Dr Leonard Taitz (1935-91), the first Chairman of Transport 2000, was convenor of the Conservation Society's national transport working party. He was also a distinguished paediatrician and co-author of *Handbook of Child Nutrition* (OUP, 1989).

26 *Hansard*, 16 December 1972, column 621W.

27 *On the Rails*, p55.

28 Ken Marks (1920-88) was the Labour MP for Manchester Gorton from 1967-83, having formerly been a head teacher and LNER office worker.

29 Sir Ian Bancroft (1922-96) was a career civil servant who entered the Treasury in 1947 and became head of the Home Civil Service and Permanent Secretary to the Civil Service Department from 1978–81, after serving at the DoE. Ennobled in 1992, he was also director of the Rugby Group (formerly Rugby Portland Cement) 1982-93.

30 Sir Idwal Pugh (1918-2010) was a career civil servant who rose to Second Permanent Secretary in the Department of the Environment from 1971-76, and subsequently became the Parliamentary Commissioner for Administration (or Ombudsman).

31 David Lipsey (born 1948) was a journalist and research assistant to the GMWU before becoming political adviser to Anthony Crosland. He was ennobled as Lord Lipsey in 1999.

32 Richard Pryke, an Oxford academic, was co-author with J. Dodgson, of *Rail Problem: An Alternative Strategy*, published in 1975, which argued that over-manning was the cause of most of the railway's difficulties.

33 Richard Marsh. *Off the Rails: An Autobiography*, Weidenfeld & Nicolson, 1978, pp199-202.

34 By coincidence, the 'pigeon policy' fell within the responsibilities of John Palmer – then recently appointed to the railways division of DoT, but later to join BR, become the Chairman of Eurostar and work with John Welsby on rail privatisation.

35 Included in Anthony Crosland's private papers, deposited at the London School of Economics.

36 Ann Carlton (born 1943) was an adviser to Labour Cabinet Ministers Tony Crosland and John Silkin, and previously the party's Local Government Officer. She is the daughter of the late Sir Stanley Holmes, Chief Executive and Town Clerk of the City of Liverpool, and is married to former Labour Minister and MP Denzil Davies.

37 Included in the Anthony Crosland papers at the LSE.

38 *In the Corridors of Power* by David Lipsey, Biteback Publishing, 2012, pp71-72.

39 The Rt. Hon. Peter Shore MP (1924-2001) was Secretary of State for the Environment, 1976-79, and MP for Stepney 1964-97. Ennobled as Lord Shore of Stepney in 1997, as head of the Labour Party's research department, before entering Parliament, he had also been the author of most of the party's manifesto for the 1964, 1966 and 1970 elections. He was Harold Wilson's Parliamentary Private Secretary in the 1964 Government and then Secretary of State for Economic Affairs. Following Labour's defeat in 1979 and the subsequent resignation as leader by James Callaghan, Shore was a serious candidate to succeed him. He was initially promised the support of Michael Foot, who changed his mind overnight and stood himself, winning the position and relegating Shore to third place behind the favourite, Denis Healey. Shore was described in his obituary by Conservative journalist Patrick Cosgrave as 'between Harold Wilson and Tony Blair, the only possible Labour Party leader of whom a Conservative leader had cause to walk in fear.' (*The Independent*, 26 September 2001.)

40 *In the Corridors of Power*, pp72-73.

41 *On the Rails*, p53.

42 Labour Party National Executive Committee Research Paper RE 725, July 1976, p3.

43 Orange Paper paragraph 7.37, p55.

44 *An Opportunity for Change: Comments by British Railways Board on the Government Consultation Document*, British Railways, July 1976.

45 Dr J.D.C.A. Prideaux CBE (born 1944) rose from the BR policy unit to become Managing Director of InterCity, under BR, and Chairman of Angel Trains after privatisation. He is currently Chairman of the Ffestiniog Railway.

46 *An Opportunity for Change*, p44.

47 '"*Replacement bus service*" – arguably the most depressing three words in the English language.': Marina Hyde writing about football fans' travelling problems in *The Guardian Sport* (1 September 2011).

48 Michael Foot (1913-2010) was the veteran Labour politician first elected to Parliament in 1945 as MP for Plymouth Devonport, which he represented until 1955. In 1960 he won Ebbw Vale at a by-election, following the death of Aneurin Bevan, and represented it until his retirement in 1992. Foot served in the Wilson and Callaghan Governments of the 1970s, first as Secretary of State for Employment and then as Leader of the House of Commons. He was deputy leader of the party from 1976-80 and in 1980 unexpectedly became leader, following Callaghan's resignation (see footnote on Peter Shore). He stood down after Labour's landslide defeat in 1983. Foot was one of the most cultivated and well-read politicians of the modern age, with a prodigious literary output of his own including biographies of Jonathan Swift and Bevan. His obituary by Michael White (*The Guardian,* 3 March 2010) called him: 'the most improbable literary romantic to lead a major British party since Benjamin Disraeli … A brilliant orator, steeped in Swift, Byron, Shelley and the great political struggles of the 17th century, Foot was first an incorrigible rebel who helped foster the left-right Bevanite split that damaged Labour throughout the 50s.'

IX

THE 1977 WHITE PAPER

There are three eternal lies. The first is, 'There's a cheque in the post.'
The second, 'Darling, I'll respect you even more in the morning.' And the third,
'I'm from the Department of Transport and my job is to help the railways.'

ANON AND UNATTRIBUTED, BUT COMMON CURRENCY IN BRITISH RAILWAYS IN THE LATE 1970s

The Regressive Railway?
Lines such as that running to Kyle of Lochalsh belied Tony Crosland's assertion that rail subsidies favoured the better off. The line brings backpackers to Wester Ross
as well as taking local people to Inverness. A parcels train is seen at Kyle in June 1978 with Skye in the background.

Despite high-level lobbying, there were still fears that the White Paper, when it appeared, was going to be even tougher on the railways than the orange consultation document had been. Shortly before its expected publication in May 1977, *The Observer* ran a major piece by Robert Taylor headed 'Big rail cuts on the way':

> The Government is determined to make British Rail pay most of its way by 1981. The railways therefore face massive cuts in services, and widespread redundancies. Passengers face huge fare increases – or no rail services at all. The rail unions, local authorities and environmental groups will be angry to discover that their counter-proposals have been completely ignored by the civil servants in the Department of Transport. Under the public expenditure cuts the Government has already decided to freeze its cash support for the railways at 1975 price levels until 1981.

According to Taylor, the Government believed that commuters to and from London in the South East could afford to pay for the full cost of rail travel, while people elsewhere should get used to their local rail services being closed down and replaced by buses: 'Over 2,500 miles of track could go.' BR's freight deficit would have to be eliminated by the end of 1978, forcing more goods off the rails onto the roads: 'a complete reversal of the policy in Labour's last election manifesto'.

September 1976 saw a number of important political changes. Not only did Richard Marsh resign as Chairman of the Railways Board, to be succeeded by Peter Parker, but James Callaghan also replaced Harold Wilson as Prime Minister. Callaghan decided that transport should be hived off from the Department for the Environment and receive its own Cabinet minister, in the shape of William Rodgers.[1] While Peter Shore remained Secretary of State for the Environment through to the end of the Parliament in May 1979, he no longer held responsibility for transport. One minor consequence of the change on 10 September 1976 was that Shore's plan to appoint William Camp to the board of British Railways was blocked by Rodgers. Less than five months later, however, Peter Parker appointed Camp as a part-time public relations consultant to British Rail, with his colleague Richard Faulkner, with whom he had worked on the rail unions' No Rail Cuts campaign. In a piece in *The Guardian* on 5 February 1977, headed 'BR post causes a stir', Hazel Duffy reported:

> Mr Camp has held several top publicity posts, most notably as adviser to Harold Wilson during the 1970 election campaign, which Labour lost. He was director of information at the British Steel Corporation during the sixties, and before that was given much of the credit for launching the 'High-speed gas' campaign when he was public relations adviser to the Gas Council. He also advised British Leyland during the time of the Ryder inquiry. He has written several novels and is a director of the publishing firm, Quartet Books. He is a part-time member of the British National Oil Corporation.

Camp remained an adviser to the British Railways Board until his retirement in the early 1990s. Faulkner maintained his professional links with them until after privatisation.

The Sunningdale conference

Rodgers' approach to the railways was a great deal more pragmatic than Crosland's. The principal event during his time as Secretary of State was publication of the transport policy White Paper at the end of June 1977. Prior to that, the weekend of 5 and 6 March 1977 was devoted to a secret conference at the Civil Service Staff College, Sunningdale Park (now the National School of Government) for ministers, officials and advisers, where the White Paper was discussed in great detail. The authors have been given private access to papers for the Sunningdale weekend (all marked either 'Secret' or 'Confidential'), which provide a fascinating insight into how Government policy was then formulated.

As far as the railways were concerned, the stage was set in a memorandum dated 28 February 1977 from Peter Baldwin[2], Permanent Secretary at the Department of Transport, to Bill Rodgers, entitled 'Cost-ineffective railway passenger services'. This paper formed a crucial part of the documents amassed for the Sunningdale conference. It shows clearly and unambiguously how the conspiracy to close significant parts of the railway network still dominated the thinking of senior civil servants, despite protestations to the contrary. In case readers may be tempted to give officials the benefit of the doubt, Baldwin's covering paper makes clear their starting point: 'We believe it to be most important that closures should become possible again in time to have substantial results within the next five years.' The main paper reveals a series of astonishing assertions:

Railways play a very small part in the movement of passengers and freight throughout the country; why, therefore, are we 'bothering so much about this small part of our apparatus of transport?' (para 3)

The case for forgoing the 'economic and environmental gains' of building new roads and improving existing ones by meeting 'the cost of maintaining railway services which are uneconomic because, even with subsidy, they are little used is very weak indeed.' (para 9)

'We had better try to find quickly the parts of the system in which it is no longer sensible to invest … So long as an unnecessary, unprofitable railway passenger service continues, we are paying subsidy to make good the loss; and this is money down the drain from the point of view of the economy, the population at large and possibly even the local community.' (para 11).

Baldwin confirms in paragraph 13 that there was a 'Chairman's List' of proposals for closure, amounting to 1,416 miles of track, 'which BR prepared in Sir Richard Marsh's time, which leaked to the rail unions and on which action by BR and the Government was stalled.' The list consisted mainly of 'small provincial lines in England (with small stretches of London commuter line as well) and long rural lines in Scotland and Wales … None of them comes within the system for which BR has installed or, plans to install, continuous welded rails.'

In paragraph 14, Baldwin says, 'We know also of 57 other passenger services about which BR are doubtful. In England, these are usually longer stretches than those in the Chairman's List, and they are partly outside and partly inside the system of continuous welded rail. At least where they are within that system, BR are presumably thinking not of closure of the line but of withdrawal of passenger services and closure of stations. These lines amount to 2,707 miles, mainly in England.' In paragraph 15, Baldwin refers to a further 1,065 miles 'outside the system of continuous welded rail', mainly provincial lines, but 'not apparently considered seriously by BR for closure in any form'.

So Baldwin arrives at a 'total of 5,188 miles as candidates for consideration', formulated largely on the basis that BR had not got around to equipping the lines with continuous welded rail – a novel criterion for closure which had not previously featured in any transport legislation.

Identifying the lines was the easy bit. Implementing a closure programme was going to be much more difficult. Baldwin devotes four paragraphs to describing 'the obstacles to closure', which variously include the statutory closure procedure, the role of the rail unions (who had 'made common cause with some of the environmental or anti-road lobbies' – Baldwin presumably had Transport 2000 in mind here), the emergence of the TUCC as 'an organised lobby for the consumers' interest' and a British Railways Board which 'can blame their inability to move on the Government', while simultaneously keeping in with the rail unions 'by taking credit for not trying to move'.

The remainder of Baldwin's paper was devoted to finding a new procedure to effect a closures programme. The ingenuity of the approach was matched by its dishonesty. The 'package' would include higher levels of tax on road haulage – while sparing the haulier a cut in drivers' hours or restrictions on the size of lorries, and going 'gently on tachographs' to keep the Transport and General Workers Union (TGWU) sweet. The TGWU membership would also benefit from bus services replacing rail, while the rail unions, in return, would benefit from the restoration of Freightliners to British Rail ownership.

On the rail network, Baldwin suggests that the Government guarantee part of the system (say 70 percent) 'for 10 to 15 years', while a commission would be charged with determining how much of the remainder should be retained:

> Their recommendations would take effect on approval (without power of amendment) by the Secretary of State. Thereafter the board could withdraw, without further ado, from any service not within the guaranteed system and the extra lines within the commission's definitions.

Baldwin acknowledged that this procedure would not relieve the Secretary of State of responsibility for closure, since he would have to approve the commission's proposals. This, along with the commission's non-elected status, would 'attract the full weight of the national, defensive campaign of the rail unions and their allies'.

So instead of a national approach, Baldwin suggested handing over life-and-death decisions on non-guaranteed lines to county councils, which would be given a specific sum by the Exchequer of 'not less than, say 75% of the sum … of the subsidy to the railways which would have been required to meet the deficit on operating any specified existing rail service in the area'. His expectation was that most local authorities would conclude that bus services offered better value for money than rail, and would therefore be willing to take responsibility for shutting down rail services.

Anticipating the argument that difficulties would arise with lines that crossed local authority boundaries, Baldwin said that in the majority of these cases the same political party controlled the councils concerned. (Why he should think that councils of the same political hue were bound to see eye to eye on a subject as controversial as closing rail lines remains a mystery.)

The 'local option' approach was put forward in a further paper – described in a note by Baldwin to Rodgers as 'interesting and provocative' – considered at the Sunningdale weekend. It was submitted by the Transport Policy Review Unit (TPRU) at the Department of Transport and written by Messrs Holmes, Girling and Welsby[3] (the latter would later become Chairman of British Rail). The gloomy tone was set in paragraph 2:

> Most public passenger services can now operate only at an overall loss. They already provide a largely worse service than before, at a cost which is or seems higher than people have been used to: in some areas, they provide no service at all. They can

only look forward to a doubtful future, in a period of declining public expenditure and falling patronage. They will have to rely increasingly on public funds for revenue support to keep services going, and for investment to replace basic facilities and vehicles as well as for technological advances. For the next 10-20 years, and perhaps longer, they will lose ground further to private transport.

The comments on 'unremunerative local rail services' (para 33) were predictable and depressing:

> Many local lines serve only vestigial, or at best seasonal, travel needs which no longer meet their cost. These local provincial services carry only 6% of all rail passenger traffic (2% of all travel by public transport). They fail to cover their allocated costs by well over £100m a year. The subsidy per passenger ranges from 4p to well over 20p per mile. However, only a small proportion is provided by local authorities (about 10% of the overall subsidy to rail, and about 16% of investment). Local authorities outside PTAs have every incentive to argue for the maintenance of these services rather than to replace them by bus services entailing substantial local authority subsidy, or to take on the procedural agonies at present suffered by BR, TUCCs and the Secretary of State. Yet a decision on whether a branchline should close is surely, in any practical sense, 'local'.

The TPRU paper then enthusiastically embraces the 'local option' put forward by Baldwin. Responsibility for public transport services would be put 'squarely on local authority shoulders', with said authorities then given 'the power to withdraw or rejig services if desired, and replace them with alternative services to meet identified needs and the responsibility for funding the resultant services. Central Government might provide extra pressure by actually identifying candidates for closure through some sort of network commission; or it might ask BR itself to prepare schedules of services to be considered for closure, on the basis of guidelines set by Government (perhaps with the agreement of BR and the unions). But in either case, the final decision would be taken by the local authority in the light of local needs, alternative modes, and the resources available.'

The following paragraph does, however, concede that it would not all be plain sailing:

> First, it is often the case that the importance of a local line does not begin and end within the boundaries of the county in which it lies; it will sometimes have important contributory revenue implications for the network as a whole. A local authority would not be inclined to take such extra-territorial considerations into account when deciding the future of a line and paying for it.

Then there was the problem of lines which crossed county boundaries:

> … it is very difficult to get even two counties to co-operate over supporting or providing an alternative to a rail service. In fact, 53 out of the 99 branch lines which lose most money lie within more than one county or Scottish region.

The authors offer no real solution to this problem. They suggest that 'local consultative machinery', with the Secretary of State as the final

Cost-Ineffective Railway
The train for Haltwhistle leaves Alston a few weeks before closure in 1976.

arbiter, could deal with local cross-boundary services. But that would not apply to inter-city services or London and the South East (LSE) commuter services: 'There needs to be a basic strategic network which would not be nibbled at by reason of the aggregate of individual local authority decisions.'

Another option put forward is 'regional authorities large enough to take the wider view necessary (particularly for the financing of the rail system)', i.e. grouping counties together, but they admit 'it is unlikely that now is the right time to attempt major and expensive new legislation, particularly so soon after the major local Government upheavals of 1974'. Unsurprisingly, little more was heard about the regional option.

There were numerous papers discussed at Sunningdale Park over the weekend of 5-6 March (including those from Baldwin and the TPRU). One on future requirements of public service obligation (PSO) support for the railways, arising from a joint DTp and BR study, concluded that to keep PSO support at its 1977 level would require real fare increases on the LSE services. BR said that if fares went up 5-7.5 percent in real terms, that could improve net earnings by £50m-£55m, with a loss of 4-12 percent of traffic. The actual size of the required increase depended on wage costs, productivity gains and the scope for cost escapement. Interestingly it was felt that little could be gained by replacing rail services with buses – perhaps 'up to £5 million by 1981 and more in later years'.

The railways directorate within the DTp submitted a paper on bus-rail substitution, stating uncompromisingly that 2,400 route miles of railway would be replaced by feeder bus services to the remaining rail network ('*only* [our emphasis] 1,400 miles would close completely'):

> Between 8,500 and 11,000 jobs would be lost … Both the Railways board and NBC (National Bus Company) are favourable to the proposition subject to various conditions. The rail unions oppose the idea because they are worried about redundancies. They prefer the existing network to have an assured future, a view shared by the Labour Party, CTCC (Central Transport Consultative Committee), ACC (Association of County Councils), and Scottish and Welsh Ministers.

The plan was that legislation would be introduced which would allow BR to contract for feeder bus services with the NBC, pay for them out of the PSO and also be responsible for their marketing and integration with rail services. As a *quid pro quo*, BR expected NBC to give up running express coach services which competed with InterCity rail. The legislation would also have to waive the statutory rail closure procedure where bus feeders were to be provided.

One interesting piece of unpublished information in the paper concerned 22 rail replacement bus services introduced as conditions of closure consents between 1969 and 1975. Eight had been withdrawn, seven remained in modified form and seven were unchanged: 'The South West TUCC has estimated 60% of rail replacement bus services introduced in their region since 1962 have been withdrawn.' Among the reasons given for their failure were unreliable connections with the remaining rail network, longer journey times compared to the previous rail service and poor interchange facilities, especially for old people, mothers with prams and passengers with heavy luggage.

This book's authors have not seen a detailed account of the discussions which took place that March weekend in 1977, but the summary of points 'generally agreed' contained a number of highly relevant statements. The afternoon session on Saturday concluded:

Railways

The central problem. The present passenger rail system is not a good buy. There should be closures of many cost-ineffective passenger services and other services should come closer to paying their way.

Subsidies should be reduced somewhat, perhaps significantly.

For those services which rail *can* do well we should see that they are enabled to do them efficiently.

Political Difficulties

1. The Government is not anxious for controversy at present.
2. It will not be possible to achieve a more cost-effective railway without some trade-off elsewhere in the railway package (and in other areas, e.g. lorries).
3. The Rail Unions seem ready to accept the substantial redundancies publicly foreshadowed by the Board and might accept more provided they are not set as a target. But there must be some tangible recognition of the continuous role of the railways.
4. Redundancies will be especially difficult over the next two years, with high unemployment.

Perennial target
The Heart of Wales line was on every closure list from around 1962 onwards, and was certainly in the consciousness of Sunningdale conference attendees. It would survive every attack, remaining a lifeline to deeply rural communities as well as an important tourist attraction, with active support from the innovative Heart of Wales Line Forum. This class 153 unit from Swansea is seen heading across Knucklas viaduct on its way to Shrewsbury in 2008, branded with the line's own livery. *Photo courtesy HOWL Forum*

It is clear from the notes of the second session, which took place from 4:45-7:30pm on the Saturday, that the participants made efforts 'to construct a railway "package" which BRB and the unions would find reasonably acceptable'.

Among the points made was the need to 'give a positive verbal vote of confidence in the future of the railways, which would not depend on the cost or the precise size of network, and which gave an assurance that there would be a railway system which served public need as far ahead as we could see.'

On cost-ineffective services, delegates liked the idea of placing the onus upon local authorities to decide their future and it was agreed that necessary legislation should be kept 'as simple as possible'. The issue was intractable, however, and the arguments lacked substance and intellectual rigour; even Baldwin's covering paper acknowledged, 'The paper itself does not come to any firm conclusion,' but this did not stop his concluding plea to Rodgers: 'We now need your political direction on the approach which seems to you most readily practicable and advantageous.'

One further startling conclusion was that 'a prestigious inter-city service' was felt to be a 'less appropriate role for railways and attempts should be made to dislodge BRB from this viewpoint and to encourage the gradual thinning-out of services'. How this would square with BR's suggestion that NBC give up long-distance coach services which competed with Inter-City was not explained. The proposal was followed up by pressure from the Department to reduce the successful half-hourly Euston-Birmingham service to hourly to test the elasticity of demand for Inter-City services. The board wisely decided not to conduct such an experiment.

However, the mandarins were attracted by Parker's idea of a 'contract' with BRB, which would establish a framework to provide guidelines and a budget for the board within which they would take decisions.

The White Paper

When it appeared, the White Paper took as its basis the supposed need for further closures. In his covering paper to the Cabinet on 13 June 1977, Transport Secretary Bill Rodgers wrote that its purpose was 'a reallocation of resources to give higher priority to public transport', but then went on to say that it included 'a £20m reduction in subsidies [the equivalent today of £300m] to British Railways' passenger operations', stressing 'the impossibility of maintaining the present network indefinitely, without a substantial and continuing increase in provision for investment and subsidy, and the difficulty, under present procedures, of making any significant progress on closures'.

Rodgers went into more detail in a five-page annex which accompanied the main document, which began as follows:

The most difficult and controversial proposal in the White Paper relates to the new procedures for deciding the future of certain cost-ineffective railway lines. Its origins lie in the impossibility of maintaining the present network indefinitely without a substantial and continuing increase in provision for investment and subsidy; and the difficulty, under present procedures, of making any significant progress on closures, even of services which at high cost make a trivial contribution to meeting transport needs. To maintain the existing network unchanged would require expenditure over and above present levels amounting to some £200-250 million by 1985. *Local decision* [our emphasis] may show that perhaps only half of that is necessary to maintain adequate public transport.

The procedures I propose would focus on making the best use of expenditure on public transport and on local people judging their own priorities … I do not underestimate the delicacy of any steps in this direction. If no more money is found for the railways, the proposals in the White Paper will simply not be credible without indicating how cost-ineffective lines are to be tackled. Amongst alternatives I have considered the possibility of an independent commission, with local inquiries if necessary, in effect to settle the size of the railway network and to propose closures. But this would sound too much like the Beeching Report all over again and would leave the present unsatisfactory procedures unchanged. We should get the worst of both worlds.

Another possibility would be to prescribe a massive rundown in manpower (over and above the 40,000 reduction by 1981 at present assumed). But apart from obvious difficulties while unemployment remains high, I cannot believe that this solution would be more acceptable, politically and to the trade unions, than my current proposals for dealing with cost-ineffective lines.

Rodgers went on to explain that his proposals had been accepted 'on balance' by the Chancellor of the Exchequer's ministerial group. He said that some colleagues may have wished him 'to go further in defining the national railway network', but was against it because it would 'not only prejudge the Board's detailed examination of local services, which will take some time to complete, but would immediately provoke questions about the future of all services not within the definition'.

Anticipating reaction, Rodgers said the railway unions would regret the absence of a commitment to increase investment and 'will be apprehensive about the consequences of the local option on rail closures':

The NUR and the TSSA will probably feel a fair balance has been struck (whether they say so is another matter), bearing in mind the action I propose on the road programme and heavy lorries; ASLEF will take a less generous view. The British Railways Board may also be relieved although cautious in its public statements.

Rodgers then described a series of other likely reactions to the White Paper, from organisations such as the CBI, the TGWU, the TUC, freight transport operators, bus operators, motoring organisations, the construction industry, environmentalists and local authorities. At the very end of this long list was the Liberal Party – the Government's partner in the Lib-Lab pact – who were 'aware of the broad approach of the White Paper and of the particular line it takes in areas in which they have shown an interest but they have not seen a draft'.

The White Paper demonstrated that, to some extent at least, ministers and officials had learned from the success of the No Rail Cuts campaign that public opinion would not allow them to propose another round of closures in which they took life-or-death decisions on particular lines. The solution they came up with was 'local democracy' – giving local authorities the power to specify train services in their areas to be paid for out of a transport budget allocated specifically to them. What they did not spend on the railway would become available as bus subsidies. The expectation in central Government was that once councils had responsibility for deciding how budgets would be spent, many would opt to support buses rather than trains and the lines could be closed.

One further element in this conspiracy was to have been the abolition of transport users' consultative committees' powers to hold public inquiries into closure proposals.

Unfortunately for the Government, the Railways Board declined to play ball. They had gone along with ideas for bus substitution because they had believed, naïvely, that if they saved money on rural rail services the Government would allow them to keep the cash to develop more profitable parts of the railway, such as InterCity. They even hoped that the Government would give all the InterCity traffic to them, via halting the operation of competitive long-distance coaches.

However, the Board realised there would be no such pay-off if local councils acquired control of the purse strings. It was not far-fetched to imagine that large parts of the network might eventually be abandoned or truncated, if district or county authorities declined to pick up the bill for running services in their areas. One could envisage, for example, a line such as Waterloo-Exeter, which runs through six local authority areas outside London, being supported by one council and abandoned by the next.

Ingenious as this approach appeared, it required primary legislation. But by 1977 – when they had lost their majority in the House of Commons and were reliant on the support of the Liberal Party to stay in office – the Labour Government had lost their appetite for introducing controversial transport bills.

1 William Rodgers (born 1928) was a Labour politician, later SDP/Liberal Democrat, who served as MP for Stockton-on-Tees from 1962-83. He was Secretary of State for Transport from 1976-79 and a passionate pro-European, later joining Roy Jenkins, Shirley Williams and David Owen in the SDP's 'Gang of Four' in 1981. Ennobled as Lord Rodgers of Quarry Bank in 1987, he was leader of the Liberal Democrats in the House of Lords from 1997-2001.

2 Peter Baldwin (1922-2010) was a civil servant who worked in the Treasury from 1954-62 and 1964-76, becoming Second Permanent Secretary at the Department of the Environment and, immediately after, Permanent Secretary in the Department of Transport until 1982. While still an Oxford undergraduate, Baldwin had been recruited to work as a code breaker at Bletchley Park, and achieved particular success with Japanese codes. In 1980, he led the first British trade mission to post-Maoist China and came back with a 'KF7' class British-built steam locomotive dating from 1934 – now on display at the National Railway Museum at York, upon whose committee he served from 1983-87. Baldwin also served on the Railway Heritage Trust for many years, and was a successful campaigner for accessible transport for disabled people, serving as the

first chair of the Disabled Persons Transport Advisory Committee (DPTAC). He was knighted as a KCB in 1977. In a letter to the authors, William Rodgers recalls: "My guess is that he was a liberal in politics... a sympathetic man and not hostile to the railways. But he worked in difficult times and he was deeply puzzled – sometimes in despair – by the trade unions, which seemed to impede the future of the railways rather than assist it. He understood the NUR and TSSA and could work together with them, but ASLEF was impossible; a view I shared."

3 John Welsby (born 1938; awarded the CBE 1990) was the Chairman of the British Railways Board from 1995-99. He was also its Director of Provincial Services, 1982-84; Managing Director of Procurement, 1985-87; Member of the Board, 1987-99; Chief Executive, 1990-98. Welsby also worked for the Government Economic Service, 1966-81; as Director of London and Continental Railways Ltd, 1999-2007; and as President of the Institute of Logistics and Transport, 1999-2002. He was the first Chairman of BRB not to receive a knighthood, despite his key role in turning the Government's inconsistent and inadequate plans for privatisation into a practical reality.

X

LIFE UNDER THATCHER

Never travel under my name again!

THE RT. HON. WILLIAM WHITELAW MP

Selling the family silver
BR, like its predecessor companies, was a huge vertically integrated organisation running ships, hotels and
workshops as well as trains. The Thatcher years saw the sale of many BR subsidiaries, including Sealink in 1984.
The sale included the Windermere lake services and its ships, of which the graceful MV *Tern* of 1891 is seen
here approaching Bowness pier in 2010.

On 28 March 1979, the Labour Government led by James Callaghan faced a vote of no confidence in the House of Commons and lost by one vote – 310 to 311. Parliament was dissolved in April (around six months before its five-year term was up) and a general election held on 3 May 1979. This resulted in a Conservative victory by a majority of 44 over all parties. Margaret Thatcher[1] became Prime Minister.

It was believed that Thatcher had not travelled on a train for years and the Railways Board, though disillusioned with Labour, were apprehensive about what was to follow. In his memoirs, Peter Parker recalled the one occasion Mrs Thatcher came to lunch with the Board in 1976, not long after she had become leader of the Conservative Party – along with Norman Fowler[2], whom he described as 'the shadowiest of Transport Ministers'. Her view of nationalised industries was not complimentary:

> … to be nationalised was an industry's admission of failure. She did not spell out the implications that – well chaps, it must follow surely – only failures would work in the public sector.[3]

During the meal she asked Clifford Rose, the board member responsible for industrial relations, a complicated question. As he embarked on a lengthy answer, Thatcher turned to the person on her right and started talking to him. Rose faltered and stopped in mid-sentence. 'Carry on – I can listen to two people at once,' she snapped.

Much of the Conservative election manifesto was devoted to strikes and trade union law reform. The only reference to railways came at the end of a section on nationalisation:

> High productivity is the key to the future of industries like British Rail, where improvements would benefit both the work force and passengers who have faced unprecedented fare increases over the last five years.

Unsurprisingly, there was nothing on closures, but that did not deter Peter Parker from continuing to promote bus substitution and, by implication, a programme of rail closures. In a speech entitled 'Towards a Commonwealth of Public Transport', at the conference of the Confederation of Passenger Transport (the bus and coach operators' trade association) in Bournemouth on 19 September 1979, he said:

> … the blunt fact is that if bus competition, particularly on medium-distance, limited-stop services is to increase, this is bound to have a bad effect on the finances of the rural BR services, and losses there are bad enough now. At the moment we have a statutory commitment which means that there must be no change in the size and nature of the passenger system … inexorably the pressure of decision is forced by the illogic of our railway situation, running a fixed route network within a fixed financial framework … Surely there are certain jobs done inadequately by railways. Surely a better set of services could be developed by, and with, buses and coaches. Surely this would be better value for the community's money … I foresee the development of a contractual basis between BR and bus operators for the provision of such replacement services, and a start has already been made with the National Bus Company in thinking through the terms of such an agreement.

In February 1979, before the change of Government, the board had presented the unions with their latest thinking on bus substitution, which proposed replacing the largest loss-makers with BR-run buses, crewed by rail union (not TGWU) members.

The Department of Transport had not given up either, as officials once again pressed for major closures. Also in February 1979, its internal transport policy and management board had recommended there should be early legislation in the next parliamentary session 'to enable local transport needs to be better served than by highly cost-ineffective local rail services', claiming that 'expenditure running to £25 million a year could be avoided'. By this point, the board and the Department of Transport were very wary of producing lists of closures or maps showing cuts. Nonetheless, press reports (which were not denied) appeared saying that around 700 miles of network were targeted.

The 41 services

Experts got to work on analysing what savings of £25 million would mean. The first exclusive was claimed not by a giant Fleet Street newspaper but by a tiny monthly environmental magazine, *The Vole*, edited by the eccentric but hugely entertaining Richard Boston[4] (the pen-name for his regular diary column was 'C. O. Jones' – even those with no more than a smattering of Spanish can get the joke). Indeed, back numbers of this sadly defunct but excellent magazine have been the authors' *aide-mémoire* for these events.

It immediately became clear that far more than 700 miles would need to close. *The Vole*[5] put the figure at 2,000 miles:

> … and it would mean decimation of rail services in much of rural Britain – East Anglia, Cumbria, Central and North Wales, Highlands of Scotland, and a huge number of local feeder services carrying passengers to the main lines. With Government support for British Rail running at around £450 million, a saving of £25 million is pathetic, taking into account the hardship and aggravation another round of Beeching-type closures would cause.

One of the constituent members of Transport 2000 – the Ramblers Association – then decided to conduct their own research into the threat facing the rail network. They claimed to have identified a total of 41 local rail services, accounting for about 900 miles, which they believed were threatened by plans for bus substitution, many of the lines being popular with their members. Alan Mattingley, the Ramblers' secretary, was reported in *The Vole*[6] as saying:

> These 41 services are merely the tip of the iceberg. If the Government allows these to close, the hatchet men in the Department of Transport will be pressing for the future closure of scores of services, achieving the maximum reduction in the national rail network which certain officials have striven for since the time of Beeching. We welcome Transport Minister Norman Fowler's categorical assurance that 'there will never again be another Beeching'. We therefore call on him to instruct his officials to cease conspiring against the railways and his own statement, and to abandon their blackmail against the British Railways Board.

(The 41 services are shown in Appendix E, which also details what happened to them subsequently.)

Lord Fowler of Sutton Coldfield
As Secretary of State in 1979, Normal Fowler robustly rejected the suggestion that 41 lines were on a DoT 'hit list', ensuring the survival of most of them until the present day. *(Photo courtesy Aggregate Industries).*

The Vole claimed an exclusive for their coverage of the Ramblers Association's report and *The Guardian* paid them the compliment of lifting the story for their front-page lead, written by David Hencke[7], on Wednesday 7 November 1979. The newspaper also published a leader by Frances Cairncross[8] which began as follows:

> It is increasingly probable that British Rail will decide to close down some more local rail services. Plans to shut some 41 services, running over 900 miles, have been circulating between Whitehall and BR.

Having confirmed the threat, the article went on to support the closures with a series of inaccurate and misleading assertions:

> ... it is not easy to defend the full panoply of British Rail's rural network on any grounds other than nostalgia or a wishful belief that the day of Thomas the Tank Engine will one day return ... On some branch services ... the costs of transporting each passenger are indefensibly high ... most buses are quite simply cheaper to run than most rural rail services.

Attention shifted to the House of Commons where, by a happy coincidence, Norman Fowler was due to answer transport questions that day. BR expected a cautious response from the Minister. They thought he would confirm that talks had been held with officials about some rail services being replaced by buses – Peter Parker had, after all, gone on the record about discussions with the National Bus Company in his speech in Bournemouth less than two months previously – and the occasion would also give Fowler the chance to say

again that there would not be 'another Beeching'. But Fowler's answers to MPs went far beyond that sort of equivocation:

> Let me make it absolutely clear that the report in *The Guardian* is untrue and I read it with astonishment. I see no case for another round of massive cuts in the railways. I have no list of passenger services for closure such as is printed in *The Guardian*. There have been no secret talks between my officials and the Railways Board to discuss any such list of closures. I deplore the groundless anxiety which such inaccurate reports cause.[9]

British Rail issued a self-contradictory statement that same day:

> No list of railway services with proposals for closure has been discussed by British Rail and the Department of Transport. The discussions that are taking place with the Department of Transport have centred on the inadequate level of current financial support and the need to consider ways of serving rural areas at a lower cost possibly by replacing some lightly used railway services by guaranteed bus services running to railway timetables.

On the following day, 8 November, David Hencke wrote another piece in *The Guardian*, claiming to have got hold of BR's confidential corporate review:

> It discloses the background to plans to axe 40 passenger services published in *The Guardian* yesterday. The document confirms that British Rail has evaluated 40 out of 85 branch lines and provincial services. It lays down a timetable for closures, covering two stages, up to 1984 and up to 1989 ... Specific action should be initiated to put these closures in hand.

In case his answer to Parliament had not been clear enough, Fowler followed it up with a letter to Peter Parker:

> I thought I should write to you immediately following the stories in *The Guardian* yesterday and today about the board's Corporate Review to make it quite clear that it is my firm policy that there should be no substantial cuts in the passenger rail network. I thought it only right to make absolutely clear to you and to your colleagues that this is the policy I shall pursue. I shall want to talk to you about the Corporate Review that you sent me on October 25. But you will understand that the option of closing 40 passenger services is one that the Government have rejected.

And that appeared to be that. All the effort that had been put into drawing up the list of 40 or so services, in which the British Railways Board and the Department of Transport had clearly colluded (though neither had apparently thought fit to tell the Minister) had come to nothing.

Fowler's account of these events is illuminating. In his autobiography, *Ministers Decide*, he gives an accurate description of the relationship between Sidney Weighell and his opposite number in ASLEF, Ray Buckton:

> Whenever they came to meetings at the department they sat at opposite ends of the table. Whatever reservations they had about dealing with me were as nothing compared to the reservations they had about dealing with each other.

On one point they were united. They wanted to see a positive statement from the Government which demonstrated our commitment to the railways. With the election of Margaret Thatcher, the assumption among some lobbyists had been that we would institute a new round of 'Beeching cuts' … Indeed in 1979 *The Guardian* had published a wholly imaginary story about 900 miles of railway being under the axe. For all its note of fantasy, however, the article was widely read and well-timed. It appeared on the day that I was answering questions on transport on the floor of the House and there was a question of the future of railway services on the order paper. As I rose to answer there was a roar of laughter from the Labour benches. I looked behind me to see what appeared a solid forest of Tory MPs from county constituencies anxious to ask questions about their own particular rail lines. I repeated that I saw 'no case for a further round of Beeching cuts' and there had been no secret talks or plans. The House settled back more or less reassured.[10]

More than 30 years on, virtually all of the 41 services are still running and most are thriving. Only two of those listed were closed and one service (March-Doncaster) was diverted to start from Peterborough. Two lines have been electrified, one is being converted to light rail and 21 are now supported by community rail partnerships.

The new Conservative Government elected in 1979 had little appetite for bus substitution, while the option of handing over control of rural and secondary lines to local authorities had died with the previous Government's manifesto. However, there was still insufficient money being provided to invest adequately in the railways' future. Peter Parker's last attempt at a solution lay in another high-level inquiry into the state of the railways' finances. How close that came to going catastrophically wrong we shall see in Chapter 12.

Parker had worked hard at building up a relationship with Norman Fowler while the latter was in opposition, and hoped to gain support for the changes he wished to make. One powerful ally in the Government was Deputy Prime Minister William Whitelaw, whose grandfather (and namesake) had been Chairman of the London & North Eastern Railway and had an 'A4' steam locomotive named after him. On one memorable occasion, Whitelaw had been guest of honour at one of the dinners Parker hosted during the Conservative Party conference. During a brief after-dinner speech, Whitelaw recounted how, as a boy of 12, he had caught the sleeper train from Aberdeen to London. He had sent word ahead to the station that William Whitelaw was travelling and found that the stationmaster was there in his top hat, ready to escort the great man to the train. To the railway servant's great credit he turned not a hair, gravely showing the boy to his sleeping berth. He wished him goodnight but, reaching under the pillow, removed a bottle of whisky, saying, 'I don't think you'll be needing this, sir.' To gales of laughter, Whitelaw said he then heard nothing for a few days until his grandfather wrote to him: 'Don't ever travel under my name again, but here's half a crown so long as you don't tell the family about the whisky.'

The electrification review
Despite the difficult political climate, the case for railway development was effectively made to Norman Fowler and a major study on network electrification was so well put together that it was endorsed by the Government in 1981 – even though each case still had to be made on its merits, with the usual pressure from the mandarins to pare back to the minimum.

Level playing field
In 1982 the Kessock Bridge (paid for by the taxpayer) was opened, cutting journey times on the A9 to the north of Scotland. Meanwhile, the railway continues to make long detours around the water gaps, with many speed restrictions on its Victorian infrastructure – as seen here at Clachnaharry, where a Wick/Thurso train slows to 10mph to cross the Caledonian Canal on its approach to Inverness in May 1991.

The electrification review also gave enemies of the railway another opportunity to argue for significant closures. Fowler lifts the lid on the machinations of another notorious anti-rail hardliner in his book, describing how, in March 1981, he circulated a paper 'which enthusiastically backed electrification'. A meeting was set for mid-April, but just before it, the whole strategy was challenged by an adviser to the Government, Sir Alan Walters[11]:

Walters had two main points. First he argued that the railway system should be reduced. Many experts, he said, believed that we should aim for a smaller, more concentrated and more efficient network. Second he challenged the forecasts on electrification and said that competition from cars, the newly deregulated coaches and the airlines could all erode rail traffic. The case for widespread electrification was not plausible, he thundered. It was based on assumptions that were not credible. I strongly disagreed with both arguments.

Fowler went on to say he did not believe there were large savings to be made from reducing the size of the rail network, as over two-thirds of the railways' costs were the cost of labour:

The obvious policy to follow was one of improved productivity, and I proposed with the agreement of British Rail, a reduction in the workforce of 38,000. With electrification I could achieve that goal.

If I simply concentrated on reducing the network, I would involve myself in a long and profitless public, political and industrial row. There would be public enquiry after public enquiry – for the law ensured that no closure could be made without one – and many areas would be deprived of valued rail services. I believed the case for electrification to be overwhelming.

Triumphantly, he goes on to say that these arguments prevailed with ministerial colleagues: 'There was no support for reducing the network.'[12]

(This was to be the last time the railway industry put forward a combined proposition for electrification for over a quarter of a century, until ATOC and Network Rail put the case strongly to Ruth Kelly[13] as Secretary of State in 2007, which were eventually accepted by Lord Adonis[14] in 2009. It was left to a Conservative Secretary of State, Philip Hammond[15], to approve the first major project: the Great Western Main Line in 2010, to Oxford and Newbury, and in 2011, to Bristol and Cardiff.)

Ironically, the 1981 electrification strategy was approved at the same time as the 1955 electrification scheme, Manchester-Sheffield and Wath via Woodhead, was closed. Having lost its through passenger service in 1970, the route remained an important freight carrier, particularly for coal to Fiddler's Ferry power station. However, declining demand and the existence of alternative routes allowed the Woodhead route to be sacrificed in pursuit of the cost-base reduction needed to persuade the Government that BR could be trusted with a larger investment programme.

In 1983, *New Scientist* magazine reported that the Department of Transport had commissioned a study by Professor Peter Hall[16] of Reading University on converting the Woodhead route into a road, paying two-thirds of the £30,000 cost with the balance met by a transport research fund. It looked at two alternative means of ventilating the tunnel but came to the conclusion that there would not be enough traffic to justify the costs of conversion.[17] A campaign to reopen the Woodhead route would later begin in 2008, when the National Grid announced that its electricity cables would be transferred from the original site to the newer 1954 tunnel at Woodhead, thus precluding its future use as a railway line.

1   Margaret Hilda Thatcher (born 1925) was Britain's first woman Prime Minister and the 20th century's longest serving. The product of a grammar school education in Grantham, Lincolnshire, she studied chemistry at Oxford before becoming a barrister. Elected Conservative MP for Finchley in 1959, she represented that constituency until her retirement from the Commons in 1992 – whereupon she was ennobled as Baroness Thatcher. Thatcher also served as a junior minister in the Ministry of Pensions and National Insurance from 1961-64, and as Secretary of State for Education and Science from 1970-74. Following the Conservatives' defeat in the two 1974 elections, she challenged Edward Heath (*qv*) for the leadership of the party in 1975 and won. Thatcher led the Conservatives to power in the 1979 general election, winning two further elections in 1983 and 1987. She was ousted in 1990, as a result of a revolt by her ministers, and replaced by John Major. Thatcher was Britain's most divisive Prime Minister of recent times, adored and reviled in almost equal measure. Dubbed 'the Iron Lady' by a Soviet journalist, she received credit for leading Britain to victory in the war with Argentina over the Falkland Islands in 1982, and succeeded where Heath had failed in an industrial confrontation with the miners in 1984. While a great proponent of privatisation, Thatcher never tried to apply this approach to the railways – although, during her tenure of office, many BRB subsidiaries were sold, including support services such as ships, hotels and railway workshops.
2   Now the Rt. Hon. Lord Fowler of Sutton Coldfield, where he was MP from 1974-2001, having previously served as MP for Nottingham South from 1970-74. Born in 1938, he was Minister of Transport from 1979-81 and Secretary of State for Transport in 1981. Fowler became a peer in 1981 and Chairman of the Conservative Party from 1992-94. He is now Non-Executive Chairman of Aggregate Industries, suppliers to both the road and rail industries.
3   *For Starters*, p277.
4   Richard Boston (1938-2006) was a writer, journalist and humorist. In his obituary (*The Independent*, 30 December 2006), Jeremy Bugler wrote: 'He was once a regular presenter of the television programme *What the Papers Say*, a task for which he and his producer had to travel from London to Granada's Manchester studios. On the early Euston train, their enjoyment of the breakfast was spoiled regularly by an officious and bossy chief steward. One day, Boston slipped onto his plate, among the rashers and sausages, a plastic fried egg. He then complained about his inedible egg. The steward, puzzled and poking at the inert egg, was for once on the defensive. When he had suffered enough, Boston picked up the egg off his plate and calmly folded it into his wallet.'
5   *The Vole*, Volume Three Number One, 12 October 1979, pp5-6.
6   *The Vole*, Volume Three Number Two, 8 November 1979, pp2-3.
7   David Hencke (born 1947) is a journalist and author. He has been the planning correspondent for *The Guardian* from 1979-81 and its Westminster correspondent from 1986-2009. Winner of the 1994 Journalist of the Year award, he is a frequent and influential writer on transport issues.
8   Frances Cairncross (born 1944) is a journalist, economist and academic who worked

on *The Guardian* from 1973-84. Now rector of Exeter College, Oxford, she is the daughter of distinguished economist Sir Alec Cairncross.
9   *Hansard volume 973*, column 379.
10 *Ministers Decide: A Personal Memoir of the Thatcher Years* by Norman Fowler, Chapman's, 1991, p137.
11 Sir Alan Walters (1926-2009) was full-time economic adviser to Margaret Thatcher from 1981-83. He had been Cassell Professor at the London School of Economics, was an expert in cost/benefit analysis, and an advocate of road-user charging. He was knighted in 1983.
12 *Ministers Decide*, p138.
13 Ruth Kelly (born 1968) was the Labour MP for Bolton West 1997-2010. She was also Economic Secretary to the Treasury, Minister for the Cabinet Office and Secretary of State for Education and Skills for the period covering 2004-06, as well as Secretary of State for Communities and Local Government, 2006-07, and Secretary of State for Transport 2007-08.
14 Andrew, Lord Adonis (born 1963) was formerly the Secretary of State for transport 2009-10 and Minister of State for Railways 2008-09. He is widely regarded within the industry as the most successful governmental champion of the railways of all time. During his year as Secretary of State he delivered the plans for the High Speed 2 rail line and won all-party political support which survived the change of Government in 2010. He also approved the principle of a major programme of electrification of the Great Western main line and routes in the North West. He is believed to be the only senior parliamentarian who, when given a choice of ministerial appointments, asked for transport because he believed – correctly – that he could make a difference to the nation's railways.
15 Philip Hammond (born 1955) has been the Conservative MP for Runnymede and Weybridge since 1997; he was also Secretary of State for Transport from May 2010 to October 2011, at which point he succeeded Liam Fox on his resignation as Secretary for Defence.
16 Professor Sir Peter Hall (born 1932) is Professor of Planning and Regeneration at the Bartlett School of Architecture and Planning, University College London. At the time of the railway conversion studies he was Professor of Geography at the University of Reading. He is a prolific writer on town planning issues and has been awarded a string of awards, honorary degrees, doctorates and professorships from around England and abroad. Hall was knighted in 1998, received the Gold Medal from the Royal Town Planning Institute in 2003 and the Deputy Prime Minister's Lifetime Achievement Award in 2004. He was co-author of the report of the Better Stations task-force established by the Secretary of State for Transport in 2009 and is an enthusiastic supporter of High Speed 2, serving on the board of advisers of Greengauge 21 (a lobbying organisation dedicated to development of a high-speed rail network in Britain). There is no reference in either his *Who's Who?* entry or his biographical details published by UCL to his work in the 1970s on converting railways into roads.
17 *New Scientist*, 4 August 1983 – see also Chapter 14 on railway conversion.

XI

THE RISE AND FALL
OF SIDNEY WEIGHELL

There is no doubt that Sidney Weighell was an exceptional leader.
He was awkward, arrogant, unclubbable, and he was decisive,
visionary and convincing.

SIR PETER PARKER, *FOR STARTERS*

Making Tracks
Sid Weighell had worked as a driver out of Northallerton, including this section of the Wensleydale line to
Garsdale on the Settle & Carlisle line. He had seen at first hand the effect that closure had on communities in the dale.
The formation of the line near Castle Bolton is shown in 2004. (Photo courtesy Wensleydale Railway Association)

There are few individuals who played a greater – or indeed more successful – role in the battle to maintain the railway network than Sidney Weighell, General Secretary of the NUR from 1975-83. Having joined the railway at Northallerton, he had been a driver on the Wensleydale line and had seen at first hand the effect that its closure to passengers in 1954 had had on the communities in the dale. He was the first to realise that in order for the railways to win the argument for their existence, they needed to enlist a coalition that extended well beyond those who depended on them for their employment. Environmental campaigners, passenger groups, amenity bodies, heritage enthusiasts – even trainspotters – all needed to be part of the 'railway lobby' (a concept that had scarcely existed since the Big Four railway companies were running their 'square deal for the railways' campaign in the 1930s).

As we have seen, Weighell's vision led to the formation of Transport 2000 in 1973, and he was the driving force behind the astonishingly successful No Rail Cuts campaign in 1975. At the same time, he appreciated the need for the NUR to pull its weight politically and persuaded the union to change its rules so that it could sponsor a number of influential Labour MPs who had not previously been members. He also made sure that the NUR maximised its influence in the labour and trade union movement and believed passionately in expanding educational opportunities for its members, via creation of an education centre at a country house in Frant, East Sussex.

Weighell's loyalty to the Labour Party was visceral and he repeatedly spoke of the need for the NUR to remember its role in the formation of the party at the turn of the 20th century.[1] It was this which drove him so passionately to oppose the Crosland orange paper – and the *Socialist Commentary* philosophy underlying it – in 1975-76. Here was a *Labour* Government which not only seemed willing to tear up the entire transport policy on which it had fought and won two elections in 1974, but was proposing a course of action which would irrevocably destroy a large part of the railway network, damage the nation's transport infrastructure for ever and decimate his union's membership. No wonder Weighell felt betrayed.

By 1979, Labour were out of office (and would be for all but five years of the remainder of Weighell's life) and the battle for control – some would say the soul – of the party had begun. No one was in any doubt where Weighell stood. In his political report to the delegates at the NUR's annual conference in 1981 at St Andrews, he wrote:

> After a period of covert activity [the infiltrators] now feel themselves well enough entrenched to proclaim quite openly their Trotskyist[2] and revolutionary allegiances … We should be in no doubt about their determination to convert the Labour Party into a Bolshevik-style organisation paving the way to physical confrontation on the streets. With such people there can be no compromise, there can be no hope of genuine unity in the party. That is why the NUR has proposed that the party should now take the measures necessary to protect itself from those who would destroy it.[3]

By the 1980s, however, Weighell was not just battling against the far left. Margaret Thatcher's Conservative Party had won the 1979 election following the 'Winter of Discontent', determined to introduce laws limiting the freedom of trade unions to call strikes. She did not intend to make the same mistake as her predecessor, Edward Heath, and lose an industrial battle with the miners, whom she later described as 'the enemy within'. There would be only one winner in any dispute. Another huge additional problem for Weighell and the moderates of the NUR was the attitude of the train drivers' union, ASLEF.

The strikes of 1982

The mixture of potentially explosive materials came together in 1982, with a succession of industrial disputes on the railway involving pay claims, 'flexible rostering'[4] and the introduction of driver-only operation on the newly electrified Bedford-St Pancras commuter railway. Weighell accused Ray Buckton and ASLEF of dishonouring agreements, while Peter Parker and the Railways Board were said to be obsessed by the desire to achieve productivity gains without implementing awards made by the Railway Staff National Tribunal (RSNT)[5], and David Howell[6] (new Secretary of State for Transport) and the Government were starving the railways of money.[7]

Parker and the board certainly took the view that if they could not demonstrate improvements in productivity, they could forget about favourable decisions from ministers on issues such as the Advanced Passenger Train and further electrification. Nicholas Jones, then BBC Radio's labour correspondent, recalls how, 'in November 1981 British Rail advised Balfour Beatty Power Construction that it could offer no more work to the company's electrification team after completion of the Bedford to St Pancras line; plans to extend electrification from Hitchin to Huntingdon on the East Coast Main Line would have to be abandoned as the Department of Transport was refusing to give consent.'[8]

The NUR finally reached agreement on flexible rostering in December 1981 and Howell responded by giving the go-ahead to electrify the routes from Colchester to Norwich and Harwich. ASLEF, however, declined to play ball and the board retaliated by withholding a 3 percent pay award due in January 1982. ASLEF's response was to call two one-day strikes in mid-January, which were to be followed by others in succeeding months.

This industrial action ceased as the result of intervention by Norman Tebbit[9], then Secretary of State for Employment. The Chairman of the British Oxygen Company had complained to him about the damage done in the transhipment of gases from Merseyside to its depot at North Wembley for use in London hospitals. Tebbit asked the board to back off and find another way of dealing with ASLEF, which they did by referring the issue to RSNT – effectively 'kicking the ball into the long grass'.

As we have seen, the railways' enemies were looking for opportunities to demonstrate they were no longer an essential part of the nation's transport infrastructure. There was now a strong belief (in the media and elsewhere) that much of the board's industrial relations strategy was being directed by ministers and civil servants. The board recognised the dangers in that perception, and so Parker encouraged the formation by Bob Reid[10] and Cliff Rose of a small 'back room' strategy advisory group. Under the initial Chairmanship of Syd Hoggart, the members were John Nelson (then Bob Reid's PA), Richard George (who had just joined the board HQ from Freightliner as Rose's new PA) and Alan Marshall.

Marshall describes how it worked:

> Our aim from the outset was to separate the various issues concerning NUR and ASLEF and which were all in danger of getting muddled together (e.g. pay, driver-only operation, flexible rostering); to find ways of influencing rank and file opinion to put pressure on union reps up to executive committee members; and to monitor rank and file opinion through weekly 'dip stick' polling outside their workplaces, the latter being undertaken by Tommy Thompson's Opinion Research Centre, whom Cliff Rose had brought on board. During that summer

I subsequently spent much time at Tommy Thompson's house and office off Marylebone High Street. He was an amazing character, and also extremely useful in backward briefing to his Government and media contacts.[11]

For the NUR, the crunch came in June 1982. They had taken the decision to strike in support of a pay claim from midnight on 28 June unless the board improved their offer. Parker had responded with a letter (drafted by Tommy Thompson) to every BR employee which started with the words, 'It is now one minute to midnight,' and concluded, 'Make no mistake. If there is a strike, you may well have no job to come back to.' On behalf of the Government, Howell said the railwaymen had 'declared war on the nation'.

The railway's friends were aghast at what might happen. For the first time since 1955, it looked as though the entire system could be shut down for an indefinite period. It stood to reason that if it were demonstrated that the nation could manage without the railway for even a couple of weeks, then the case for retaining anything like the existing network would be fatally undermined.

The NUR's executive committee appeared not to care. By then there was already a strong (and still growing) hard-left presence which saw a railway strike as part of a much wider display of union militancy against the Thatcher Government. For a while it looked as though Weighell was their prisoner, not their leader.

Fortunately for him – and for the railway – the cavalry rode to the rescue in the shape of the NUR's annual general meeting. This was the one mechanism which could override the executive and it was scheduled to start in Plymouth on 28 June, coinciding exactly with the start of the strike. Although Weighell never admitted it, there is strong circumstantial evidence that he worked hard during the weekend to persuade delegates not to back the strike and saw to it that a motion would be tabled to call it off.

Which is precisely what happened, when a delegate proposed that the strike be suspended and the matter referred to the RSNT. The resolution was carried by 47 votes to 30 and the strike was abandoned after just two days. *The Guardian* leader the following day put this outcome down to tough talking by BR and the Government, who 'got their message across. They were prepared to sit out a long, bitter strike – whatever the cost in lost business, lost subsidies and, inevitably, lost jobs … Those who did strike demonstrated that they could reduce the system to supportable chaos anyway – at the price of endangering their jobs, jeopardising public investment and, in the ultimate, precipitating a general election which the Prime Minister would almost certainly win.'[12]

But no sooner had peace broken out between the board and the NUR – at least a temporary peace until both sides would have to consider what to do with the RSNT recommendation – than a very serious dispute with ASLEF blew up over flexible rostering. The dispute had already dragged on for months, with a series of weekly one-day strikes. ASLEF had rejected the RSNT findings published on 7 May, which urged its members to accept shifts varying between seven and nine hours and effectively end the guaranteed eight-hour day. The board responded by saying that they would introduce the new rosters whether or not ASLEF agreed.

As the scale of the disagreement widened, the Board said it would hold back from imposing flexible rostering if ASLEF dropped their proposed strike action and agreed to try out the new rosters in two areas. Despite initial indications from Buckton that the ASLEF executive might agree, they announced an all-out strike from 4 July,

just days after the NUR had called off their strike over pay.

Weighell accused ASLEF of 'tearing up agreements like confetti' and its executive of being 'misguided, stupid and inconsiderate'. Nor did he hide his view that the ASLEF dispute was politically motivated, and that 'hard-Left political influences were focused in the summer of 1982 to provoke a confrontation on the railways by one means or another'.[13] Margaret Thatcher obviously agreed with him, making 'a ferocious speech on Cheltenham racecourse against the drivers, calling on the so-called "Falklands spirit" to crush them.'[14]

We are no longer prepared to jeopardise our future just to defend manning practices agreed in 1919 when steam engines plied the tracks of the Grand [*sic*] Central Railway and the motor car had not yet taken over from the horse.[15]

Despite protestations from ministers that they were leaving BR to manage the dispute, there is evidence of very considerable interest in the negotiations and the board's tactics. Gourvish comments on how 'it is puzzling that Howell should have attended so many BRB/DTp meetings to discuss the strikes, for example, on 22 and 30 June, 6, 7, 9, 12 and 16 July.'[16]

The ASLEF strike started on 4 July, as planned. Although some trains continued to run and a few drivers disobeyed the strike call, it caused massive disruption. Parker wrote another letter, this time to ASLEF members, which started by referring to the decision to suspend strike action taken at the NUR's annual conference:

Earlier this week, the good sense of ordinary railway workers pulled us back from the brink of a real disaster. Now your union has put us back there. I need your help to save the railway.

We are back to the same issue on which you went on strike in January, flexible rosters. You lost wages. The industry lost customers and freight. There were no winners.

He concluded by appealing to the union's members over the heads of its leadership:

What we are asking for is not unreasonable. And it is vital. Give it a chance.

Convince your union leaders to see sense. Your strike will drive customers away and wreck this great industry. Let us work together for a good future.

The strikers' determination was reinforced by an unwise intervention by Michael Foot, then leader of the Labour Party. The text of a speech to the Durham miners' gala was distributed in advance, in which he was quoted as saying that the board showed 'an extraordinary desire to pick a fight with the rail unions'. ASLEF had 'offered a sensible way out of the problem. But the board – with the Government pushing them – were adamant that they would have a strike and they got one.'[17]

Foot's actual speech notes contained nothing on the ASLEF dispute (see David Howell's explanation for this, below). But the damage was done, as the passage was in the text delivered to the London media in advance. Foot's support for ASLEF was the lead story in the *Sunday Times* the next day, together with a bitter riposte from Peter Parker:

The Railways Board has never needed politicians of any colour to tell it how to run a railway, and Government ministers have played no part whatever in the board's handling of the present crisis.[18]

On the following day, *The Times* contained a report which implied Weighell had complained to Foot about his speech:

The job of the leader of the Labour Party is to look at the facts before he makes a statement. What I have been saying is what I would expect him to say.[19]

This was picked up in the House of Commons first by the Prime Minister, on 13 July, and then by David Howell the following day. Thatcher said:

I noted the Leader of the Opposition's support for ASLEF. Indeed, he seems to have become the strikers' friend.

In an exchange with Foot, she added:

I am more in agreement with Mr Sidney Weighell than with the right honourable gentleman, when Mr Weighell said: 'No amount of smokescreens can hide the fact that the train drivers have refused to accept a decision on flexible rostering, which my union is operating. This is a narrow, stupid, sectional dispute and it is causing untold damage to the railways.'[20]

Howell followed this with his own statement one day later, containing the clearest warning yet of the consequences of a continuing ASLEF strike:

The path ahead for the railways of this country is now very dark. Vast resources are being bled away. Thousands of jobs could disappear for good. Travellers and holidaymakers are being caused much bitter misery and suffering.

Those who called this unnecessary strike, as well as those who have given comfort and succour to the strike, carry an immense and direct responsibility for all this damage and all this suffering.

It remains in the hands of the ASLEF executive to call a halt to the destruction; and it is the duty of all those who believe the public should be protected and the railways and those who work in them saved from disaster to urge the executive of ASLEF to desist from its futile course.[21]

Responding to a request from Shadow Transport Secretary Albert Booth[22] that he intervene, Howell said:

The right honourable gentleman asked about an initiative. I believe that a good initiative by the right honourable gentleman and his right honourable friend the Leader of the Labour Party would be for them to go back on their bizarre statement at the weekend and the announcement at Durham racecourse – which apparently was not given because the right honourable gentleman ran out of time – which gave comfort and support to ASLEF and instead to listen to the wise words of Mr Sidney Weighell, who urged the Leader of the Opposition to behave like a leader. When I hear the right honourable gentleman apportioning blame for the railway crisis, I feel that we should all refer to the words of Mr Sidney Weighell: 'We have grave doubts about you and Albert.'[23]

Alongside the Prime Minister's comment the previous day, this was all too much for Weighell and he dashed off a furious letter to Howell:

I want to state categorically that I made no such remarks at that meeting [the one which he had with Foot and Booth], nor did I say anything that remotely approached them. In the present rail crisis I find it deplorable that you should waste your time in attempting to stir up phoney divisions on the basis of untruthful reports of a private meeting, whatever the source ...

I take great exception to you and the Prime Minister having the temerity to pray me in aid in defending your position in the present dispute.[24]

Before these arguments raged in Parliament, the BRB and its public relations operation had been busy. As Alan Marshall has told us, once the dispute with the NUR was out of the way, 'we now had the fight we had planned for, with ASLEF.'[25] His email continues:

All along, the policy was to encourage drivers to come to work so when, on the first strike day (a Sunday), several on the Southern Region broke the strike Syd Preston (BRB's Chief Press Officer) and I were manning the press office and milked the situation for all it was worth. And every day thereafter we had a regional round up of the growing number of trains BR was able to run.

As we got to mid week, the question arose of what to do about the following weekend, in terms of keeping routes open and therefore scheduling and paying staff, such as at stations and in signal boxes. Our recommendation was that we should keep open any line or route where footplate staff reported for duty up to and including the Friday late turn. This was agreed by board exec on the Thursday morning and communicated by conference call to the regions.

Throughout the dispute we kept the press office open from about 06.00 to midnight, particularly to monitor media activity and stories. So it was that at about 23.00 on that Thursday night we found a story on the Press Association teleprinter stating that BR Western Region would be shutting down for the weekend. This was clearly incorrect, as no final decision could be taken until the last possible booked-for-duty driver did or did not turn up the following afternoon.

I got Ron Drummond, the WR public affairs manager, out of his bed in Northampton – but he simply repeated that his office had issued a statement as instructed by his General Manager, Leslie Lloyd[26]. I tried phoning Lloyd at home near Slough, but got no reply.

At about 01.00 I called the Press Association and explained the board's position – and they put out a correction withdrawing the original story and repeating that BR would keep open any route where drivers reported for work up to and including Friday afternoon.

Marshall says that he reported on the events of the previous night at 06.00 on Friday morning to James Urquhart, who had taken on the industrial relations role from Cliff Rose (by then unwell):

I felt somewhat uneasy that I had unilaterally countermanded the Western Region's public statement. Urquhart told me not to worry and that I had done the right thing.

A little later that morning, at about 11.00, John Nelson phoned me to say a motor cycle messenger was on his way down to my office with a letter, which I should read with interest, then replace it in the envelope, seal it, and hand it back to the messenger for delivery. The letter was on Bob Reid's personal notepaper and addressed to Leslie Lloyd, General Manager at Paddington, and briefly asked him to confirm by return his retirement from BR, and signed 'Yours, aye, Bob.' Leslie Lloyd left his office at Paddington by lunchtime to start his 'gardening leave', never to return.

As the dispute dragged on into a second week, Parker and the board got tough. They said they would sack all 23,000 ASLEF members and close down the network within seven days unless the union returned to work and accepted the principle of flexible rostering. Weighell records his own reaction on hearing this:

> We are now at the crossroads. The future of British Rail will be decided this week. Thousands of jobs and thousands of miles of railway track will go down the plughole.[27]

One complication was that rostering staff for duty to operate only a few trains was costing a small fortune, with the board's cash reserves dwindling rapidly. While keeping up the momentum of encouraging drivers to return to work, the board decided that operations staff would have to be given protective notices.

After this strategy was approved by the board executive, the letters were prepared at Rail House and run off in some secrecy to be dispatched to area managers around the country. They were put on night trains with instructions to guards to deliver them to the stations indicated. The regions had been alerted to what was happening, with specific instructions that area managers were to collect and receive the packages, but under no circumstances to open them until or unless instructed. However, one of them didn't follow instructions and the contents were observed at Leicester.

The scene then switched to the TUC, which intervened as the result of pressure from other unions. Rumours of the dismissal letters (stemming from the leak in Leicester that Friday morning) helped to accelerate the process.

Late on Friday afternoon, Parker, Urquhart and Richard George set off for the conciliation service ACAS, following the TUC developments. The machinations at ACAS went on into the small hours of Saturday morning and then it seemed the deal was done, subject to ASLEF's executive. Parker and George retired to the Charing Cross Hotel for some breakfast, with Parker telling Nick Jones of the BBC that he was going to have his eggs 'sunny side up' and then go home. When the ASLEF executive reached its decision, Buckton would communicate with Len Murray[28] who had been asked to contact Marshall so he could break the news on behalf of BRB. Murray did so at about 11:30, with the words, 'Alan, it's all over. We've [sic] won.'[29]

Meanwhile, several of the industrial relations correspondents had gone to 'doorstep' Arkwright Road and await ASLEF's decision. They waited in vain, as no one came out to see them. It transpired that, once the executive members had taken their decision, they left over the back garden fence.

Eventually, on Sunday 18 July, Ray Buckton announced that the ASLEF executive had agreed to accept the TUC's terms. Harsh criticism was aimed at Weighell for assisting the board and for acting contrary to the spirit of trade unionism. This agreement meant that the board's threat to dismiss all drivers who failed to report for duty on 20 July did not need to be implemented.

ASLEF's monthly newspaper, *Locomotive Journal*, claimed that Parker controlled 'the biggest and most professional public relations effort a nationalised industry has ever known'.[30]

We shall never know exactly what would have happened had ASLEF not called off the strike of July 1982, but it seems certain the board would have gone ahead with their threat to dismiss all striking drivers and close down the network. It would have become the moment when the railways' enemies argued that Britain was able to manage without a rail network of anything like the size it was then; as a result, large parts of it would never have reopened. That is why the 1982 disputes were a turning point in the postwar history of Britain's railways.

'Flexible voting'

Weighell was used to being attacked by the Left, and took their abuse philosophically. However, the near-humiliation of ASLEF had increased the determination of his enemies to drive him from office – though few would have predicted just how they would achieve that.

His downfall came about as a result of the 1982 Labour Party Conference, which took place less than three months after the drama of the ASLEF strikes, when he went against an instruction from the NUR's executive to support the National Union of Mineworkers' candidate (Eric Clarke) for election to the trade union section of the Labour Party's National Executive Committee. Instead, Weighell gave the union's vote to the electricians' union candidate, taking the view that he was entitled to do this as he had not received a promise of reciprocal support from the NUM for the NUR's own candidate (Assistant General Secretary Russell Tuck). Had there not been an unusual secondary scrutinisation of the ballot, he would probably have got away with it.

Once Weighell was found out, all hell broke loose. At last, the hard left on the NUR's executive had the grounds they needed to get rid of him. They planned to suspend him from office and get him out of the way while the NUR decided what to do with McCarthy's[31] recommendations on the union's pay claim and about their refusal to allow driver-only operation of the Bedford-St Pancras trains.

Not for the first time, however, Weighell outwitted them. He knew that if he resigned in advance of any move to suspend him he'd stay in post for three months – until 5 January 1983 – rather than being shown the door immediately. He reasoned that this might allow him to speak at a specially convened recall conference at the AUEW office in Birmingham to consider the findings of the McCarthy tribunal on the NUR's pay claim, already in his diary for 13-14 October. There was also a chance that the moderate majority among the delegates might ask him to stay on as General Secretary and withdraw his resignation.

The full story of what happened next is described in a letter sent to *The Guardian* by Richard Faulkner, following Weighell's death in 2002, correcting a number of crucial errors in their obituary of Weighell published that 15 February. Some of Faulkner's letter was published on 18 February 2002; he had been present at the conference and this extract contains more information than appeared in *The Guardian*:

> Weighell hoped that the rank and file members of the union would assert themselves and seek to persuade him to stay. It nearly worked. Emergency resolutions were tabled asking the General Secretary to reconsider his resignation, and for a while it appeared at the meeting that one of these would be carried. Sid Weighell stayed away from the debate, and awaited the outcome in the nearby Albany Hotel. I was the first to get to him to say that the vote was lost by 41 to 36.
>
> Had he chosen to address the delegates, he would probably have won. Had that happened he would have secured a huge victory over his enemies in the union's executive, who wanted

to fight the Thatcher Government, alongside the train drivers and the miners.

Despite the crushing disappointment of the morning's vote, Weighell went into the afternoon conference to argue the case for accepting the tribunal's pay award, and rejecting strike action. It was a display of political and personal courage greater than I had ever seen before. Sid's combination of invective, wit and passion won the vote easily, and this proved to be the turning point in the union's relationship with the British Railways Board.

Sid Weighell never apologised for the way he cast the union's votes at the 1982 Labour conference. He believed that the party was a whisker away from oblivion, and that a start had to be made by changing the composition of the party executive. His public position was that he had received no undertaking from the NUM that the miners' votes would be cast for the NUR candidate, and that he needed to protect the NUR's position. This he was able to do by doing a deal with the electricians' union.

At least one other General Secretary did the same as Weighell with his union's votes at the 1982 conference (I know this, because the individual concerned told me). He and Weighell shared what was then a widespread view that the party was finished unless it moved back to the centre.[32]

While he was a socialist who believed passionately in public ownership, Weighell was also a pragmatist who realised that, however great one's idealism, politics and industrial relations were about the art of the possible. This was why he developed such a good working relationship with Peter Parker ('from Day One', as he says in his autobiography[33]), for Parker's approach to these issues was remarkably similar. It says much about the qualities of these two men that they managed to stick together throughout the periods of political danger described in this book. Both saw the truth in one of Parker's favourite aphorisms: 'Never forget that a halo is only nine inches away from becoming a noose.'

1 'No trade union played a greater part in the creation of the Labour Party than the NUR. The parent body of the union – the old Amalgamated Society of Railway Servants – sponsored the original TUC resolution in 1899 at the Plymouth Congress which led to the creation of the Labour Representation Committee the following year. The union was one of the first two to affiliate to the committee, which in 1906 was converted into the Labour Party.' Sidney Weighell, On the Rails, p130.

2 After Leon Trotsky (1897-1940), Lenin's second-in-command during the Bolshevik revolution of 1917 and proponent of 'permanent revolution'. Trotsky was assassinated on Stalin's orders while in exile in Mexico, with an ice-pick.

3 On the Rails, pp139-140.

4 Flexible rostering provided for abolition of the fixed eight-hour working day, which had been established as an outcome of the railway strike of 1919, and its replacement by rosters of seven or nine hours to increase train-crew productivity.

5 'The Railway Staff National Tribunal was established under part six of the machinery of negotiation for railway staff, which was agreed in February 1935 between the railway companies on one side and the National Union of Railwaymen, Associated Society of Locomotive Engineers and Firemen, and the Railway Clerks' Association on the other. The agreement covered weekly paid traffic employees and salaried staffs within certain salary limits; it set up negotiating machinery, of which the tribunal acted as the final resort for settling questions of major importance left unresolved at earlier stages. The tribunal consisted of three members, one chosen by the unions and one by the railway companies, with a permanent independent Chairman appointed by the Government.' (National Archives website) Between 1973 and 1986, the RSNT was chaired by Labour life peer and Oxford academic Bill McCarthy (ennobled as Lord McCarthy in 1976).

6 David Howell (born 1936) was the Conservative MP for Guildford 1966-97 and Secretary of State for Transport 1981-83. He also served as Secretary of State for Energy 1979-81 and Junior Minister 1970-74, becoming Chairman of the Foreign Affairs Select Committee in 1987. He is an author and journalist, ennobled as Lord Howell of Guildford in 1997, and returned to Government as Minister of State in the Foreign and Commonwealth Office with the 2010 coalition government, retiring in 2012. Howell is also the father-in-law of George Osborne, Chancellor of the Exchequer since 2010.

7 On the Rails, passim.

8 Quoted in 'Make or Break Confrontation' by Nicholas Jones, Railnews, July 2011, pp19-21.

9 Norman Tebbit (born 1931) was a Conservative politician who held a series of posts in the Thatcher Government, including Secretary of State for Employment, Trade and Industry, and Chancellor of the Duchy of Lancaster. He was Chairman of the Conservative Party from 1985-87 and served as MP for Epping 1970-74 and Chingford 1974-92. Ennobled as Lord Tebbit in 1992, he is a former RAF and civil airline pilot, as well as having served as a union official.

10 Sir Robert Reid (1925-93) was a career railwayman who joined the LNER in 1947, after war service as a captain in the Royal Tank Regiment. He became Chairman of British Rail in 1983, having previously been Chief Executive (Railways), responsible for the highly successful sector management reorganisation. He re-established trust with ministers on BR's ability to manage its resources and in return for meeting cash limits, secured investment in East Coast main line electrification completed in 1991.

11 Email from Alan Marshall to the authors, 3 June 2012.

12 The Guardian, 29 June 1982, p10.

13 On the Rails, p95.

14 Ibid p95.

15 Reported in The Times, 5 July 1982, p1.

16 British Rail 1948-1973, p168.

17 In Michael Foot's papers deposited at the People's History Museum, Manchester.

18 Sunday Times, 11 July 1982, p1.

19 The Times, 12 July 1982, p2.

20 HC Deb volume 27, 13 July 1982, cc850.

21 HC Deb volume 27, 14 July 1982, cc1035.

22 Albert Booth (1928-2010) was a left-wing Labour politician who served as Employment Secretary from 1976-79 and as MP for Barrow 1966-83, which he lost largely as a result of his commitment to unilateral nuclear disarmament – the principal employer in the constituency was Vickers, which built the Polaris submarines. He refused a peerage and subsequently became Executive Director of the South Yorkshire Passenger Transport Executive. Among Michael Foot's papers deposited at the People's History Museum in Manchester are several handwritten notes produced by Peter Mandelson, Booth's 1980-82 political adviser, on aspects of the dispute including a private telephone conversation with William Camp: they show clearly how very difficult it was for the Labour front bench to adopt a line which did not cause offence to either of the trade unions involved or the travelling public.

23 HC Deb volume 27, 14 July 1982, cc1036.

24 Unpublished letter from Sidney Weighell to David Howell, 15 July 1982, deposited in Michael Foot's papers at the People's History Museum, Manchester.

25 Email from Alan Marshall to the authors, 3 June 2012.

26 Leslie Lloyd (1924-2004) was the General Manager of BR Western Region 1976-82. He joined the railway as a management trainee in 1949 and served as Operations Manager at BR HQ before becoming WR General Manager.

27 On the Rails, p96.

28 Len Murray (1922-2004) was General Secretary of the TUC from 1973-84, ennobled as Lord Murray of Epping Forest in 1985. He was described in his obituary (The Independent, 22 May 2004) by Tam Dalyell as one of the 10 most influential people in Britain in the 1970s: 'For a decade and a half he stood at the very centre of British public life.'

29 Alan Marshall's email to authors, 3 June 2012

30 Quoted from Locomotive Journal by Nicholas Jones in Railnews, July 2011, p21.

31 William McCarthy (born 1925) chaired the Railway Staff National Tribunal from 1973-86, and numerous other industrial tribunals and committees of inquiry. A working-class boy who went to Ruskin College Oxford on a trade union scholarship, and then to Merton and Nuffield colleges, he is the author of numerous books and papers on industrial relations. He was ennobled in 1975.

32 From Richard Faulkner's unpublished papers. Extracts from this letter were published in The Guardian on 18 February 2002, p15.

33 'I wanted to work with him to make a success of British Rail.' On the Rails, p50.

XII

THE SERPELL REVIEW

A really rotten report.

THE GUARDIAN LEADER, 21 JANUARY 1983

Threatened by worms

In 1980, it was discovered that Barmouth bridge, a timber viaduct across the Mawddach estuary, was under attack
by teredo worms which bored their way into the timber piles supporting the structure. This resulted in a ban on
locomotive-hauled trains until repairs had been carried out. Seen here in April 1971, Class 40 locomotive *Aquitania*
hauls a charter train for the Wirral Railway Circle across the bridge on its way to Portmadoc.

In 1980, Peter Parker had sufficient confidence to ask the Government to set up a major review of the board's objectives, in the hope it would help create a fresh financial framework and allow the railway to escape from the 'crumbling edge of quality', as he called it. He characterised the Government's approach to post-war rail policy as only ever having the puff to run from A to B:

> A was for *per ardua ad hoc*; it would be dangerously embarrassing in parts of the country, in rural areas particularly, to let railways die – so keep them alive, just, but certainly not kicking. B was for Beeching.[1]

His hopes for the future aimed higher. Eighteen months after the request was made, in May 1982, Transport Secretary David Howell set up a review chaired by Sir David Serpell, a former Department of Transport Permanent Secretary who had become a non-executive member of the BRB. (As we saw in Chapter 3, he had also been a member of the Stedeford committee.)

Parker had seen the inquiry as an opportunity for him and the board to make the case for the sort of modernised, electrified, cost-effective railway they had described in *Rail Policy*, a board document published in March 1981. In practice it did not work out like that at all. Parker's difficulty was that the review had been conducted at a time when his position was at its weakest. (As we have also seen, 1982 had been the worst year for strikes on the railways since the General Strike of 1926.)

Serpell did not deliver the blueprint for modernisation which Parker had been hoping for, but neither did the review contain a list of recommendations. Instead, it set out a series of options purporting to show what sort of railway could be delivered, depending on the level of support available.

Unfortunately for Serpell – but immensely helpful to BR – virtually every option contained a fatal political weakness. One such was huge fare rises for commuters – perhaps as great as 40 percent in real terms. (British Rail subsequently said that to cover the true costs of providing commuter services on some routes, fare increases of above 100 percent would be required). Another option was a basic network of just 1,630 route miles (down from 10,500), consisting of just three major trunk routes plus seven London commuter routes. A third option was to save money by reducing the railways' very high level of safety, as had been specified by rail engineers.

To add to the confusion, one member of the Serpell review committee, Alfred Goldstein, decided to produce his own minority report. It claimed that a political decision needed to be made on the size of the network, from which other decisions would naturally follow: 'The real issue is what size and quality of railway should the nation decide to support having regard to the many demands on taxpayers' money.' The obvious targets for cuts were the provincial services which were very heavily subsidised. 'Ultimately, if change is desired, the trade-off may be between a larger railway operating under severe investment constraints or a rather smaller railway at a high quality of service to the customer.'

The report leaks

The report was delivered to Howell just before Christmas 1982. Parker and the BR board received their copies shortly afterwards. Well-informed pieces started appearing in the media prior to its publication, including allegations that two members of the committee – Alfred Goldstein and James Butler – had conflicts of interest, as firms for which they worked had both been engaged by the Government during

the review. *The Observer* reported on 23 January 1983 that Goldstein was a senior consultant with R. Travers Morgan, which had been paid £370,000, and Butler held a senior consultancy with Peat Marwick Mitchell and Co, which had received £182,000 for work commissioned by Serpell. Neither of these jobs, both commissioned by the Department of Transport, had been subject to public tendering. A study of British Rail Engineering carried out for Serpell by Travers Morgan was, according to *The Observer*, 'the subject of a savage critique' by BR Vice-Chairman Ian Campbell. 'It is difficult to understand why better consultants, of which there are one or two, were not chosen,' he was quoted as saying.

The official publication date for the review was 20 January. Media comment was almost uniformly hostile. *The Guardian's* leader of 21 January was headed 'A really rotten report':

> There is always a danger with reports which are well leaked in advance that the leaks are selective and that the report is damned unfairly. Not so with Serpell on the railways … For example, the report's option C3 shows two lines all the way to Taunton and Exeter, where they then stop. But even a schoolboy could have told Serpell and his colleagues that a large part of the justification for those lines is Plymouth and Torbay, connections beyond Exeter which would be scrapped. One of Serpell's options even suggests closing the March to Spalding line in Lincolnshire. One small snag: British Rail has already closed it.
>
> Take another example: Serpell foresees a minimum option in which passenger services continue to lose a small amount of money but freight services compensate with a £66 million profit. But the maps showing the shrunken network for that option reveal almost exclusively a London-centred passenger railway network. Some of the most profitable freight operations BR currently runs, including the merry-go-round coal deliveries from the mines to power stations, would go.
>
> Serpell is, in short, the worst report which it has been the taxpayers' indignity to fund for a very long time.

There was a lot more press coverage in the same vein.

A similarly critical view of Serpell came from an unlikely source at the opposite end of the political spectrum. One of the Prime Minister's advisers at that time was a former Marxist turned Thatcherite by the name of Alfred Sherman.[2] He was in the habit of firing off memos to her on almost every conceivable subject and kept copies of most of them. Sherman also had a particular aversion to publicly owned corporations such as the British Railways Board and endlessly sought ways of putting it out of business. (He reappears in Chapter 14, on converting railways into roads, which was a particular obsession of his.)

He wrote privately to Prime Minister Thatcher on 7 February 1983:

> I think setting up the Serpell Committee was a major tactical error, bound to cause political embarrassment fairly close to an election. There are lessons to be learned.
>
> Only the Government can decide what to do about British Rail. Committees of the Serpell (or Scott) variety can tell the Government little it doesn't know already, or which should be available from BR's own files.
>
> If the Government is not prepared to make decisions, a mediocre committee headed by a man who made no great impact on events at the head of the Ministry of Transport cannot help them, least of all when its brief is so restricted.

End of the Joint Line
A train from Newcastle to Norwich approaches March from the Spalding direction in 1972. The Serpell report listed this line in its report ten years later, but by then it had already been closed. The line is now blocked by a new prison, while Whitemoor Yard is a major Network Rail infrastructure depot. On the right is the Wisbech line, out of use now, but a potential reopening for the future.

Had the Government known what it wanted to do, the Serpell Committee could only act as a hindrance. For it was bound to create counter-waves, alerting all vested interests led by Peter Parker to begin a campaign of propaganda against any new ideas. They know what they want: more public money; while the Government does not know what it wants, and is therefore in no position to fight.

I note that the idea of the Serpell Committee originated with Peter Parker in the first place. He knew what he was doing. He is hopeless at industrial management but very good at political intrigue. David [Howell] was sold a pup, not for the first time.

It was fatal for Transport then to hand the report to Parker and then sit on their hands while he deliberately leaked a distorted version to the press in order to whip up feeling against the report for weeks before it appeared, by which time, no one really troubled to read it. BR had the media 'debate' almost all their own way, because Transport made no effort to have any other case put or to counter Parker's machinations. It was a supreme example of how to kick an own goal without really trying.

The great question which someone must eventually have the political courage to ask is: do we need railways, and are they the best way of using the huge network of rights of way through town, suburb and country developed during the nineteenth century, and if not, how can be [*sic*] initaite [*sic*] the transition to the twenty-first century? This is a challenge matching the Falklands. I cannot see dear David facing it.[3]

Happily, we have now answered Sherman's question and decided that we, as a nation, *do* need railways – a decision that has been taken in all advanced economic societies. Nor did all Conservatives share Sherman's view that Parker was a hopeless industrial manager. In his autobiography, Norman Fowler, Margaret Thatcher's first Secretary of State for Transport, described Parker as 'an industrial star … He had taken over the railways at a difficult time, with morale at rock bottom after the resignation in 1976 of the former Chairman and Labour minister, Richard Marsh. One of his first priorities had been to restore the workforce's self respect, and thanks to the bounce and energy Peter has, that is precisely what he did.'[4]

We can leave the last word on the Serpell review to *The Guardian* and its splendid editorial of 21 January 1983: 'the best thing that could happen to the Serpell report would be a short, sour journey along the branch line of no return'.

And that is more or less exactly what happened to it.

More bus substitution

The Government returned to bus substitution in the early 1980s. One of the workstreams arising from the Serpell Report in 1982 was the replacement of rail services by guaranteed bus routes designed to connect with rail services. Work started in September 1982 on a joint study between BRB (Director, Provincial Services) and the National Bus Company. Recognising the difficulties, seven pilot schemes were proposed without commitment to withdrawing the parallel rail services. The routes were:

1. Darlington-Bishop Auckland
2. March-Doncaster (the 'Joint Line')
3. Norwich-Sheringham
4. Morpeth-Berwick (local services)
5. Shrewsbury-Chester
6. Leamington Spa-Stratford upon Avon
7. Newport-Gloucester

In retrospect, the choice of such busy routes as Norwich-Sheringham and Chester-Shrewsbury seems strange, but in 1982 they were moribund and on the list of 'usual suspects' for early closure.

The report, which was not published, concluded that bus substitution on these routes could be cheaper, but there were too many qualifications for it to be a recommended solution. Instead, its authors recommended some more limited experiments.

But bus substitution stayed in the minds of policymakers as a possible way forward on a limited number of routes until the early 1990s and remained a recurring theme, as illustrated in Appendix E. In Scotland, however, it was ruled out from a slightly earlier date by political sensitivities. In November 1988, Secretary of State for Scotland Malcolm Rifkind[5] met BR Chairman Sir Robert Reid and afterwards put his clear views on the record:

You said that British Rail had no plans for any line closures and bus substitutions in Scotland. You also said that no work was being done on this within your organisation. I am very glad to hear this … I consider that it would be unwise to examine possibilities such as line closures or bus substitution which you do not plan to pursue.[6]

In fact, work had been put in hand by BRB just a year beforehand on a number of lines, including Ladybank-Perth, but nothing more was heard of this subsequently. (The line then carried one train a day, which has turned into one train an hour today.)

Finally, bus substitution was killed as a concept by privatisation – and franchises which specified the *rail* services to be run – and by the subsequent growth in traffic. Passenger numbers have doubled on the Norwich-Sheringham line, for example, and risen threefold on the Chester-Shrewsbury line, with additional trains run to cater for demand.

Structural threats

The pre-publication treatment of the Serpell report had the effect of preventing any further programme of closures, but a threat to some routes was manifest as major structures required renewal. The Barnstaple line was threatened during the 1980s, when the bridge over the River Exe at Cowley Bridge Junction near Exeter required renewal as a result of flood damage. Similarly, the future of the Castle Cary-Weymouth route looked uncertain when it became apparent that expensive repairs to Frampton tunnel would be required.

The most dramatic example of this occurred in 1980, when tests showed that the long timber viaduct over the Mawddach estuary on the Cambrian Coast line was being attacked by teredo worms and, for a period, locomotives were banned from the bridge. Peter Parker used this to highlight some of the difficulties faced by the railway and, after much thought by the engineers, an affordable solution was found to repair and protect the timber piles that supported the viaduct, completed six years later. More dramatic still was the collapse of the Ness viaduct at Inverness as a result of a tidal surge in 1989, cutting off the routes to the far north and the Kyle line. Determined action by ScotRail General Manager John Ellis[7] and Chairman Sir Robert Reid ensured that public commitments were given the following day about the board's intention to rebuild the bridge. In the event, the bridge was closed for 15 months and rolling stock transfers were made by road and a temporary depot established at Muir of Ord, to provide a service to the north of Scotland while reconstruction took place.

Today, the method of funding Network Rail, regulated through the expenditure for each control period agreed by the Office of Rail Regulation, includes contingencies for such risks. This has removed the threat of closure under such circumstances, as was evident in the replacement of extensive flood damage on the Conwy Valley line in 2005 and of a costly bridge on the Esk Valley line in 2009.

1   *For Starters*, p262.
2   Sir Alfred Sherman (1919-2006) was a member of the Communist Party until he was expelled in 1948, and had fought for the Republicans in the Spanish Civil War. Following a spell of teaching and journalism, he founded the Conservative think tank the Centre for Policy Studies with Margaret Thatcher and Sir Keith Joseph in 1974. He was a major contributor to Thatcher's speeches and introduced her to Sir Alan Walters, who then became her economic adviser (see Chapter 10). However, Sherman lost influence in the mid-1980s, as well as his position as a leader writer on the *Daily Telegraph* when Max Hastings sacked him in 1986.
3   From Sir Alfred Sherman's papers, bequeathed by him to Royal Holloway, University of London. Ref. AR MT/M/7/3 Box 8.
4   *Ministers Decide*, p94.
5   Sir Malcolm Leslie Rifkind KCMG, QC (born 1946) represented Edinburgh Pentlands from 1974-79 and has been the MP for Kensington and Chelsea since 2010.His ministerial posts include Secretary of State for Scotland 1986-90 and Secretary of State for Transport 1990-92, where he is remembered both as an advocate of privatisation and for rejecting the advice of BR in his choice of route for the Channel Tunnel Rail Link (now HS1).
6   Letter of 2 December 1988, National Archives of Scotland, BR/RSR/4/1399.
7   John Ellis (born 1938) joined BR as a graduate management trainee in 1962. He was Chief Freight manager, 1980-83; General Manager of ScotRail and then Southern Region; Deputy Managing Director of InterCity, 1992-93; Director of Production, Railtrack, 1993-95; Managing Director of ScotRail, 1995-97. He has been a Director of GB Railfreight, since 2001 and is a trustee of the Transport 2000 Trust, as well as Chairman of the National Railway Heritage Awards and the Cotswold Line Promotion Group.

XIII

APPRAISING PETER PARKER

Peter Parker, widely regarded as one of the greatest chairmen of British Rail …

CHRISTIAN WOLMAR, *FIRE AND STEAM*, 2007

Press Button for Attention
The Chairman launches the Ayrshire electrification project in January 1983. Parker's flair for publicity helped boost morale and raise the image of the railway from its nadir in the 1960s. Here he is with Scottish Region General Manager Leslie Soane (on his left), as well as Convenor of Strathclyde Regional Council James Burns (left), Scottish Office Minister Allan Stewart MP (on Parker's right) and the Provost of Kyle and Carrick (right).

As we have seen, Peter Parker was one of those rare public figures who attracted, in equal measure, respect for his leadership qualities and affection from those who knew him well. Geoffrey Goodman, the doyen of the industrial correspondents, described him in an obituary for *The Guardian* on 1 May 2002:

… one of the outstanding industrial leaders in postwar Britain. Had he continued to run British Rail after 1983, he would – given essential Government financial support – have turned it into the finest railway system in the world … Parker was a prophet in advance of his time. His fertile, artistic, imaginative and, yes sometimes, eccentric brilliance put him well ahead of virtually every other industrial chief in the land. He was years ahead of Tony Blair, with his own, special third-way concept of partnership between public service and private enterprise.

Parker remained as Chairman of British Rail after the change of Government in 1979 – indeed, he had his contract extended by two years, not stepping down until September 1983. By surviving the industrial relations turmoil of 1982, in particular, he was able to hand on the railway in a far better state than it had been in at the time he took on the Chairmanship in 1977. The fact that his successor, Robert Reid, was overwhelmingly his preferred candidate helped secure his legacy. (Parker describes in his autobiography how a nameplate unveiling ceremony for a locomotive named after Airey Neave,[1] at which Margaret Thatcher was the guest of honour, helped smooth the path for Reid to follow him[2].)

Parker's misfortune was that, throughout his term as Chairman, retrenchment and cost cutting mattered far more to ministers and civil servants than developing the railway. It was only much later – in July 2001 – that distinguished City correspondent and Railway Heritage Committee member Christopher Fildes could write in *The Spectator*:

Railways are a growth industry. Their most sustained attempts to drive away their customers have not succeeded.

Twenty years earlier, however, choking off demand by fare increases well above the rate of inflation was not only talked about but implemented – particularly for London commuters, who it was believed could make their own contribution to reducing the railways' deficits by paying through the nose for their season tickets.

Despite all these vicissitudes, Parker pressed on. By a series of high-profile advertising and marketing campaigns, he got the railways talked about again. Jimmy Savile[3] presented a particularly effective (though much parodied) TV campaign based on the slogan, 'This is the age of the train.' Guided by William Camp, Parker initiated a series of corporate advertisements aimed at 'opinion formers' in

Age of the Train
Parker's flair raised the profile of BR through striking offers such as the Senior Citizens Railcard, a £1 ticket which elicited packed trains on the day it became available. Fronted by Jimmy Savile, this advert includes the famous 'age of the train' strapline.

broadsheet newspapers and political journals, asking how British Rail could go on running 'the most cost-effective major railway in Europe', drawing attention to its achievements and the need for new money if it was to do more. The advertisements also pointed out:

… on average the eight biggest European railways received twice as much in relation to their countries' gross national product as BR did. Furthermore, in Germany and France, Government paid normally between 35 and 45% of total costs, in Italy nearly 70%. Our 27% of turnover looked skinny, even 'mean' in the words of the *Financial Times*.[4]

On 5 March 1981, the *FT* had reported:

In just eight months British Rail's corporate advertising campaign has created the right impression in high places … The BR campaign is almost certainly the boldest, most vigorous and most skilled use of corporate advertising by a nationalised concern seen in Britain to date.[5]

As the principal subject of this book is the successive attempts by Government and the railway itself to reduce the size of the network (and the efforts made to counter them), it is essential to gauge where Peter Parker stood on these matters. On the negative side, he was an enthusiastic advocate of replacing the lesser used rural rail services with buses. We have already given an account of his speech to the Confederation of Passenger Transport in Bournemouth on 19 September 1979, and he did nothing to draw back the enthusiasm of some senior rail colleagues in formulating the board's response (*An Opportunity for Change*) to Crosland's orange consultation paper on transport policy, in which bus substitution featured heavily. A charitable viewpoint would have it he was under such pressure from DTp officials to acquiesce in a closure programme that he felt he had to go along with it, in the hope they would deliver the investment the railway needed for projects such as electrification and the Advanced Passenger Train. However, had he seen Sir Peter Baldwin's secret paper, prepared for the Sunningdale conference in March 1977, he might have been less trusting and perhaps not have described Baldwin as 'a godsend to me'[6].

On the other side of the balance sheet are his achievements in finally seeing off Sir Alfred Sherman's absurd plans to concrete over the railways and turn them into busways (see Chapter 14), and in giving his public affairs advisers full rein in discrediting the Serpell Report in advance of its 1983 publication. The warmth and closeness of his relationship with Sidney Weighell also worked to the railway's advantage through the appalling crises of 1982. Both men believed that if just the two of them had been in charge, with neither having to look constantly over their shoulder (to civil servants in Parker's case, to the NUR's executive in Weighell's), it would have been possible to create a really great railway.

Meanwhile, the railway had to get by as best it could. Parker decided to face head-on the negative arguments about regressive subsidies, and developed the concept of the 'social railway'. The White Paper had clearly identified the commercial railway, with the ultimate target (achieved by BR) of self-supporting InterCity and freight operations. Parker argued in turn that the PSO grant was not a subsidy for the rest of the passenger railway but a contract payment from Government, in return for which they got the railway they had specified (i.e. that operating at the end of 1973).

This transformed the argument. Not only was the stigma of 'subsidy' removed, but the onus for deciding which parts of the network should be kept and which closed became the responsibility of Government. Parker rightly judged that there would be little political appetite for further closures and the mandarins would have to go carefully if closure decisions were no longer seen as the responsibility of the board. The word 'subsidy' was replaced by 'support' or 'contract payment' in the vocabulary of railwaymen. Parker was the master of the apposite one-liner and coined the quip, 'Subsidies are sickening, contracts are quickening.'

He also invented the phrase 'the crumbling edge of quality'. This related to the rundown in maintenance on secondary routes which, if unchecked, would have inevitably led to their closure. At one stage the board had warned that a small number of lines would have their rail services suspended if work was not carried out. Signalling renewals were postponed, station refurbishments abandoned and economies made in track renewal, so that perhaps only one sleeper in six would see replacement.

For a non-railwayman, Parker was remarkably skilled in understanding the railway culture. He was determined to promote two aspects of this: the first was the railway as a profession – an industry in which the brightest university graduates would be as keen to work as the ambitious school leaver. He also wanted to tap into the public mood, which could be summed up as 'It's our railway and we care about it.' The concept of the railway as both profession and community was not appreciated by everyone, however.

The Government, and perhaps especially DfT officials, hated both – the 'profession' because it supposedly represented a selfish provider interest; the 'community' because they associated it with sentimental nostalgia; and both because they obstructed 'progress' – or rather, what the Department intended to do.

Every so often, outsiders would come in to the British Railways Board determined to change this culture. One such was a controversial industrial relations director called Trevor Toolan, who arrived in December 1986 from Land Rover. He succeeded a career railwayman, John Palette, who had taken over after the untimely and much-mourned death of Cliff Rose in 1983 (see Chapter 10 for an account of Rose's encounter with Margaret Thatcher).

Toolan's confrontational style did not go down well and he resigned in July 1990, after the board was outmanoeuvred by the NUR when it failed to obtain an injunction against a strike. On one occasion, Toolan was heard saying to colleagues:

You know what's wrong with this industry? It's a community.

In Chapter 19, we will explore how the concept of 'community railways' has developed – a further demonstration of how the British people have been able to both connect with and share the ownership of their railway.

---

1 Airey Middleton Sheffield Neave (1916-79) was a World War 2 hero (despatches, MC, DSO) who was wounded and taken prisoner in 1940, and escaped from Colditz in 1942. He was a member of the British War Crimes Executive, 1945-46, serving indictments on Goering and major Nazi war criminals. Neave was the MP for Abingdon from 1953 until his death (resulting from an IRA car bomb) and the head of Margaret Thatcher's private office from 1975.
2 *For Starters*, pp278-9.
3 Sir James Savile (1926-2011) was a disc jockey and TV presenter. This wartime Bevin boy was knighted for his charity work in 1990, but his reputation was destroyed a year after his death by revelations about his private life.
4 *For Starters*, p269.
5 *Financial Times*, 5 March 1981.
6 *For Starters*, p129.

XIV

RAILWAY CONVERSION

The frequent call by environmentalists to transfer freight from road to railway can be achieved if the railway is converted into a road.

THE HALL/SMITH REPORT, 1975

Connel Ferry road bridge
This train from Ballachulish in 1959 had priority over cars, which were stopped when a train was due. Now the cars
have it all to themselves as the rails have been lifted. The magnificent structure remains, however, still linking
Ballachulish to the south.

One of the curious side-effects of the debate over railway closures was the establishment of fringe organisations with their own solution to the 'railway problem'. One of the most vocal – but least influential – was the Railway Conversion League, which believed not only that Beeching did not go nearly far enough in closing the lesser used lines, but that the entire railway network could be converted into roads.

Its founder was one Brigadier Thomas Lloyd[1], who argued in 1954 that 3,433 buses could make all rail passenger journeys obsolete: there would be one bus at each railway station which would set off when it was full of passengers. The Institution of Civil Engineers held a debate on this in April 1955, when the notion was rejected by 10 road and rail experts and supported by just four. In January 1958 *The Engineer* reported that the Railway Conversion League had been formed, with Major Angus Dalgleish[2] as its first Chairman.

Converting the Great Eastern – the Hall/Smith report

From time to time, the 'conversionists' received encouragement from road lobbyists, Government officials, and academics. In 1972, Peter Hall, Professor of Geography at Reading University, wrote in *New Scientist*:

> There is a perfectly simple answer to the problem, which could give Britain's rural areas a more effective public transport system than now. *The key lies in the conversion of railways to roads*: a process advocated by a body called the Railway Conversion League. In recent years, as the League shows, hundreds of stretches of former rural railway have been incorporated into the road system. The technical problems are not great: a 24 foot single carriageway, well aligned, can provide smooth and fast traffic flows. In countries like Holland, for instance, many motorways are built to this specification. Railway conversion on this model would give hundreds of miles of well aligned rural main roads as an alternative to the present road system. New bus services, replacing the trains, would share the roads with ordinary traffic. The economic benefits from this solution should be self-evident. Of course, because of tired thinking and institutional barriers, it may not happen. But at least it would be worth a detailed look at the technical and economic implications.[3]

The railway conversionists' influence continued to grow to the point that, in 1975, Hall and his fellow Reading University academic Edward Smith[4] were commissioned by the Department of the Environment to carry out a study into six railway lines in the east of England. These were the main London-Harwich route and its branches to Walton-on-the-Naze, Clacton and Southend, Colchester-Sudbury, Witham-Braintree, Romford-Upminster, Tottenham Hale-North Woolwich and the Crouch Valley line from Wickford to Southminster. They came to the following conclusion:

> … converting the six lines in this study to roads will save the community about £31,042,000/year at 1973 prices, and also possibly 63 lives yearly.
>
> The saving from converting the whole BR network may be between £700,000,000/year and £1,800,000,000/year at 1973 prices, say £5,000,000/day at 1975 prices. Probably at least 1200 lives now lost in road accidents each year would be saved with the new limited-access road network. These extrapolations are only a rough indication, and are no substitute for a study of the

whole network, but they give some idea of the extra cost to the nation of continuing to use the BR network as a railway.[5]

It was not explained how taking people off the railway – the safest form of land-based transport – and forcing them to use roads – the least safe – could possibly *save* lives.

Michael Baily, *The Times'* transport correspondent, contributed the following to the argument on 17 December 1975: 'Express buses with a terminal in Liverpool Street Station could offer faster and more frequent services than trains and still make a profit at about a third of the present railway fares.'

The best quote of all came towards the end of Baily's piece: 'The frequent call by environmentalists to transfer freight from road to railway can be achieved if the railway is converted into a road' – a statement which turns out to have been lifted verbatim by Baily from the Hall and Smith report.[6]

Angus Dalgleish, writing to the editor of *The Times* on behalf of the Railway Conversion League, was ecstatic in his response: '… it has long been obvious that there is no role for modern railways in a small island surrounded by all-weather ports.'

The Department of the Environment did not share his enthusiasm, however, three days later announcing 'major reservations' about some of the calculations in the study and that they would not be publishing it. Professor Hall was free to publish it himself and did so in January 1976, with the aid of a grant from the Nigel Vinson Charity Trust[7].

In the week leading up to 1 April 1976, the Institution of Civil Engineers held a meeting of their members to discuss the issues. The Planning and Transportation department of the GLC costed the conversion of the Romford-Ilford route. According to a *New Scientist* article of 1 April 1976, the GLC's 'estimate of cost was £260,000 per km for a 6m wide roadway and £350,000 per km for an 8m route. These compare with Smith and Hall's estimates of £40,000 and £60,000. Figures from Norfolk … show that the cost of its latest project – a 6km roadway – is running out at over £200,000 per km.

'That Smith and Hall's figures for conversion are a factor of four lower than those from Norfolk and London is perhaps not so surprising when seen against Smith's revelation last week that his costings were based on data produced by the Railway Conversion League.'[8]

The Government poured cold water on this impractical idea in its 'Orange Paper', also published in April 1976.[9] Richard Marsh, then Chairman of British Rail, dismissed the Reading University research as 'fatuous', writing in his autobiography:

> Buses would need to run together at high speeds to provide capacity equal to that of a train. After they had been running for a few months, they would be so close together they could be linked and then all one would have to do would be to remove all the drivers apart from the front one, and, hey presto, at vast public expense, Reading University would have reinvented the train![10]

Sir Alfred Sherman

It looked as if the railway conversionists had gone away, but the election of the Conservative Government in 1979 gave the issue a new lease of life, thanks to Sir Alfred Sherman.

In an unpublished memo to Margaret Thatcher dated 14 September 1980 and marked, like most of his correspondence, 'Highly Confidential', he wrote:

Rail is an anachronism, and has been since the pneumatic tyre, let alone the internal combustion engine. It is run simply to keep Sidney Weighel [*sic*] turning, to keep the unions going and the staff happy. The same is true in Europe, but is no reason why we should suffer it. Rail carries only 10 per cent of freight and passenger mileage. Most working people never use it. Rail uses its segregated track (right of way) to less than five per cent of capacity which road makes of similar segregated track. If we convert rail to road, we can have the best road system in the world, and the best system of public transport (first class bus-coaches with WC's, springing, etc) as well as utility ones, with much lower petrol costs, greater convenience for car-users who now constitute over half the electorate, and a growing half at that.

The pro-rail rationalisations are easily destroyed. My group would be happy to attend such a disputation, or do it by documents. Prof. Peter Hall, leading member and past-president of the Fabian Society, is wholly with us too. So we gain better roads, vastly reducing costs to firms, and cut out the huge rail subsidy, which will grow when capital back-log is made good. Conversion costs are quite low.[11]

What Sherman did not reveal in this note to Thatcher was the personal reason he had for wanting railways converted into roads. He lived in Pimlico, near Victoria coach station, and was concerned at the noise and congestion caused by coaches, particularly following the 1980 deregulation of long-distance coach services.

This was a point picked up by Peter (now Lord) Snape, a Labour MP and former Government whip who had served as a signalman at Stockport and a guard at Manchester Victoria before being elected to Parliament.

Writing to the authors, Snape recalls a conversation with *Guardian* political correspondent Simon Hoggart about the Railway Conversion League 'in which I'd joked about Dr Beeching being reincarnated as Dr Strangelove in the shape of Alf Sherman, former Southern Region boss Lance Ibbotson and some retired Major General or other.

'I pointed out to Simon that Sherman's enthusiasm for the principle of railway conversion did not extend to the wretched vehicles passing his front door as he had recently been quoted in the *Evening Standard* as having written to Westminster Council about the number of coaches passing his house "and loitering in the vicinity" waiting their turn to pull in to Victoria coach station.'

Hoggart took up the story in his weekly 'On the House' column for *Punch* on 1 February 1984:

> Fresh tidings of Sir Alfred Sherman, the Prime Minister's friend and favourite guru. Sir Alf has taken exception to remarks made by Mr Peter Snape, the dapper legislator who serves as one of Labour's Shadow Transport Ministers.
>
> I fear I cannot repeat Mr Snape's words, which might one day be the subject of legal action. But I can quote from Sir Alf's letter. This is typed (rather badly, as if by the proverbial team of monkeys which comes up with *Hamlet*) on Sir Alf's famous letterheaded writing paper. This has his house number in huge letters at the top left, thus: 'TEN', and the name of the street in tiny little letters next to it. It also includes his telegraphic address 'Shermania'. Quite why Sir Alf should have a telegraphic address when there are no longer any telegrams to send to it I do not fully understand ... Sir Alf gets straight to the nub. 'You have,' he writes to Snape, 'grossly libelled and defamed me, accusing me of impropriety and bias.' He follows this with the deathless line:

> 'No one will impugn my integrity with impunity.'

In his letter to the authors, Snape adds the following:

> The letter was written on what looked to be pretty expensive headed notepaper but was rambling, ungrammatical, laced with crossings out, sentences written above the original typeface, and scrawled notes in the margins. His address was prefaced with the numeral 10 in very large red letters and he mentioned therein that he was 'very influential' and 'an adviser at 10 Downing Street'. He used the phrase 'I have the resources for litigation and will not hesitate to deploy them' unless he received 'an apology and an undertaking not to repeat' what he described as 'slanderous comments', in future. He also set out what he described as 'my many achievements in the business and political worlds.'
>
> I wrote in return addressing him as 'My dear Alf' (we'd never met), something on the lines of 'some ill educated nutter has obviously stolen your notepaper, and judging by the letter to me (copy enclosed) it's a wretched secondary modern boy incapable of writing or indeed spelling the Queen's English.'
>
> I went on 'I do however admire your very stylish letter heading and note particularly the prominence of the numeral "10". Having recently seen a film with the title *10* I wonder if you got the idea from the cinema? The film was very funny although it did contain some rather bawdy scenes. The very energetic star of this film is Mr Dudley Moore who is like you a tiny little chap and I wonder if you are by any chance related.' (I was obviously into *Private Eye* clichés in those days.) I heard no more.
>
> I was introduced to Sherman at some function years later. To my 'how do you do?' came the glittering-eyed reply 'I suppose you think you're funny' as he swept away.

Converting the West London line ...

Sherman's next attempt at converting a railway to a road came in 1981, when the Centre for Policy Studies gave evidence to the Commons transport select committee on building a system of ringways over existing railways. The main example they chose to illustrate this idea was the West London line, which was – and remains – the chief rail freight route from the north and west to the south of England. Back in 1982, it carried 60 freight trains a day, the equivalent – according to Mick Hamer, writing in *New Scientist*[12] – of 1500 juggernauts on the road. Today the line is extensively used for passenger trains as well, with 10 off-peak services an hour, and three new stations have opened between Clapham Junction and Kensington Olympia.

The CPS claimed erroneously that 'in a wide cutting lie the four tracks, almost disused, of the West London line', yards away from the juggernaut-laden Earl's Court Road. Most of the line is in fact two-track.

Hamer reported that the press conference at the CPS was chaired by Sherman, and that the authors of the report were Dalgleish ('the epitome of the country squire, grey-haired, a military moustache and a slightly clipped, precise voice'), and Nigel Seymer ('a more complex man. His full name is Nigel Victor Evelyn Seymer. Seymer has previously written pro-rail articles, while "Victor Evelyn" has advocated turning railways into roads').

... and the Great Central

Sherman's particular enthusiasm was for a dedicated busway from Gerrards Cross, using the formation of today's Chiltern Railway, to a coach station at Marylebone. Rather than telling Sherman to get lost

The quietest spot in London?
'Have you tried Marylebone station, my son?' was the reputed response by a father confessor to a novice monk, who complained he could find no place in London to contemplate in peace and silence. The 12:10 to Aylesbury is seen waiting at Marylebone for a handful of passengers in May 1981, at the height of the controversy about its future. The missing roof glass results in puddles on the platform, as the ageing, smoky diesel train hints at the malaise that affected the line after the opening of the M40 to Oxford and before its complete modernisation a decade later. Only two trains per hour left this station at off-peak times in 1981, compared with eight per hour today. Marylebone is now a bustling terminus rather than a place for contemplation.

– and against the advice of almost everyone around him (the authors included) – Peter Parker agreed to meet him and Professor Alan Walters over dinner on 23 June 1983, to discuss setting up yet another study to look at the possibility of converting some under-utilised railways into roads.

According to *New Scientist* (which reported these events on 4 August 1983, claiming it had seen an internal BR memorandum dated 19 July), the group directing the study included Sherman, Michael Posner[13], who was a director of BR as well as being Chairman of the Social Science Research Council, and Professor Christopher Foster, who was a director of Coopers & Lybrand:

> The consultants' brief is 'to examine the extent to which it would be possible for BR to profitably convert [*sic*] insufficiently used railway lines into toll or metered roads.
>
> The idea is that BR would run coaches instead of trains on these roads, and perhaps open them to other traffic for tolls. At present BR does not have the legal power to operate roads.
>
> The study brief mentions two specific areas for studying

conversion. One is in Greater London. 'As part of this exercise we would also examine the potential of converting at least one major commuter route such as some or all of the services on the central division of the Southern Region into Victoria.' BR is spending £30 million on resignalling these lines.

The other option is to convert the line from Marylebone to Leicester. BR is going to close Marylebone, which will be announced this year [*in fact it wasn't*], but north of Aylesbury the old main line to Leicester is largely disused.[14]

This description of the lines to be studied seems to have been slightly wide of the mark, as the main focus would be on whether trains on the High Wycombe line could be diverted to Paddington, with Aylesbury served by extending the electrified Metropolitan Line from Amersham. The study would also look at the feasibility and costs of conversion of a number of other routes with different characteristics, including the North London line, the West London line, the Hounslow loop line, Elmers End-Sanderstead, Wimbledon-Sutton and Wandsworth-Chiswick.

Meanwhile, the National Bus Company – presumably following pressure from Sherman (who was paid by them as an adviser) – had conducted their own study into conversion of the first 10 miles of the old Great Central railway line out of Marylebone. Their report came out first, in February 1984, and was breathlessly enthusiastic about how 'it could handle two-thirds of present National Express Bus traffic into Victoria, cutting up to an hour off journeys into London at peak times' (*Bus News*, February 1984).

The most astonishing sentence in the report read:

Perhaps most importantly the proposal offers the chance to British Rail to turn a line which has long since outlived its usefulness in the London transport scene into a profit-making venture. It would also please conservationists by preserving the much revered façade and concourse buildings of Marylebone intact.

The BR study

The British Rail/Coopers & Lybrand report was a rather more serious piece of work. This was a proper engineering study of the feasibility of converting routes, rather than of the political and commercial effect of their conversion. The results varied by line, but some of the common features which demonstrated the impracticality of conversion are summarised below:

In general, a two-track railway is too narrow to support anything other than a single carriageway road. It proved just possible to fit a route for coaches (but not private cars) into the route approaching Marylebone through the tunnel under St John's Wood, for example, but it involved coaches passing each other in the tunnel with no safety barriers to separate them, at high closing speeds and with close headways.

The principles of drainage for rail and road are quite different, and part of the cost of conversion is to provide a new drainage system to cope with the fast run-off of surface water from a concrete or tarmac carriageway.

Significant costs were involved in diverting through rail traffic away from the routes to be converted. While buses would have substituted for local services, fast peak services using the Hounslow loop would have had to be diverted via Richmond where peak capacity was already (even in 1981) fully used, with pressure on the level crossings along this busy route. Extensive diversions for freight were required to release the North and West London lines.

The costs of slip roads to connect to the rest of the road network were high, particularly in densely packed inner urban areas where property demolition would have been required to provide the links.

The logic was clear and the report well argued. It should also be remembered that the exercise was carried out at a time of low demand on the routes, with a run-down rail service to Marylebone failing to compete with the newly opened M40. It was clear that no capacity would have been available on the Metropolitan Line for any future growth in demand from the Aylesbury corridor, and so BR and LT wisely decided not to pursue the idea. Parker's boldness in taking the risk to commission the study was triumphantly vindicated. Chiltern Railways has been a huge success story and now runs six trains an hour off peak on the High Wycombe route, compared with British Rail's one at the time of the study in 1980.

If there had been little stomach within Government for railway conversion before, then following the report the movement just died away and the campaign was wound up following the death of Dalgleish in 1994. Proponents of converting rail lines into roads still turn up occasionally at public enquiries, as at a hearing into Chiltern Railways' plans for a new Oxford-Marylebone service.[15]

Guided busways

Notwithstanding the demise of the Railway Conversion League, the concept has been kept alive in two counties in the east of England. In Bedfordshire, there are plans to convert the Luton-Dunstable railway into a busway, and a similar but much more controversial scheme has been implemented in Cambridgeshire, taking over the old Cambridge-St Ives railway. Two years late and substantially overspent, the busway finally opened on 7 August 2011. The final cost turned out to be £160m for conversion of 10 miles of railway, with the contractors (B.A.M. Nuttall, the same as in Luton) forced to pay daily penalty charges for non-performance.

It proved necessary to sink piles to support the track where the alignment crosses the fens near Swavesey and additional work was needed to meet the tight tolerances required on the system. The top speed on the route is 55mph, but the need to slow for road crossings and reversion to conventional streets in Cambridge, where traffic congestion is worst, means that journey times are the same as before the investment was made. At this stage it is used by a standard off-peak service of only nine buses an hour and, while initial loadings are exceeding expectations, some of the patronage appears to come from riders trying out the new system for themselves (particularly as concessionary passes for senior citizens are accepted). It is hard to see what benefits are being delivered, although peak journey times are more reliable than previously.

The Liberal Democrat MP for Cambridge, Julian Hippert, described the busway as 'a white elephant'. Local pressure group Cast Iron, which was established to oppose the busway and reinstate the railway, now claims that it would have cost less than a third to reopen the railway (around £50 million) compared with the cost of the busway.

On the Luton-Dunstable scheme, the Conservative MP for South West Bedfordshire, Andrew Selous, was quoted in local online newspaper *Luton Today* (6 August 2010) as demanding sight of the contract between Luton Borough Council and construction company B.A.M. Nuttall:

Ever since the Busway was announced by Luton Borough Council I have had a stream of letters and emails from my constituents objecting to the spending of £90 million of public money on this project.

Only one person has written to me to say they support the Busway. This scheme is already having an impact on my constituency and many people have asked me what the cancellation clause in the contract states.

The high capital costs, need for special buses to be fitted with guide wheels and limited quantifiable benefits suggest that this new mode is not the pattern for the future. It is certainly not a cheaper alternative to rail.

Rail closures for roads

Following the departure of Dr Beeching, with no strategic plan or vision to follow, the Department of Transport spent six years worrying about the tactical issue of saving costs on new road construction where the formation of a railway was to be crossed, or used by the road scheme. In 1968, the Department issued a circular, drawing attention to potential savings in the construction costs of roads if the railways or canals they crossed could be closed first.

Very little came of this policy, although many sections of closed lines have subsequently been incorporated in new road schemes. (It was one reason for the timing of the closure of the Lewes-Uckfield line in 1969.) In other parts of the country, narrow bridges built for single track now inhibit track doubling to take traffic with which the motorways can no longer cope.

Estuarial crossings

The huge investment in road building, particularly in new estuarial crossings, during the 1960s also had an effect on closures – although it was more a question of timing rather than whether or not the lines would close.

The importance of the Callington branch line in Cornwall was that it gave a much more direct route to Plymouth than was available by road. The opening of the Tamar road bridge in 1961 meant that a direct bus was introduced with a shorter journey time than the train (particularly as the latter involved a change at Bere Alston). The line was cut back to Gunnislake two years later, with the rest of the branch to Bere Alston and the line into Plymouth reprieved because of the lack of direct road links deemed capable of taking buses.

The Newport on Tay-Dundee local service was suspended to enable works to be undertaken for the Tay road bridge. Following the opening of the road bridge in 1966, the branch closed permanently in 1969. The Tay road bridge was also the principal reason for closure of the line to St Andrews in the same year.

The Humber crossing opened in 1981, at the same time the railway-owned ferry service from New Holland to Hull was withdrawn and the short section of line to New Holland Pier closed. A bus service was introduced from the end of the branch at Barton on Humber across the bridge to Hull.

The opening of the second Dartford Tunnel in 1980 saw a decline in the number of passengers using the Tilbury-Gravesend ferry, leading to the closure of Tilbury Riverside station (but not until 1992). The ferry service continues, however, supported financially by Thurrock District and Kent County Councils.

1 Brigadier Thomas Ifan Lloyd CBE, DSO, MC (1903-81) founded the Railway Conversion League in 1958 and was the author of *Twilight of the Railways – What Roads they'll Make!*, Forster, Groom & Co, 1957.
2 Angus Dalgleish was a retired engineer employed by the Greater London Council (GLC). A former major in the army, he died in 1994.
3 *New Society*, 23 November 1972.
4 Edward Smith was the co-author of *Better Use of Railways* with Peter Hall (see above, note 16, Chapter 10). A research officer in the Department of Geography, University of Reading, he was later a member of the GLC's Department of Planning and Transportation. He also wrote *An Economic Comparison of Urban Railways and Express Bus Services* while working for the GLC, which went to some trouble to say that it accepted 'no responsibility for the author's opinions or conclusions'.
5 *Better Use of Railways*, Peter Hall and Edward Smith, Department of Geography, University of Reading, 1976.
6 Ibid, p17.
7 Nigel Vinson (born in 1931, ennobled by Margaret Thatcher as Lord Vinson in 1985) was one of the founders of the Centre for Policy Studies with Thatcher, Sir Alfred Sherman and Sir Keith Joseph, working for it between 1974 and 1980. He is a vocal opponent of High Speed 2, which he has called a 'vanity project' (*Lords Hansard*, column 233, 16 March 2011).
8 *New Scientist* editorial, 1 April 1976: 'Rail into road won't go'.
9 *Transport Policy* – a consultation document, HMSO 1976, paragraph 6.46, p44.
10 *Off the Rails*, p169.
11 From Sir Alfred Sherman's papers, deposited at Royal Holloway, University of London. Ref. CN AR MT/S/3/8.
12 *New Scientist*, 21 January 1982, p141.
13 Michael Posner (1931-2006) was a member of the British Railways Board from 1976-84, where his other main contribution was the preparation of the report on railway electrification.
14 *New Scientist* editorial, 4 August 1963.
15 The Chiltern Railways (Bicester to Oxford) Order Public Inquiry, 2010-11.

XV

THE DECLINE OF RAIL FREIGHT

It was relatively easy to pick off branch lines, even unprofitable main lines or to close small freight stations and depots. But behind the scenes lurked those huge bastions of restrictive practices where enormous economies could have been made.

BEECHING: CHAMPION OF THE RAILWAY?
BY R.H.N. HARDY, ON THE MAIN FREIGHT TERMINALS SUCH AS BISHOPSGATE

Pick-up goods train on the Bordon branch
The morning branch line goods train from Farnham to Bordon in Hampshire, in June 1948. Delightfully framed by the trees, the locomotive is already almost half a century old, while the small box vans and open wagons are of a design suited more to the previous century. They have limited capacity and the cost of staging them through marshalling yards – with delivery by short trains such as this, requiring three train crew as well as depot staff – had already set a cost base higher than that of the competing road haulier. The branch exchanged traffic with the Longmoor Military Railway as well as serving the needs of the town.

The conspiracy to run down the rail freight network was very different from that against the passenger network. It was set against the background of decline in Britain's industrial base, Government complicity in road haulage interests, a powerful industry and union lobby, and trade union rivalries where the rail unions came off worst. It is a story of the privatisation of the electricity supply industry and the collapse of the UK coal industry; of radical changes in logistics and the replacement of home production by imports; the consistent failure of Governments to oblige the road haulage industry to meet the costs it imposed on the road network and on society; and of remarkable innovation by rail freight companies and their staff in order to recover and rebuild after privatisation.

For years, the story of rail freight in Britain was one of decline compared with continuing demand elsewhere in Europe. Sadly, this is no longer true. In every European country now, the evidence of abandoned depots and marshalling yards tells of a dramatic decline in rail freight.

The key aspect is that 'freight does not vote', and developments in rail freight did not attract the high level of media scrutiny to which passenger services were subject.

Wagonload traffic

This is not to deny that some flows of goods traffic were clearly uneconomic. Delivery of domestic coal to stations in the Isle of Wight was the classic example. Sacks of coal were delivered to homes by lorry from station sidings to which they had been tripped by goods train from Medina Wharf. It had been unloaded there by grab from a barge that brought it from Southampton, to which it had been transported by rail. From loading at the colliery to delivery to the customer, it was handled no fewer than five times.

A simpler example was the rail transit of guano, imported from South America through the little port of Topsham in Devon, where it was used in the manufacture of glue. Movement to the nearby factory involved hauling it up the quay branch on which a special lookout vehicle was required, running round at Topsham station and then tripping it across the River Clyst to the factory's private siding, a distance of about 1.5 miles, including two reversals, which involved extended engine hours, poor wagon utilisation and around four staff, while the rate earned by such traffic was low.

The pattern of goods traffic until the 1950s was of universal provision to around 6,500 goods yards and depots around the country. The unit of production was the individual consignment, either a wagonload or a parcel sorted by hand and transported by small 12-ton rail vans. Where the demand was even smaller, one of these vans was attached to the pick-up goods train which contained the individual consignments for each local station, neatly stowed to make unloading at the platform easy.

However, the predominant traffic at local goods depots was coal and the small wagon size was determined by the constraints of the sidings and loading facilities at the collieries. The pattern of goods train services was based on the movement of individual wagons tripped to the nearest marshalling yard, formed into longer trains and then staged from yard to yard until the yard serving the destination was reached, when it would be tripped again to its unloading point. Costs were high, delays rife and the contents of wagons liable to pilferage or damage. Demand was also erratic and required a large wagon fleet to give sufficient flexibility, as well as spare locomotives and crews to move them around the country and haul the special trains to meet variable demand. A hierarchy of clerks supervised the collection of data, and control offices struggled to balance supply and demand.

Mixed train
Many branch lines combined passenger and goods services in a 'mixed' train to save costs and meet customers' requirements on long single-track lines with limited capacity. Here, a mixed train from Tollesbury in Essex approaches the junction with the Great Eastern main line at Kelvedon. The Victorian locomotive pulls a train of two tramway coaches (originally used on the Wisbech & Upwell tramway in Cambridgeshire), a box van, an open wagon and a brake van. The box van doubtless contained boxes of the excellent Tiptree preserves, then a staple traffic of the line.

The removal of common carrier obligations under the 1960 Act allowed some of the more uneconomic traffics to be abandoned, but in particular allowed the process of freight concentration to start. The objective was to focus rail services on larger towns and cities where mechanised handling facilities could be provided, with delivery to smaller towns and villages by van or by the iconic Scammell Scarab three-wheel 'mechanical horses' which were a familiar sight in high streets of the 1950s and 60s. Much of this retrenchment took place between 1955 and 1965.

By the end of the 1970s, the move to eliminate unbraked wagons and investment in air-braked vans and 'opens' spelled the end of the wagonload network. It was replaced by Speedlink, limited to principal routes based mainly on grouping portions of trains rather than individual wagons, with faster schedules and planned connections between services. However, it was not able to make the step change hoped for and declined to vanishing point by the time of privatisation.

National Carriers and parcels

National Carriers inherited a network of rail-connected depots served by regular trains. Throughout their existence, they set about closing these down and selling off the assets. Initially this involved closing smaller depots, with traffic handled by road from the larger rail-connected counterparts. Soon, road trunking replaced rail and the rail connections were progressively removed. Today, many of the depots have gone, replaced by office development, as at the mighty Bristol goods depot, or housing, as at Paddington. In a few cases, the huge buildings with warehousing above, served by wagon hoists, remain – as at Huddersfield. At Manchester Liverpool Road, the buildings now form the excellent Museum of Science and Industry.

The Didcot scandal and the TGWU conspiracy

To most people, Didcot is a dormitory town from which its residents commute to Oxford, Reading and London, with many also working at the Atomic Energy Authority's establishment at Harwell. It is also the home of the Great Western Society's splendid railway heritage centre. Its principal landmarks are the six cooling towers of its coal-fired power station, which are fed by long merry-go-round trains bringing imported coal from the port of Bristol.

The town itself only came into being because it is located on Brunel's Great Western main line to Bristol and the West, becoming the junction for Oxford, the Great Western's original main line to Birmingham, and Worcester.

In 1977, Didcot was the location for a disgraceful piece of pro-road industrial action on the part of the Transport and General Workers Union, which led to one of the most non-fraternal and unpleasant rows ever seen within the Labour Party. Its relevance to our story in that the row was about carrying more freight on the railway and the frustration of plans to establish a rail-based freight distribution centre.

At this point we should remind ourselves that the Labour Party manifestos for both general elections in 1974 unequivocally supported the transfer of freight from road to rail. In February 1974, the manifesto read: 'we must do two things: one, move as much traffic as possible from road to rail; and two, develop public transport to make us less dependent on the private car.' This was reinforced in the October manifesto: 'The energy crisis has underlined our objectives to move as much traffic as possible from road to rail and to water.'

The events of 1977 first came to light in *The Times* on 11 July, when it was reported that Bryan Minks, Marketing Division Manager of BR Western Region, had written to an MP saying 'managements of big companies have been reluctant to discuss the possibility of moving traffic to the railways because the consequences might halt distribution and production. The spread of membership of the TGWU covers many aspects of total business, and aggravation in one sector can readily spread to others in a demonstration of industrial muscle by the TGWU.'

The article alleged that freight forwarders planning to use the new distribution centre at Didcot had been warned by dock workers at Southampton (all TGWU members) that if they went ahead they would be 'blockaded' at all British ports. Minks said:

> … there are now no major forwarding agents left at Didcot with a long-term future. None of the agents operating at Didcot could possibly take on the TGWU and hope to survive.

For good measure, the Railway Invigoration Society (now Railfuture) was also quoted in the article by Christopher Thomas, labour reporter, as saying that Rowntree Mackintosh had to abandon plans for sending 'scores of tons of confectionery a day by rail from York to Norwich'. The RIS also claimed: 'The British Leyland car train from Cowley to Bathgate [Scotland] has been stopped and the proposal to move grain by rail to the new Courage brewery in Reading has been rejected due to TGWU pressure.'[1]

TGWU General Secretary Jack Jones issued an angry denial and told *The Times* he would protest to Peter Parker about Minks' letter. However, the paper reported the next day that 'road car transport workers at Southampton, members of the TGWU, had told companies that if they transferred deliveries from road to rail to the Didcot inland port near Reading, their goods would be blacked throughout the country'. Charles Turnock, NUR Assistant General Secretary, was quoted directly: 'TGWU members have blacked NUR freightliner drivers from moving traffic out of the overseas container depot in Birmingham.'[2]

The Labour Party's own transport sub-committee decided that the matter needed to be investigated. If the allegations turned out to be true, it would represent a blatantly obvious attempt by one element within the party to frustrate a key aspect of party policy.

The secretary of the sub-committee, Liz Atkins (whose father Ron Atkins[3] was then a Labour MP, as her twin sister Charlotte would later become) wrote a paper entitled 'Note on the Didcot Distribution Centre and Transfer from Road to Rail'. This went rather further than the original *Times* piece, referring to a journal published by TGWU shop stewards at Southampton Docks and written by Ron Moulsdale, Chairman of the Container Committee, entitled *The Hook*. One of its articles was headed 'Didcot Shutdown' and described how the Container Committee had heard about 'a big depot just this side of Oxford, in a place called Didcot'. Members of the branch 'took a trip to Didcot, and there was a depot, some three times the size of 201 Depot [*in Southampton*], some 40 acres and what a location … Also a railhead off the main line, we had to admit it was the best depot we have seen but we had a job to do, and that was to close it.'

The Hook then described how it had obtained the names of agents who had offices around the Didcot depot ('not saying who we were') and returned to Southampton:

> We went straight to everyone in turn and told them straight they had a choice to either use Southampton or Didcot, and if it was Didcot they would not get another container through Southampton Docks, or any other port. Most made up their minds there and then not to use Didcot.

A number of firms – Kwikasair, Transtec, Inter Route and International Express – all put in writing confirmation that they would not use Didcot: 'So after two years and about 1000 miles of travelling it looks as if we have closed down the biggest threat to our future.'

The Labour Party note contained a lot of this information and also referred to 'The 100 Company study', a list of firms that had been warned by the TGWU that if they moved freight from road to rail they would face 'retaliatory action [which] would affect their distribution and production capabilities'. Some of the firms listed were household names:

Aberthaw Cement
Allied Breweries
Bass Charrington
British Leyland
Ford Motors
Guinness
Metal Box Co
Raleigh Industries
Rank Hovis McDougall
Scottish & Newcastle Breweries
Watney Mann & Truman
Vauxhall Motors

With masterly understatement, Liz Atkins concluded:

> Clearly the issues raised in this paper are very sensitive ones. Since the committee have not heard the Transport and General Workers' response to these allegations it is hoped that Jack Jones or another official will be present to give their case.

No member of the committee could recall the last time Jones had attended one of its meetings, but he was certainly there, on 22 September 1977, for what those present felt was a most extraordinary occasion.

He was livid. The minutes of the meeting (drafted by Liz Atkins) reported that he began by saying: 'the Transport Committee should not be discussing the issue of Didcot and any allegations of rail blacking by TGWU members since it was not within their terms of reference'. On that he got short shrift from the committee's Chairman, Tom Bradley, a TSSA-sponsored MP who ruled that the discussion was in order.

According to Liz Atkins' minutes:

Jack Jones said that the TGWU had nothing to do with the situation at Didcot, though he admitted that Southampton dockers were worried about losing their jobs because of developments at the Didcot Distribution Centre. He insisted that though therefore there was some objection to Didcot, the TGWU was not using physical tactics to stop the transfer from road to rail.

The minutes show that committee members were not satisfied by Jones' answers. Ron Atkins MP said that the paper on Didcot and newspaper reports gave details of companies intimidated by the TGWU, which, if the allegations were true, would be acting against Labour's manifesto commitment of February 1974 to move as much traffic as possible from road to rail. When he raised what had appeared in *The Hook* and Ron Moulsdale's description of how Didcot had been shut down, 'Jack Jones said he had no knowledge of Ron Moulsdale or the publication.'

The above exchange was reported in the minutes. What did not appear was a further exchange between Jones and another member of the committee, the distinguished professor David Wiggins. Pressed by Wiggins to confirm that the TGWU supported Labour Party policy, Jones snarled at him: 'Who are you? Some academic I suppose.'

He was not wrong. Wiggins was at the time Professor of Philosophy at Birkbeck College London, and went on to become Wykeham Professor of Logic at Oxford University. He was also Chairman of the Transport Users Consultative Committee for the South East. The discussion came to an inconclusive halt with Jones demanding that the party's note on Didcot be destroyed. In a spirit of compromise, the committee agreed it should 'lie on the table'.

The minutes also omitted how, at one point during the meeting, the lights failed and the room was plunged into darkness. Kelvin Hopkins[4], who was then the TUC officer servicing the transport industries committee, recalls for the authors how this wound Jones up even more. He claimed that the Labour Party were the tenants of his union in Transport House (where the meeting was taking place): 'They can't even pay the electricity bill; if they didn't like the T&G they could move out and find somewhere else.'

According to Liz Atkins in a letter to the authors:

> Jack Jones didn't give up his fight on Didcot lightly. When Jack read the reference to the 'blacking of rail freight at Didcot' in the minutes of the transport sub-committee which I drafted he was furious. I was told that he demanded that Ron Hayward the then general secretary of the Labour party should sack me. Ron did not agree.

Ron Atkins recounts his own subsequent encounter:

> I believe my meeting with Jack Jones took place after the sub-committee. He tried to persuade me to change my stance. I remember distinctly that he said I should be grateful that his members in Preston supported me in my efforts to keep Preston Dock open and that I should return the favour. I pointed out that all my efforts were in support of his members' jobs in the docks. He must have been very annoyed because he contacted the T&GW branches in Preston and requested that they withdraw any support for me. When I heard this, I asked the regional organiser to call a meeting of his members, to which I explained my case. They made it clear that they would not withdraw their support. This conduct of Jack Jones was so

different from the attitude of Frank Cousins, when General Secretary, who supported Labour's transport policy despite opposition from some of his members.

I remember writing, in longhand, to Tony Crosland, a plea for Government action to transfer as much freight as possible from road to rail. The only part of his reply (also in longhand) which I can remember was: 'Dear Ron, I glossed through your letter.' So it is safe to assume that he did not commit himself or I would have remembered. I know that I was disappointed. On other matters he was always co-operative and helpful.

These extraordinary goings-on did not remain unreported for long. Environmental magazine *The Vole* had many reliable sources at this time, and one of them was able to keep it briefed on what was going on in the Labour Party's transport sub-committee. The first extensive piece on Didcot appeared in 1977[5]. *The Vole* would enthusiastically return to the charge a month later[6].

'Our report,' said *The Vole*, 'was taken up by the national press – in particular by *The Observer*, the *Daily Telegraph* and the *Financial Times*. But what was the reaction of the protagonists? Of the T&GWU, which stands accused, and of the injured parties – the rail unions, British Rail and the would-be customers of the depot? Almost without exception the response has been a silence as revealing as in Sherlock Holmes's case of the dog that didn't bark.'

The Vole described how it tried to get comments from these various parties: they were not surprised that they got nothing out of the TGWU; British Rail said there was no evidence; the NUR 'made mild complaint in the *Financial Times*', but took the view that 'a public row would not be in the interests of the Labour movement'. (Sid Weighell makes no reference at all to this dispute in his autobiography.)

The Vole didn't have much more success with the companies kept out of Didcot: 'Only Howard Tenens, the firm running the blighted Didcot depot, has spoken out.' It concluded with a demand for an official inquiry: 'We cannot appeal to the Department of Transport whose White Paper on transport is a monument to the TGWU's threats (no mention of tachographs, nothing on company cars, no real action to transfer freight to rail).'

Unsurprisingly, no such inquiry was held. Indeed, on 4 January 1978 a van was driven across the tracks at Didcot to prevent the delivery of 114 cars from the Cowley depot of British Leyland, on the

first of a number of trains scheduled to deliver 500 such vehicles.[7] This report seems to have prompted the Chairman of the BBC, Sir Michael Swann, to write an internal memo to the Director of News and Current Affairs, Richard Francis, on 20 January:

Reading the *Sunday Times* (I think) a week or two back, I was reminded of the extraordinary and scandalous matter of the new British Rail Didcot depot, being scuppered for years on end by the road interests, mainly the T&GWU.

Have we ever done a programme on this? Not that I remember, but of course I may have missed it.[8]

Francis replied on 2 February:

It would be nice to say 'No sooner said than done.' But already in the pipeline last week. *Tonight* are this evening putting out 'The Didcot Dossier' (BBC-1 11.05).

He added a handwritten addendum: 'Chairman, Jack Jones is not pleased!'[9]

Following a request from the authors, the BBC found a copy of the programme and kindly made it available to them. (The archives contain the complete transcript, and quite a lot more besides.) Presenter Denis Tuohy sets the scene, describing Didcot as:

… the site for one of our newest and biggest freight terminals and inland ports … That was four years ago. But today Didcot's inland port, centrepiece of the whole development, stands largely idle, brought to a standstill by the men from the T&G.

Vincent Hanna then takes over:

The Didcot Distribution Centre should have been the money spinner of the decade … Now the dream is shattered. Didcot the super inland port has become the prime casualty in a bitter

THE DECLINE OF RAIL FREIGHT • **107**

struggle for control of the British transport industry. It was a demonstration of the power of a single union: the Transport and General Workers Union. This film is about what they did, and how they did it.

There then follows a series of comments by interested individuals. First up is John Swanborough, Chairman of Howard Tenens, the company which managed the depot. He confirms that it would be a marvellous facility because of the rail link which came right into the site. Hanna then reports what dockers' magazine *The Hook* said about having to close Didcot down. A succession of comments are made by actors speaking the words of businessmen too frightened to be identified. The first says his company's directors have been to Southampton to see the dockers and as a result are pulling out of Didcot. The second describes how his manager 'burst through' and shouted: 'Now the shit's really hit the fan! I've been sacked and the place is going to be closed down.'

The dockers' Chairman, Ritchie Pearce, is next on, confirming the dialogue with the companies: 'What we said was that if they did use Didcot as a depot, we would not allow them to use the port.'

Hanna then switched to the movement of cars from Cowley, just 12 miles away, all of which had been moved into Didcot by road on the orders of the T&G shop stewards. Between 1974 and 1978, only two car trains had left Cowley for Didcot. Then, on 4 January 1978, Leyland persuaded the T&G to allow them to take 500 cars to Didcot by train, 'because of the Christmas rush,' says Hanna. When the train arrived at Didcot, there was a white van in the middle of the track with a man sitting on the bonnet. As Hanna is interviewing the driver of the train, 'who should appear but the man on the van bonnet, still shifting cars. I asked for some reason for the incident.'

> **Hanna:** Before that day was there ever a car in the middle of the track?
> **interviewee:** Never.
> **Hanna:** That was the first one.
> **i/v:** The one and only.
> **Hanna:** Does it strike you as somehow a bit of a coincidence that the only day, indeed the first you ever have a car on the track, was the day a train came down?
> **i/v:** Yes.
> **Hanna:** That's a coincidence?
> **i/v:** It's an absolute coincidence, you see.
> **Hanna:** Forgive me for sounding a bit sceptical about that.
> **i/v:** I don't mind. You can believe me or believe me not – I couldn't care less. I was involved in the incident.
> **Hanna:** Are you a member of the T&G yourself?
> **i/v:** I am, sir.

Hanna then explains that the train was eventually offloaded at Didcot, 'and flushed with success two days later, Leyland tried it again … They got the cars as far as the Didcot rail siding, whereupon the T&G shop stewards sent it back again.'

The programme also contains interviews with senior local ASLEF official Amwell Williams, David Buckle from the TGWU and Bryan Minks, British Rail's Western Region freight manager who had been the original whistleblower. Minks is adamant that Didcot is 'the tip of an iceberg' and there are many other examples of the TGWU preventing the transfer of traffic from road to rail.

Hanna refers to the 12 companies 'whose trade union officials say were subjected to T&G pressure about shifting business from road to rail', and accurately describes what happened at the meeting when Jack Jones blew his top, claiming, 'the entire thing was a table of lies and tittle-tattle and suggested that the Labour Party group was being used as a venue for union-bashing'. Ron Atkins MP is then interviewed and confirms the accuracy of the minutes of the meeting.

The programme's transmission produced a furious response from Jack Jones, who by then had been awarded the Companion of Honour. He wrote to the Chairman of the BBC, Sir Michael Swann, in the following terms: 'There can be no doubt that the effect of this programme was to heavily imply that the TGWU has been guilty of improper and even illegal conduct in the matter of bringing pressure on firms to, in the one instance, not use the Didcot depot and in the other instance, to require the transfer of freight traffic from rail to road.'

Jones went on – over three pages – to demand a public retraction and 'an investigation of the manner in which this programme was constructed and presented'.

The BBC Chairman replied by saying that 'the item left a public curiosity about the official policy of your union and I very much hope that you will accept the programme's invitation to take part in future discussion.'[10]

As the minutes of the BBC's Board of Management meeting on 13 March reported: 'It was noted that Jack Jones had refused to appear in a follow-up discussion with Ray Buckton of the ASLEF and Sidney Weighell of the NUR (Jack Jones asked for a meeting with the Chairman – yet to be arranged).'[11]

The BBC archive also contains a copy of an undated minute from Roger Francis to Swann, rebutting Jones' letter and robustly defending the programme. Dealing with an allegation made by Jones in his letter that he can 'hardly believe' Sidney Weighell would confirm the BBC's account of his union's attitude to the issue, Francis says, 'At the time the statement was checked out carefully with Weighell's press officer and then with Weighell himself.' As far as ASLEF is concerned:

> Buckton, it is said unprintably, has been threatened with removal from the TUC General Council if he rocked the boat. That being the case, I do not think we should be seen to be checking any further with either, since neither has complained about the original item.

Francis adds in a postscript that transmission was delayed by one day so that Jones knew of it in advance.

Jones' meeting with Swann eventually took place on 22 March. There appears to be no official minute of this encounter, but the BBC archive contains a handwritten note by Francis, presumably after a debriefing by Swann. It is notable for a number of vitriolic attacks on Vincent Hanna and a remarkable statement attributed to Jones, who told Swann it had been 'effrontery to tell me my chaps were like the Teamsters.'[12]

It was left to Jones' successor as TGWU General Secretary, Moss Evans, to reach an eventual agreement with Weighell and the NUR after talks held during the Scottish Trades Union Congress on 18 April 1978. A statement was issued which restated support for 'the principle of an integrated transport policy in which each mode is judged on the same criteria and is encouraged to do what it can best in terms of economic, social and environmental costs. We believe that the old road versus rail controversy is a barren argument.'[13]

Fine words, but the Didcot distribution centre never came anywhere near meeting its potential as an inland terminal providing customs clearance for containers brought by rail from Southampton docks. The A34 continues to be battered by juggernauts from the port.

One further example of Jack Jones' touchiness about Labour Party transport policy resulted from the party's response to the Government's transport policy consultation. The party had proposed the abolition of vehicle excise duty and the raising of petrol tax (this has long been seen as an environmentally friendly policy, as it would discourage unnecessary car use, and align the perceived cost of car journeys more closely to the actual cost). Jones wrote to the Labour Party General Secretary in August 1976:

> Quite apart from the fact that the Statement proceeds from an incorrect base, it is surely wrong to adopt completely anti-motorist and anti-road transport stands. We, therefore, ask that the authors of the Document reconsider the approach as quickly as possible, including our request that the Document itself be amended or withdrawn.

Tom Bradley MP, Chairman of the transport sub-committee, wrote back to Jones. Sticking firmly to his guns, he said that the committee would uphold the views it had expressed: 'It is felt that such a change in taxation policy would benefit the poorer motorist with a small car, would create an incentive to save petrol and would encourage the car industry to concentrate on the manufacture of small models.' He also reminded Jones that the Labour Party was 'pro public transport and anti company cars'.

That was not what Jones wanted to hear at all. Ignoring Bradley, he again wrote directly to the General Secretary, saying that the letter was 'the sort of thing I was complaining about Monday last':

> When will the special Committees of the Party try to avoid interfering with the livelihood of members of unions, such as my own? ….As the committee does not seem to have given any thought to the 1.600m. (in real terms) [sic] that the Government has already committed to support motor vehicle manufacture in Britain, have they considered the reactions of the 20 million driving licence holders in this country, the half million people directly involved in motor vehicle and component manufacture, and the two million who are in one way or another dependent on the road vehicle for their livelihood?

'Highway robbery'
Although the British Railways Board had no part in preparation of the *Tonight* programme, apart from the brave contribution by Bryan Minks, it had allowed Frank Paterson[14], then their chief freight manager, to appear briefly. His contribution was to express a fear that the Didcot incident could be repeated elsewhere, with the railway trade unions following the same practices as the TGWU.

Paterson was at this stage battling to get a fair deal for rail freight from the Government and decided to take a two-page centre-spread advertisement in the parliamentary journal *The House Magazine*.[15] Its banner headline was, 'In 1978 Highway Robbery still exists on a huge scale,' and it depicted a lorry driver dressed as a burglar, extracting money from the wallet of a hapless motorist.

Writing privately to the authors, Paterson described the reaction to it:

> The cartoon created a tremendous furore principally from the Road Haulage Association, the British Roads Federation and the TGWU. In addition to contradicting the figures I'd quoted we were accused of maligning the industry and lampooning truck drivers and generated quite a lot of vitriolic letters in the press and the trade magazines.
>
> I then got a message from the DTp that Sir Peter Baldwin, the Permanent Secretary, wanted to see me. I dealt at principal level so I asked my contact, Jenny Page, to find out what it was about. Deathly silence. Bob Reid was my boss but wasn't around so I went to see Bobby Lawrence[16], deputy Chairman, and asked him if I should go.
>
> I still remember his words: 'If the Permanent Secretary sends for you, you go boy.' So off I trotted to Marsham Street. I was waiting in the outer office when the director general of the BRF arrived. I knew him quite well through the Institute of Transport. He was one of the leading public critics of the *House Magazine* entry and had also been summoned by Peter without being told why.
>
> We were then together escorted into the 'presence'. Baldwin sat us down in front of his desk and proceeded to lecture us as though we were sixth formers in front of the headmaster. 'Don't think you'll impress politicians by this kind of rabble [rousing] – go away and behave yourselves.'
>
> It was unbelievable and when I reported back to Bobby he just laughed like a drain. Sadly it didn't change anything but it was a good way to get a message across.[17]

The Peeler memorandum and the Armitage report
Once the inequality of the common carrier obligations had been removed, there still remained an uneven competitive playing field between rail and the juggernaut, so brilliantly described in Frank Paterson's 'Highway Robbery' advertisement.

The puny lorries of the 1950s were underpowered, with limited capacity, and travelled on an inadequate road network. Over the next 25 years, truck sizes increased to 38 tonnes, roads were expanded and a motorway network built. The infrastructure improvements were carried out at the expense of the taxpayer and, arguably, the rail investment programme. Road hauliers paid not a penny for this. By comparison, every rail infrastructure improvement was paid for by BR with much of the funding coming from users.

The road haulage industry was a powerful lobby, putting relentless pressure on Government to raise weight limits further and for continuous expansion of the road network. We have seen in earlier chapters how cosy the relationship between Ministry of Transport officials and road haulage interests had become since the 1950s.

Every extra tonne of permitted tare weight and every new bypass made road more competitive and, at the margin, reduced the competitiveness of rail. The problems had been highlighted in BR's *An Opportunity for Change*:

> The resource costs of heavy lorries – the infrastructure costs of road provision and maintenance – are substantially in excess of the taxes levied on their use. Heavy road haulage – Railfreight's direct competitor – is being subsidised by other road users.

In 1978, Secretary of State Bill Rodgers was under pressure to set up an inquiry to consider the case for heavier lorries. The maximum lorry weight had been set at 32 tons back in 1964, and the road haulage industry had lobbied incessantly for it to be raised. They had been rebuffed in December 1970 by John Peyton, who not only refused to raise the limit but also said that the time had come to deal with 'a growing and undoubted nuisance'.[18]

Notwithstanding Peyton's good intentions, the pressure grew for heavier lorries in Britain. The UK's accession to the EEC in 1973 provided the spur for international road haulage interests to lobby for standardised – i.e. higher – weights everywhere in the Community. Their target was 44 tonnes, and the journalist John Wardroper states in his book *Juggernaut* that motor industry records reveal how, between 1973 and 1980, nearly 73,000 lorries designed to operate above the 32-ton legal limit were registered: 'This investment mounting to nearly £2,000 million (in 1980 prices) in machinery that could not be fully exploited – not legally at any rate – was a constant incentive for British action.'[19]

Wardroper observes that, by 1978, a general election was not far off and Transport Minister Rodgers didn't dare to announce anything as potentially unpopular with the public as an increase in lorry weights. He preferred what ministers often do when faced with difficult decisions: he would support a committee of inquiry. Wardroper takes up the story:

> On 9 October 1978 the department's permanent secretary, Sir Peter Baldwin [*author of the notorious Sunningdale conference paper described in Chapter 9*] had in front of him a cutting from *The Times* about the arguments for a weight increase, with a scribbled question in the margin: 'Should we have an inquiry?'
>
> Baldwin sent a minute to his freight directorate … asking for suggestions.

Wardroper says that the under-secretary in charge of the Directorate, Joseph Peeler, talked to Baldwin on 13 October and on Monday the 16th sent a 1,200-word note via his immediate boss, Peter Lazarus, the Deputy Secretary: 'It was intended for the eyes of only a few, but thanks to an unknown traitorous dissident and a copying machine it was leaked.' It found its way a couple of weeks later to *The Guardian*, having been sent in the first instance to Transport 2000. It was revealed that Peeler had written: 'For the purpose of this note it is assumed that we wish … to move, as soon as parliamentary and public opinion will let us, to a maximum gross weight of 38 or 40 tons.' The main advantage of an inquiry was 'presentational':

> At the end of the day, recommendations would be made by impartial people of repute who have carefully weighed and sifted the evidence and have come to, one hopes, a sensible conclusion in line with the department's view … The worst risk, if not the most likely, is that the inquiry would produce the wrong answer, or come to no clear conclusion within a reasonable time.

To reduce the risk of it going wrong, Peeler argued that the scope of the inquiry should be limited:

> … it would be undesirable to allow the inquiry to get into the complex technicalities of axle weights … In general, the more the scope of the inquiry is extended, the longer it will take and the greater the danger that the main issue will be lost sight of.

He concluded by saying:

> … the establishment in the public mind of a clear and overwhelming case on balance for heavier lorry weights is seen as the main end of the inquiry. It would also help to 'do good' to their [the road haulage lobby's] now sadly tarnished public image. This would make it easier for the Government to propose legislation in their favour.[20]

Unsurprisingly, Rodgers found himself having to defend Peeler in the Commons. *Hansard* reports these exchanges on 29 November 1978:

Highway Robbery
The advertisement that spoke an uncomfortable truth to the road haulage lobby.

Hugh Dykes[21]: Since there would be a widespread explosion of anger in this country from serious environmentalists and citizens if there were any plan to make lorries heavier than 32 tons, will he now confirm that he has taken action against the civil servants who leaked to the press the fact that there was a departmental plan so to do – or will he confirm that he is still out of control of his own department?

William Rodgers: At no time have I been out of control of my own department … I personally regret that a confidential minute of one of my officials who is not in a position to defend himself became more widely available. I have complete confidence in that official and, generally, in the loyalty and the integrity of civil servants as a whole. That is how it has been and how it ought to remain.

Roger Moate:[22] With regard to the document referred to by my honourable friend the member for Harrow, East [Mr Dykes], does not the Secretary of State agree that, whatever view one takes about the heavier weight argument, that memorandum has made the situation much more difficult? Is it not the case that a Civil Service document which claims that the main end of an inquiry should be a clear and overwhelming case for heavier weights is bound to convey the impression that, far from such an inquiry being impartial and objective, it could have been cynically manipulated? As it is in all our interests that the public accept such inquiries as impartial and objective, does not the right honourable gentleman now have an obligation to take some steps to restore public confidence in the sort of inquiry which is likely to be established by his department?

Rodgers: It is very difficult to deal with a statement that there has been a loss of public confidence. I agree that there has been some disquiet, and I greatly regret that circumstances do not allow me to explain in more detail how these matters fall out. However, the proposal for an inquiry was mine and it is the task of my officials to advise me as they think fit … I have no doubt at all about the integrity of the official himself and I greatly regret that he has been the subject of some unfair criticism.[23]

Despite the obvious fury in the department over the leak of the Peeler Memorandum (as it has been known ever since), there was no police inquiry into how it had got out. In fact, it appears that the public

Parcels

Senior Porter George Jones packs the last of 800 parcels from a mail order company in Oldham, addressed to customers in Birmingham. It was a labour-intensive operation with a high risk of damage to parcels at the bottom of the pile and the risk of pilferage (the door is only secured by a pin, not a padlock). Rail was nevertheless a good way of trunking this type of traffic and in 1963, nine parcels trains left Oldham each night. Today it all goes by truck on the M6.

outcry which followed the press reports caused Rodgers to announce, in March 1979, the terms of an inquiry drawn more widely than officials had previously been advising, which meant that some environmental issues were to be taken into account.

The inquiry itself was established by Norman Fowler (Rodgers' Conservative successor after the change of Government in May 1979). Instead of the usual eight-person committee he went for one adjudicator with four assessors. The adjudicator was Sir Arthur Armitage, Professor of Law and Vice-Chancellor of Manchester University, who reported in December 1980. Despite the earlier furore,

Armitage produced a report along the lines the Department had wanted. Most critically, he accepted almost every detail of the EEC's harmonisation package – including lorries of up to 44 tonnes.

We are indebted to John Wardroper (author and journalist) for providing via his book *Juggernaut* much of the material on which this section is based. *Juggernaut* was reviewed in *New Scientist* on 2 April 1981: the writer contended that the Government 'has bowed to the pressure of the haulage and road lobbies to give hauliers an easy time', and that it 'has either suppressed or selectively used the facts about the danger, noise, vibration and cost (both monetary and social) of heavy lorries in order to show them in a better light than they deserve.'

The 'cash cow' – the last years of BR

From 1977 onwards, Government policy on freight had consistently been that it should pay its way. After huge contraction of the rail freight business and frequent restructuring, this position was reached (following sectorisation) by 1986, although the parcels sector, which at that stage included newspaper and Post Office trains, had become unprofitable. With their inherent dislike of cross-subsidy, the department encouraged BR to split freight in 1988 into a profitable trainload freight business alongside an unprofitable Railfreight Distribution (RfD), including Freightliner and Speedlink services. While the intention was to allow separate management of the successful trainload business and focus management attention on turning round RfD, the underlying intention was clearly to force further retrenchment to a profitable core, or to closure if this proved unattainable.

The financial objectives set by Government at the end of 1989 for the following three financial years required Railfreight to achieve a £50m profit by 1992/93: a 6.1 percent rate of return on its asset base, with requirement for a further increase to 8 percent by 1994/95. In effect, it was to be a cash cow to contribute to the overall limits set to the board as a whole. At a time of recession and during renegotiation of the contracts (under terms favourable to BR) with the Central Electricity Generating Board (CEGB), prior to privatisation, the strains were intense. It meant a huge reduction in rolling stock and manpower, coupled with the abandonment not just of unprofitable traffic but also of profitable traffic that did not meet the required rate of return. Much of the cement traffic was lost to road at this stage and the Railfreight Group talked of BR 'poisoning the well' prior to privatisation, even though the changes were an inevitable consequence of the objectives set by Government.

1 *The Times*, 11 July 1977, p1.
2 *The Times*, 12 July 1977, p2.
3 Ronald Henry Atkins (born 1916) was the Labour MP for Preston North from 1966-70 and 1974-79.
4 Kelvin Hopkins (born 1941) has been the Labour MP for Luton North since 1997. He formerly worked as an economist at the TUC and as Policy and Research Officer with NALGO (later UNISON).
5 *The Vole*, Volume Three, 1977, pp3-4. The inside front cover was also given over to a photocopied extract from the minutes of the Labour Party transport sub-committee meeting.
6 *The Vole*, Volume Four, 1977, p4.
7 Reported in *The Times* on 7 January 1978, p2.
8 From papers discovered in the BBC Archives at Caversham Park, Reading.
9 Ibid.
10 Reported in C. O. Jones' 'Notes from Nowhere' in *The Vole*, Volume Seven, 16 March 1978 p13. Commenting on Jack Jones' letter, 'C. O. Jones' (Richard Boston) writes: 'The Companion of Honour has an amazing prose style. Consider this sentence with its spectacularly split infinitive.'
11 From papers seen in the BBC written archives (marked 'confidential').
12 Ibid.
13 Reported in *The Times*, 19 April 1978, p2.

14 Frank Paterson (born 1930) is a career railwayman who joined the LNER in 1946 and rose to be General Manager of the Eastern Region of British Railways from 1978-85. He has been a member of the Friends of the National Railway Museum since 1988 and was its Chairman 2002-12.
15 *The House Magazine* was founded in 1977 by Mike Thomas (then a Labour MP) and Richard Faulkner (co-author of this book). Still published every week that Parliament is sitting, it is now owned by Dods. The British Rail 'Highway Robbery' advertisement ran in the 22 May 1978 edition. Other hard-hitting adverts from BR appeared at weekly intervals in 1978, but none produced the reaction that 'Highway Robbery' did.
16 Sir Robert Lawrence (1915-88) was a career railwayman who joined the LNER in 1934 and rose to be Vice-Chairman of the British Railways Board between 1975 and 1983.
17 Email from Frank Paterson to the authors.
18 Quoted in *Juggernaut* by John Wardroper, Temple Smith, 1981, p8.
19 Ibid, p8.
20 Ibid, pp9-13.
21 Hugh Dykes (born 1939) was the Conservative MP for Harrow East 1970-97. He was also an MEP from 1974-77, before joining the Liberal Democrats in 1997. He was ennobled as Lord Dykes in 2004.
22 Sir Roger Moate (born 1938) was the Conservative MP for Faversham from 1970-97. He was knighted in 1993.
23 *Hansard HC Deb volume 959*, 29 November 1978, cc 428-31.

XVI

HERITAGE RAILWAYS

Perchance it is not dead, but sleepeth.

NOTE BY CAPTAIN WOOLF, RN, PINNED TO A WREATH ON THE LAST TRAIN
ON THE LYNTON & BARNSTAPLE RAILWAY, SEPTEMBER 1935

The Bluebell Railway – the first standard gauge line preserved

The Bluebell line in Sussex was the first train line run by volunteers, in 1960. Here, an early acquisition, a North London Railway tank engine that also worked on Derbyshire's Cromford & High Peak line, is put to work for contractors demolishing the northern part of the line. It is seen working at West Hoathly, propelling a wagon of rails northwards towards East Grinstead. The section of line in the picture has now been reinstated and has progressed further, north of Kingscote, while the cutting at Imberhorne is being cleared to allow the line to be reconnected to the national network at East Grinstead.

The idea of keeping an uneconomic railway running with volunteers was pioneered by author and campaigner L.T.C. (Tom) Rolt[1] and the Talyllyn Railway Preservation Society, which started operations on the short section between Towyn and Rhydyronen on 14 May 1951. This narrow-gauge railway to Abergynolwyn had been built to carry slate from the quarries above Nant Gwernol, but when they closed, the railway had struggled on with the support of its local owner, Sir Haydn Jones. Following his death in 1950 the fate of the railway seemed sealed, but a group of enthusiasts raised funds, took over the line and made a success of it.

Tom Rolt and the preservation pioneers

The Ealing comedy *The Titfield Thunderbolt*, released two years later, undoubtedly struck a chord with many passionately committed railway enthusiasts who harboured aspirations for other lines facing closure, not least because of its authenticity. (One of the scriptwriters from Ealing Studios had visited Rolt on the Talyllyn in 1951.) Their first opportunity came in 1955, with the closure of a rural byway in Sussex from East Grinstead to Lewes which would normally have passed with little more than a token protest. In this case, however, local campaigners, led by the redoubtable Miss Margery Bessemer, discovered that the Act of Parliament authorising the railway required the provision of four passenger trains per day each way in perpetuity. British Railways had, albeit unwittingly, acted unlawfully and were obliged to reintroduce a passenger service the following year. It took a further Act to pave the way for closure of the line, which took place in March 1958 following a second TUCC inquiry. Once again, Miss Bessemer took up the cudgels. She argued that the commission had secured approval for the withdrawal of passenger services but not of goods trains, even though they had not used the line since the initial closure in 1955. In a letter to D. R. Middleton at the Ministry of Transport, Secretary of the CTCC, J. C. Chambers wrote: 'Though I admire her energy, I wish it could be diverted to something more constructive that the re-opening of a derelict railway, and the flogging of dead horses.'[2]

But this group of enthusiasts was determined that their line should not die. A short section of the route, from Bluebell Halt near Horsted Keynes to Sheffield Park, was reopened as a privately run railway in August 1960. Subsequent extensions have taken it north to Kingscote and the huge task of clearing Imberhorne cutting, which had been used as a tip for domestic refuse, will soon allow the trains to run once again to East Grinstead.

Initially, the Board's view was quite firm, as shown in the internal BR brief accompanying the first Beeching Report: 'The Board will be prepared to sell disused lines outright for cash so long as they are fully relieved of their obligations, but they will not be party to any association or company formed to operate the line, nor will they accept any obligation to provide connections or traffic facilities.'

While this appears to have been written by a lawyer rather than one of the PR team, it was clearly designed as a defence mechanism against the many requests that started pouring in to retain lines as local groups struggled to raise funds or commitments to run the trains on behalf of the community. Many of these initiatives fell by the wayside, but, in a number of cases, the vision of preserving their local railway did inspire preservation societies to take over at least a section of the route, usually some time after the withdrawal of the BR service. One exception was the Western Region line between Paignton and Kingswear, where trains continued to run until the line was transferred to its new owners, although regular operations during the winter were later suspended.

Today, there are a total of 108 heritage railways running in the United Kingdom and Eire, serving 399 stations and covering 510 route miles. This is a larger network than London Underground and the total route mileage is the same as that from King's Cross to Blair Atholl in Perthshire. Planned extensions could increase this mileage to 600 over the next few years.

In total, heritage railways carry 6.7m passengers and earn around £81m a year. They make a major contribution to the economy, employing a total of 1,993 people, as well as 17,632 volunteers, and many spend significant sums buying in local goods and services.[3]

The range of lines is vast: from the Middleton or Corris Railways, under a mile in length, to the West Somerset Railway, covering 22.5 miles from Norton Fitzwarren to Minehead, and the impressive 34 miles of the combined Welsh Highland and Ffestiniog railways between Caernarfon and Blaenau Ffestiniog. Some preserved lines became isolated from the national network as the railway shrank back in the 1960s and 70s, while others remain closely associated. In fact, 18 heritage railways have an operational link with Network Rail, with more planned.

Most heritage lines now serve an important role in the tourism economy and bring prosperity to the (largely rural) areas they serve. However, most started off with ambitions to provide a regular public transport service. Some of them did initially run a daily service throughout the year, but, when the reality of costs and the travel patterns of the 1960s and 70s kicked in, activities were cut back to a more limited seasonal service.

NUR opposition

Railwaymen have generally been interested in and supportive of heritage railways, and many enjoy working on them as volunteers in their spare time. The attitude of BR was somewhat equivocal, although in most cases it co-operated well in allowing the transfer of a closed railway to the private company or preservation society that was taking over operation. The same cannot be said of the main trade union.

West Somerset Railway
The very existence of the line was threatened by the NUR in the 1980s, but the railway has prospered and now carries over 210,000 passengers a year, with regular trains to and from the national network at Norton Fitzwarren. Seen here during a gala weekend, a Virgin Voyager brings passengers from Taunton to Bishops Lydeard where a connecting train waits to take them on to Minehead.

In fact, the NUR was responsible for heavy-handed treatment of the fledgling West Somerset Railway which was quite out of proportion to the imagined threat it posed.

The line from Taunton to Minehead was a busy holiday route until it closed in January 1971, with through trains from London, South Wales and the West Midlands supplementing the local service. A preservation society had been established by the time of its closure and the West Somerset Railway company was formed shortly afterwards. From the outset, the intention of the company was to run a regular service through to Taunton and to handle freight if possible.

Operations started running from the Minehead end to Blue Anchor in April 1976, and were extended halfway along the line to Williton later that year. Initial discussions with BR were cordial, with agreement reached in principle in 1972 on running through passenger and freight trains, although the company was concerned at the cost of the lease for the line to Taunton and access to the station (as well as expected future costs when the line was resignalled). Nevertheless, a running powers agreement was signed on 3 May 1976 and the WSR set about restoring the rest of its line towards Taunton.

In 1977, trains from Minehead reached Stogumber. The following year, talks were proposed with the NUR on through running but were declined by the union. In 1979, the WSR had been restored as far as the junction at Norton Fitzwarren, just west of Taunton, but the NUR was adamantly opposed to WSR trains running into Taunton on the grounds that it would threaten the jobs of Western National bus drivers on the Minehead-Taunton route who were also NUR members. In April 1979, the local manager for Western National at Taunton wrote to the railway to advise that even the shuttle buses planned to bridge the gap from the last WSR station at Bishops Lydeard to

Preservation pioneer
A train on the Talyllyn Railway at Wharf station, Towyn, at end of season in September 1953. At the right of the picture is the wharf where slate was transferred to the main line, now used for bringing in locomotive coal. The hikers in the foreground hint at the new market in tourism that had replaced carriage of slate as the primary purpose of the railway.

Taunton had been blacked by the union. The dispute dragged on through 1980, with even the transfer of old BR rolling stock bought by the WSR banned by the NUR. The action taken by the local branch was supported by the union's district council and endorsed by the national executive. In the annual report for 1984, West Somerset Chairman, David Morgan[4] reported that even the intervention of the TUC had failed to sway the union.

With the benefit of hindsight, we may conjecture that the sledgehammer approach which cut the railway off completely might not have been only about bus drivers' jobs, but also about the union's fear of private operators intruding on the national network. However, the original aspiration to run an all-year-round service had been abandoned in 1978 and it was evident that the WSR was going to develop as a heritage railway, rather than as a serious competitive threat to the local bus service.

In 1985, the Exeter panel signalbox was commissioned and local boxes in the Taunton area were swept away. Track rationalisation severed the WSR and the basic causes of the dispute began to fade. Five years later, the line was reconnected via a siding and the first through train – from Manchester to Minehead – ran on 16 June 1990. Today, an upgraded connection is used almost every day, while charter trains are commonplace.

1   Tom Rolt (1910-74) was a prolific writer who produced biographies of Isambard Kingdom Brunel and Thomas Telford. As a pioneer of the leisure cruising industry, he is credited with halting the dereliction of the canal system. Rolt was also a vintage car and heritage railway enthusiast and had a locomotive on the Talyllyn railway, a bridge on the Oxford Canal and a centre at the Ellesmere Port boat museum all named after him.
2   Letter of 13 May 1959. TNA MT 124/17.
3   Data from Heritage Railway Association for 2010. Passenger numbers and revenue shown are for 2009.

4   David Morgan MBE, TD, F Inst D, MCIT (born 1941) is Chairman of the Heritage Railway Association and founder president of the European Federation of Museum and Tourist Railways (FEDECRAIL) and the World Association of Tourist Trams and Trains (WATTRAIN). Chairman of Great Central Railway Plc, president of the West Somerset Railway, and president of the North Norfolk Railway. Vice Chairman, Cutty Sark Trust. Awarded MBE in 2003 for his services "to transport preservation in the UK and Europe". A solicitor, who practises as a consultant with the Westminster firm, RadcliffesLeBrasseur. Served for 32 years in the Territorial Army, ending up with the rank of Lieutenant-Colonel.

XVII

POLICY CHANGES AND THE SEEDS OF GROWTH

This is the Age of the Train.

BR CORPORATE ADVERTISEMENT, 1981

Penistone Line revival
The beginning of services via the newly reopened Penistone-Barnsley line in 1983. Prior to this date, Huddersfield-
Sheffield trains had run direct from Penistone to Sheffield via Wadsley Bridge without stopping, other than to reverse
at Nunnery Junction. The overhead line spans from the 1954 electrification remain, but no longer support their wires.

After the Serpell Report, the position was unclear. While there was to be no major programme of closures, the industry had been seriously damaged by the strikes of 1982. The Thatcher Government and its advisers, such as Sir Alfred Sherman, were quick to express the view that action was needed to prevent strikers holding the country to ransom.

Revenue had taken a big hit, and the need for costs to be cut remained. Parts of the rural network remained vulnerable, and BR skilfully used two cases to test the resolve of politicians at both local and national level to support further retrenchment of the network – or indeed, to test whether they would pay to retain the two lines in question. Although one of the services was wholly within PTE areas, the other had been part of the Midland Railway's great trunk route to Scotland.

Penistone line

The line from Huddersfield to Penistone was built by the Lancashire & Yorkshire Railway in 1850, serving that part of Yorkshire for over a century with local trains and a daily through train to London (latterly the 'South Yorkshireman'). The branch line to Meltham had closed in 1949, with that to Holmfirth following in 1959, as well as the connecting line from Penistone to Barnsley. The 'South Yorkshireman' was withdrawn from the route in 1960 and Sunday services were withdrawn the following year. The line was included in the list for closure in the Beeching Report of 1963 and it seemed like a foregone conclusion when the case was put to the Minister of Transport for approval. However, the Minister was Barbara Castle, who decided to refuse consent for six 'conurbation commuter services' in 1966, principally because approval would add to road traffic congestion.

Despite its essentially rural nature, Huddersfield-Penistone was one of the six. Nevertheless, BR closed Berry Brow station in 1966 and reduced service levels to focus on peak hours. The following year, BR was actively pursuing closure to passengers of the Woodhead route, including Penistone. While recognising it as a relatively well used station, a BR spokesman told *Modern Railways* in January 1967, 'We cannot let Penistone stand in the way of our plan to run fast freight on the line.'

The Manchester-Sheffield Victoria electric service was withdrawn from 5 January 1970 and replaced between Penistone and Sheffield by an extended diesel service from Huddersfield, running direct from Penistone through to Sheffield Midland with a reversal at Nunnery Junction. An intermediate station at Wadsley Bridge remained to handle significant football traffic to and from the nearby Hillsborough stadium.

Four years later, prospects for the route seemed better with the formation of passenger transport executives for West and South Yorkshire, covering the whole route between them. Worse was to come, however.

By 1977, West Yorkshire had agreed to support lines in the area including Huddersfield-Denby Dale (the boundary station with South Yorkshire), but not the branch to Clayton West. South of the border, South Yorkshire had declined to fund the route, saying costs were out of proportion to usage, especially if only their own passengers (Penistone-Sheffield) were considered. With no funding for the southern part of the route and the messy solution of reaching Sheffield Midland with a reversal, BR suggested rerouteing the trains via Barnsley where the line remained as a freight route.

South Yorkshire PTE's approach was then focused on buses, but they were also reluctant to be seen as conniving in closure of the

Penistone Line

The 'music train': one of the pioneering ventures by the line's community rail partnership to fill empty seats and raise the line's profile.

Woodhead route to freight, which was being planned in the late 1970s. The PTE had a strong hard left element with links to Arthur Scargill,[1] whose NUM was based in the county town of Barnsley. It was part of a united stand against what was seen as a Thatcherite agenda, although in reality the contraction of steelmaking following a strike was steadily removing much freight traffic using the route to Wath marshalling yard, which was also a major employer in the area.[2]

Discussions with BR were therefore inconclusive. In 1980, with closure to freight of the Woodhead route planned for the following year, BR posted closure notices for the line between Denby Dale and Sheffield. The public meetings, particularly those held in Huddersfield, were very well attended and this proposal holds the record for the largest number of objections received to a line closure. Ministerial approval was given in September 1982, but, to leave time for further discussion, withdrawal of the service was set for May 1983. In March of that year, just six weeks before the deadline, South Yorkshire relented. While they could not be seen to connive with the Woodhead closure, by the same token they could not be seen to acquiesce in the passenger closure either. They offered one year's support for a service via Barnsley, which replaced the service via Deepcar.

The new service was a success, but by this time West Yorkshire had withdrawn their support for the northern section of the line, fearing they would be left with the cost of maintaining an expensive and lightly used service to Denby Dale. Their argument was based on the contention that cross-boundary passengers (going beyond Denby Dale) were a BR responsibility rather than a PTE one, and that the price asked by BR for the service was too high.

So once again the closure notices went up in 1983, this time for the line between Huddersfield and Denby Dale. The wording of the notices, however, did not comply with the statutory requirement and at the insistence of the TUCC they were reissued the following year. In 1986, further uncertainty was added with the disappearance of the metropolitan counties, PTE support depending on the district councils. Nevertheless, the tide of public and political opinion had turned and the threat of closure receded, being finally removed in 1987 when WYPTE agreed to support the northern part of the line.[3] The protracted closure was a clear warning to ministers about the resistance that could be expected. Together with the example of

Settle & Carlisle (see below), it would set the Government's face against further high-profile closure cases. It was also an object lesson in what could happen if decisions on the future of rail services were devolved (as proposed in the 1977 White Paper).

The following year, an hourly service was introduced and summer Sunday trains returned. In 1990, the new station at Meadowhall was opened to serve the huge shopping centre, loadings on the line increased dramatically and Sunday services were restored throughout the year. In 1993, the Penistone Line Partnership (PLP) was formed to promote the line and ensure that the farce of the previous decade would never again undermine the confidence of the local community in its railway. With jazz trains, guided walks and 'rail ale' trails, as well as station improvements and a high public profile, the PLP has been one of the most successful of the community rail partnerships which have blossomed over the last 20 years, and which are covered in more detail in Chapter 19.

Settle & Carlisle line

The final and most dramatic demonstration that the Beeching closure programme was at an end came with the celebrated case of the Settle & Carlisle line. The line had been built by the Midland Railway in 1874, using a difficult alignment over the Pennines with heavy engineering works including Blea Moor tunnel and Ribblehead viaduct, stiff gradients and no intermediate large towns apart from Appleby. Linking with the Glasgow & South Western route via Dumfries, this formed the third Anglo-Scottish route alongside the east and west coast lines, with services running from London St Pancras to Glasgow St Enoch. Three routes were unsustainable under the Beeching criteria and plans were developed to reroute trains, paving the way for closure. Indeed, part of the financial justification for electrification from Weaver Junction to Glasgow had been the savings resulting from the transfer of freight from the Settle & Carlisle route to the West Coast Main Line. The authors Pryke and Dodgson highlighted this in their book on railway economics[4] in a very public way, with some embarrassment at BRB when it was published. Closure of this 73-mile route was going to be a complex business and would take time to achieve, as it was clear by now that it would be widely opposed by users and other action groups throughout the country.

Recognising the political difficulties, BR tempered the announcement of closure in 1983 with a commitment to keep the line open for five years and to appoint a project team under Ron Cotton, one of its very effective commercial managers, to make the most of the route for the period in which the closure process would take place. There is no doubt that, while some senior BR managers, including John Welsby, thought it the right solution for a line with such high costs and apparently limited traffic potential, they also wanted to use the case to test the resolve of ministers to face up to another round of closures.

The marketing campaign included running additional trains and reopening stations, as well as extensive publicity. The smaller intermediate stations had been closed in 1970, but some reopened with a limited number of trains, aimed at walkers, in 1975. In 1986, Cotton reopened all of them on a regular basis and encouraged charter train operators to use the line for steam excursions. It was a resounding success and, within three years, drove up ridership from just over 300,000 passengers a year to just under a million.

The five-year period was marked by a powerful lobbying campaign to save the line, involving thousands of people across the country. The case was put persuasively by Dr John Whitelegg[5] of Lancaster University and the campaign was strongly supported by the *Yorkshire Post*, whose transport correspondent, Alan Whitehouse, was subsequently the BBC's northern transport correspondent and an influential voice in the debate on rural and local railways across the north of England.

Ministers and mandarins clearly had difficulty in reaching decisions on the proposals submitted by BR. During those five years, costs were challenged and other options canvassed by civil servants, including privatisation. In a confidential memorandum to the Board's Vice Chairman, Derek Fowler[6], the head of the BR policy unit, John Prideaux, strongly advised that the board should stick to its guns, concluding, 'if the majority of objectors are in the country's heritage lobby, let us offer the route to them, after closure, with a modest sum, so that they can contemplate the expense of a 73 mile long museum.' The authors also remember BR Chairman Robert Reid (Peter Parker's successor) robustly arguing in private conversation, 'Of course the line should close.'

Conservative Transport Minister David Mitchell[7] had a strong interest in the line and was involved in seeking external funding to support what had then become a rather more busy railway and a significant tourist attraction. He reflects in his memoirs[8] on how, 'I was not the only one suspicious about BR's figures for the costs to be incurred on repair of the Ribblehead viaduct.' Mitchell had been persuaded it could be done more cheaply by a retired BR civil engineer who suggested the rubble inside the viaduct arches could be consolidated with liquid concrete to provide the stability required for many years of future operations, at around one sixth of the £6m cost quoted by BR for repairs. Despite this, in a May 1988 statement to the House he announced that the Government was 'minded to consent to BR's closure proposals on the evidence before it'.[9]

In a subsequent reshuffle that July, Mitchell was replaced by Michael Portillo,[10] who embraced a private sector approach to the S&C which did not result in privatising the line (which still required financial support), but did result in some excellent work by the Settle & Carlisle Railway Development Company which, together with the 'Friends' of the S&C, has brought continued success to the route and provided a model for other community railways around the country. In April 1989, Portillo's Secretary of State Paul Channon,[11] announced that he had refused BR permission to close because ridership had

increased and the costs of repairing Ribblehead were likely to be cheaper than forecast. It was a remarkable decision which went against the strong cost-cutting objectives set for BR, and was a clear indication to the Board that investing time in a further closure programme would be fruitless.

Following the refusal of consent to close, more positive developments took place that were encouraged both by the Government and the BR board. The Settle & Carlisle Trust was successful in raising funds for station restoration, while the development company encouraged links with local businesses and the Friends worked with train operators to promote the line. Apart from running a shop at Settle, they have uniquely shared in the staffing and running of the station, providing a wonderful welcome to visitors.

Unforeseen in 1989, but of significant strategic importance to the national network, the role of the line in carrying imported coal from Clydeport to the Yorkshire power stations would provide relief for the East & West Coast Main Lines, where capacity was limited by the increased passenger service frequency and speed. It also proved invaluable as a diversionary route during the extended upgrading of the West Coast Main Line.

The message for the board and BR senior managers was clear: further significant closures were not likely to be worth the management time and effort involved, and lobby groups were effective in ensuring that every subsequent closure became a major political and media issue. This did not prevent subsequent attempts at further pruning the network, but the S&C was a turning point.

The low-cost railway

John Welsby had become BR Director of Provincial services under Bob Reid in 1982. Given his economist's background and ruthless approach to costs, this might have seemed like appointing the wolf to guard the sheepfold. However, it proved in practice to be a huge step forward for local and rural railways. The problem he was appointed to tackle was that the Mark 1 fleet of diesel units' economic lifetime had expired, making it impossible to justify their replacement in terms of the criteria for investment set by the Department. Early experiments had produced the Pacer, based on the Leyland National bus body, and the expensive Class 210 diesel-electric unit which was trialled in the Thames Valley. Many of the old units had asbestos insulation, which

RETB signalling
Trains cross at Rogart on the Far North line in September 1989. The stop sign reminds drivers to obtain the electronic 'token' via cab radio before proceeding. The open level crossing (beyond the platform) and RETB helped to reduce the cost of the rural railway to a sustainable level, ensuring its survival into the 21st century. At the time this picture was taken, trains were terminating at Dingwall while the Ness viaduct was being rebuilt.

Far North threat
The collapse of the Ness Viaduct on 7 February 1989 – as a result of scouring by a tidal surge – cut off the line from Inverness to Wick and Thurso as well as Kyle of Lochalsh, a line that had been reprieved on a number of earlier occasions. BR was quick to announce that the bridge would be rebuilt, in the interim transferring rolling stock to a temporary depot at Muir of Ord, to maintain services

had by then been identified as a health risk to staff responsible for maintaining and overhauling the trains. Their maintenance costs were high and, while the pressure to replace them was growing, it was being resisted by the Department. But Welsby was able to develop a robust business case for replacement by using longer (23m) vehicles with a higher seating density, replacing three old vehicles with two new ones.

Not only did this break the logjam but the new trains also had lower maintenance costs and, as new trains are wont to do, attracted more passengers. More than this, they inflicted less damage on the track and encouraged some good work – particularly on routes in Scotland under ScotRail General Manager John Ellis and Chief Civil Engineer Jim Cornell – on a basic railway approach, with new trains and continuous welded rail where the initial investment was remunerated by much lower maintenance costs and higher revenue.

By 1991, when the board published its strategic review, *Future Rail*, the regional network had the newest fleet on BR and the document could promise with confidence that, over the coming decade, the railways were setting out to deliver to their customers 'a network of rural services meeting social needs and helping to promote tourism'.

Threat lifted
A train from Kyle of Lochalsh crosses the new bridge a year later, the locomotive-hauled train replacing a failed Class 156 unit.

This was almost the antithesis of the Board's view 30 years before, displaying great maturity and understanding of the role of the railway in society. The following year, however, a coherent plan would be replaced by a decade of uncertainty as the Government embarked on rail privatisation (see Chapter 18).

Reopenings

While the BTC, BRB and DoT had been working to reduce the size of the network and its costs throughout the period running from their inception up until 1989, other forces were pushing in the opposite direction. This is evidenced by the fact that, during the last 50 years, 350 stations have been opened or reopened along with 187.5 miles of new route.

Even as the Stedeford Committee was deliberating in 1960, six new stations were added to the network in Scotland and north-east London, and a further 10 were added later in the decade. From 1970, new stations have been opened in every subsequent year to date, with an annual total peaking at 26 in 1987.

These included Parkway stations, those serving airports or new towns, and funded by or with developers. The greatest number, however, have been funded by PTEs as part of a policy to encourage rail use in order to reduce chronic traffic congestion and pollution in cities. Some stations were reopened at an early date to meet local demand and should clearly never have been closed.

Line reopening started just four years after Beeching stood down as BR Chairman, with Barassie-Kilmarnock in 1969 followed by Peterborough-Spalding in 1971 (reopened just eight months after closure). Steady progress was gradually made and no fewer than seven lines, totalling 32.7 miles, were opened in 1987, while in 2003 a total length of 53.9 miles reopened (although this included the first phase of High Speed 1).

New routes have included a number of main lines:
- Temple Hirst to Colton Junction, a new section of the East Coast Main Line, built to allow coal mining under the formation of the original route via Selby (1983).

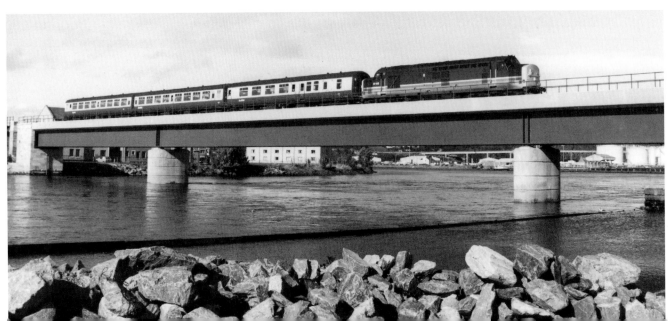

- Stansted (1991), Manchester (1993) and Heathrow (1998) airport rail links.
- Channel Tunnel (1994) and HS1 (2003 and 2007).

Most of the other lines are local in character and, once again, the majority were sponsored by PTEs or local authorities. The 'top ten' passenger reopenings, by length of new line, are listed below:

- Nottingham-Mansfield-Worksop (1993-98)   28.7 miles
- Airdrie-Bathgate-Edinburgh (1986 and 2011)   23.7 miles
- Ladybank-Perth (1975)   20 miles
- Vale of Glamorgan: Barry-Bridgend (2005)   19 miles
- Ebbw Vale Parkway-Cardiff (2008)   18.1 miles
- Crediton-Okehampton (1997)   18 miles
(summer Sunday services only)
- Peterborough-Spalding (1971)   15 miles
- Middlesbrough-Northallerton (1996)   14.3 miles
- Walsall-Rugeley (1989 and 1998)   14 miles
- Barassie-Kilmarnock (1969)   13.3 miles

The Borders Railway will eventually add 29.3 miles from Newcraighall to Galashiels and Tweedbank. Of the 81 new passenger lines introduced since 1969, no fewer than 54 use freight routes in whole or in part. The remainder are new lines or involve reinstated track.

Modern standards

When a railway is restored, it has to adopt modern standards in terms of platform stepping distances, for example, or the platform length matching the length of the longest train. When the Thornbury branch in Gloucestershire was re-laid to carry aggregates from Tytherington quarry, the local authority required that the former low bridges were raised to give better clearance over local roads. Bridge abutments had to be raised and the height of approach embankments increased. In other cases, the original location of stations was inconvenient and many reopened stations were not at their original site but were moved to improve road access, providing a park and ride as at Liverpool South Parkway or Ivybridge in Devon. Many of the original cost-saving measures adopted by the old railway companies are no longer seen as appropriate or acceptable, such as rail-level platforms with retractable steps on the train. Similarly, the civil engineer will try to use standard track components wherever possible, rather than fabricating components specially to meet the constraints of the old infrastructure. The result of this is that reinstatement is rather more complex and expensive than restoring what was there 40 or more years ago.

The Speller Act

While a number of routes and stations were reopened, BR was unwilling to try experimental services simply because of the complexity and time it took to implement the closure process if they proved unsuccessful. This was addressed by the Transport Act 1962 (Amendment) Act 1981, introduced as a private member's bill by Conservative MP for North Devon Tony Speller,[12] which allowed a new service to be designated 'experimental' – meaning it could be withdrawn without formality on six weeks' notice. He was keen to see the line from Barnstaple to Torrington (which ran mainly through his constituency) reopened, but, although the bill became law, passenger services were never reintroduced beyond Barnstaple and the route is now part of the Tarka Trail, an idyllic track for cyclists and walkers. However, the Speller Act did encourage the successful reopening of other lines, such as the Robin Hood Line

Speller Act In 1981

North Devon MP Tony Speller was successful in securing an Act permitting 'experimental' passenger services to serve local communities, such as the Barnstaple-Torrington line in his constituency. In October 1969, a year after the line lost its passenger service, a train of china clay from Meeth is seen leaving Torrington, passing a line of milk tanks in the siding. The signalbox remains open and the piles of small chippings for measured shovel packing indicate continuing maintenance. The station was some way out of the town, which lies behind the hill in the background. The line closed completely in 1983 and is now part of the Tarka Trail. Track and rolling stock remain in the platform where the train stands and the station is now a pub. It is hard to recall that this outpost was once a terminus of the 'Atlantic Coast Express' with through coaches from Waterloo.

(Nottingham-Worksop via Mansfield), Blackburn-Clitheroe, and Maesteg. Similar powers were incorporated in the Railways Act, 1993 for the privatised railway, and so Speller's good work continues.

A crop of late closures

Whilst the prospect of wholesale closures following the *annus horribilis* of 1982 was real enough, the few that actually took place in the following decade were relatively minor.

Woodside-Selsdon was a shuttle service left over from the days of competition between the South Eastern and London, Brighton & South Coast railways, providing the South Eastern with access to the leafy Croydon suburbs as well as its own route from London to the 'old main line' from Redhill to Tonbridge at Edenbridge. It was withdrawn in 1983, although the northern part of the route was used for Croydon Tramlink.

We have already seen how the Huddersfield-Clayton West service was not supported by West Yorkshire PTE. It consequently closed in 1983, most of the route being subsequently converted to narrow gauge as the Kirklees Light Railway. Similarly, and in the same year, the Kilmacolm branch lost its funding from Strathclyde PTE, although only seven years later, in 1990, the line from Glasgow (Shields Junction) to Paisley Canal was reopened with a half-hourly service.

Radipole Halt near Weymouth closed in 1984 to avoid repair costs to the deteriorating concrete slab platforms. In the following year, the rather more controversial closure of the line from Tunbridge Wells to

Eridge took place. This had been an important link in a network of lines from East Croydon, Three Bridges, Brighton and Eastbourne, all with direct trains to Tunbridge Wells and some continuing to Tonbridge. The 'Cuckoo line' from Eastbourne had closed in 1965, while the Croydon and Three Bridges services had been withdrawn in 1967. When Lewes-Uckfield closed in 1969, the role of the route from Eridge to Tunbridge Wells was substantially diminished. The planned electrification of the Tonbridge-Hastings line (completed in 1986) was based on running 12-car trains to Tunbridge Wells Central and detaching units in the platforms there, as the traction supply was only adequate for eight-car working south of this point. This required greater platform occupation time and effectively left little capacity for the Eridge shuttle to operate. The line closed in 1985, but the section from Tunbridge Wells West to Eridge has since been reopened as the Spa Valley heritage railway.

The Stratford-Tottenham Hale line (run as an extension to the service from North Woolwich) also closed that same year, although it too has been reopened for through services from the Lea Valley line to Stratford, running through the 2012 Olympic site. Its intermediate station at Lea Bridge remains closed, however.

The Broadgate development in the City of London involved the larger, more controversial closure in 1986 of the former North London Railway terminus at Broad Street and the line north to Dalston Junction. Trains from Richmond were diverted to North Woolwich as

Late closure

The line from Grove Junction (Tunbridge Wells) to Birchden Junction closed in July 1985, squeezed out by Hastings electrification. A year before closure, VSOE stock waits in the platform between services. The platforms and yard now form the site of a Sainsbury's and a Homebase superstore. The station building is a restaurant, while beyond it can be seen the former steam locomotive shed, now the base for the Spa Valley Railway which has just completed restoring the route through to Eridge.

part of a transport improvement package for the development of Docklands. This line too, from Dalston to Shoreditch, has reopened as part of the East London Line and now forms part of the London Overground network.

There were few closures in the 1990s. Holborn Viaduct station was replaced by City Thameslink and the short branch line from Derby to Sinfin Central finally closed in 1993. This spur, designed to relieve traffic congestion in Derby, had never really achieved its objectives since its opening in 1976. Employment changes meant that it served little purpose and by the end only a 'parliamentary' service was operating, latterly provided by taxi.

By 1993, however, the attention of Government was no longer focused on railway costs or reducing the size of the network. It had turned to privatisation.

---

1   Arthur Scargill (born 1938) was President of the National Union of Mineworkers from 1982-2002. He subsequently founded and led the Socialist Labour Party.

2   The authors' conversation with John Nelson, Managing Director of First Class Partnerships, is the source of this information. He was then Divisional Passenger Manager at Sheffield.

3   *The Huddersfield & Sheffield Junction Railway* by Martin Bairstow, 1993; *The Penistone Line Trail*, Penistone Line Partnership, 2003.

4   *Rail Problem – An Alternative Strategy* by Richard Pryke and J. Dodgson, Robertson, 1975.

5   Dr John Whitelegg is Professor of Sustainable Transport at Liverpool John Moores University and Professor of Sustainable Development at the University of York's Stockholm Institute. He was formerly Professor of Geography at Lancaster University, a Green Party councillor and chair of the party in the North West. Whitelegg is the author of many papers and books on sustainable transport and is a doughty campaigner for the S&C line, but critical of high-speed lines.

6   Derek Fowler CBE (1929-2006) joined BRB as internal audit manager in 1964 after a number of appointments in local Government. He rose to become Deputy Chairman of BRB in 1990.

7   Sir David Mitchell (born in 1928) was a wine shipper and owner of El Vino's wine

bar and restaurant in Fleet Street, serving as Conservative MP for Basingstoke from 1964-83, and Hampshire North West from 1983-97. He was Parliamentary Under Secretary of State at the Department of Transport, 1983-86, and Minister of State, 1986-88, before leaving Parliament in 1997.

8   *From House to House: The Endless Adventure of Politics & Wine* by David Mitchell, Memoir Club, 2008.

9   *HC Deb volume 133*, 16 May 1988, cc681-8.

10 Michael Portillo (born 1953) is a former Conservative politician who has established a successful career as a broadcaster and journalist following his departure from the House of Commons in 2005. Elected MP for Enfield Southgate in a 1984 by-election, he later served as MP for Kensington and Chelsea from 1995-2005. He was also Minister of State for Transport, 1988-90, before becoming Chief Secretary to the Treasury and Secretary of State for Employment and, later, Defence. More recently, he was the presenter of the *Great Railway Journeys* series on BBC TV.

11 Henry Paul Guinness Channon (1935-2007) was Conservative MP for Southend West from 1959-97, a member of the Guinness family selected as a candidate while still an undergraduate at Oxford. He was created Lord Kelvedon in 1997 and served as Secretary of State for Transport from 1987-89.

12 Antony Speller (born 1929) was Conservative MP for North Devon from 1979-92.

XVIII

PRIVATISATION

The curse of the railway enterprise in England.

G.W.J. POTTER, REFERRING TO LEGAL EXPENSES IN AN ARTICLE ON THE EASINGWOLD RAILWAY, *RAILWAY MAGAZINE*, VOLUME XLI, 1917

Privatisation success
Freightliner was sold to a management buyout team. One of the high-growth routes they were able to develop was the flow of deep-sea containers from Felixstowe to the North West and Scotland. Two class 37 locomotives are seen heading the 20:57 from Coatbridge, accelerating down the branch to the port in 1987. Investment by the new owners saw double heading replaced by more powerful class 66s, while lengthening the crossing loop at Derby Road, Ipswich allowed longer, more economic trains to be run.

Privatisation had been one of the major themes of the Thatcher years. It affected the ancillary businesses of the British Railways Board, with the great railway hotels being sold, mainly between 1983 and 1984, followed by the sale of Sealink and the railway workshops, as well as smaller companies like British Transport Advertising. By the end of the 1980s, BR was reduced to its core railway business. While the Thatcher government had not attempted to privatise the railway, there was lively debate amongst the Conservative think tanks on how it might be achieved and the return of the Major government in 1992 brought with it a manifesto commitment.

While not directly connected with further retrenchment of the network, it seemed likely that 'market forces' would result in further cutbacks. But the franchising model chosen by the Conservatives meant that passenger services, at least, had to be specified by government. Decisions on closures therefore remained with ministers and not with the private railway companies.

'Deerstalker express'

Continuing financial pressures did not lead to a line closure, but in a threat to the Euston-Fort William sleeper in 1995. The train was still run by BR at that stage, but the newly formed Office of Rail Passenger Franchising planned to omit the service from its franchise specification for ScotRail. Genuine anger erupted from all sides, well orchestrated by the Labour opposition and many other groups opposed to privatisation. The media were able to cover weeks of conflict over what they dubbed the 'deerstalker express'.

Faced with the risk of delaying the franchising programme before the next election, the government gave in and kept the train, which still runs today. The Scotrail franchise was awarded just two weeks before the 1997 election, which produced a landslide Labour victory.

Thereafter, closures became less relevant as passenger demand grew relentlessly and even marginal routes became busy. Indeed, only two stations have been closed since privatisation – Pendleton, following an arson attack in 1998, and Etruria in 2005, to allow track realignment for higher speeds as part of the West Coast Main Line upgrade. The Maindee curve at Newport lost its passenger service when the one train using it was diverted to Cardiff and the Oldham loop was closed for conversion to light rail. A number of other stations remain 'in limbo', however; not closed, but with their trains replaced by buses:

> Norton Bridge
> Wedgwood
> Barlaston.

To these can be added one section of line (Acton East Junction-West London Junction) which lost its passenger service when cross country services to Brighton were discontinued. Bizarrely, a bus replacement was provided between Acton Main Line and Wandsworth Road. Likewise, a number of lines remain with only a parliamentary[1] service, including:

> Stockport-Stalybridge (one train a week in one direction)
> Barnetby-Gainsborough (three trains each way on Saturdays only)
> South Ruislip-Paddington (one train a day)
> Bare Lane-Carnforth direct (one train a day). Other services from Morecambe to Carnforth and Leeds run via Lancaster.

Freight changes

The government that privatised the rail industry between 1992 and 1997 had no real understanding of how it worked, nor of the commercial framework within which it operated. Its policies were driven by economic theory and political dogma, and nowhere is this more clearly demonstrated than in their policy for privatising rail freight. The government view was that competition was needed, and to that end it split BR's railfreight businesses into six separate companies for sale:

- Trainload Freight
- Loadhaul
- Mainline
- Freightliner
- Rail Express Systems
- Rail Express Parcels

The market took a different view, recognising that the real competition was from road. Four of the companies were bought by American rail-freight operator Wisconsin Central and re-grouped as the English, Welsh & Scottish Railway. Wisconsin was itself taken over by Canadian National and subsequently sold to DB Schenker, a subsidiary of the state-owned German railways.

Freightliner was bought separately by its management, along with a £75m dowry to assist in restructuring. Niche operator Direct Rail Services (a public sector company) took over specialist operation of the nuclear flask traffic, taking spent fuel rods from nuclear power stations across the country to Sellafield for reprocessing.

The Red Star operation remained a valuable and unique service, offering reliable transits on nominated passenger trains. Cheaper than a courier and quicker than road-based services, it was sold to Lynx during privatisation, who subsequently closed down the station offices and absorbed the traffic into their own road-based business. Somewhat surprisingly, no passenger train operator has exploited the potential of this high-value 'just in time' market. Even today, empty van space still remains on many long-distance trains.

It is true that a measure of on-rail competition has developed, with Freightliner forming a heavy haul division to compete for coal traffic and operate engineering trains for Network Rail. DRS has developed other freight flows and provides locomotives for some passenger services. One successful new operator, GB Railfreight, was developed from Anglia Railways, sold to FirstGroup and is now owned by Eurotunnel. A number of other specialist operators have failed, including Jarvis Fastine, Cotswold Rail and Fragonset; it is a tough market and, while rail needs to work with road to complete the logistics chain, the real competitor remains the juggernaut.

BR's trainload freight business was thriving at the time of privatisation and was seen as having every chance of success, particularly when it was purchased by a class two American railroad. Equally, the view of both the Board and government was that if it failed to work in the private sector, further retrenchment would probably take place but would no longer be government responsibility. In fact, Wisconsin proved to be an imaginative and expansionist owner which invested heavily in 250 new locomotives and a new wagon fleet. Despite this, it suffered setbacks when the Post Office ceased to carry letter mail by rail and withdrew the travelling PO trains when their rolling stock became life-expired.

The two biggest changes for rail freight since privatisation have affected coal for electricity generation and container traffic from the ports to inland distribution depots (but not to Didcot):

Privatisation Victim
The first victim of privatisation was the successful Red Star parcels service which was bought by Lynx and closed
down, having once been a familiar sight in most towns. The Red Star office at Waterloo is pictured in 1973.

- **Coal:** The pattern of distribution changed dramatically with privatisation of the electricity supply and progressive decline of the British coal industry after the miners' strike of 1984. There has been a shift from using indigenous coal, usually moved over relatively short distances from colliery to power station, to long haul from the major coal ports, principally at Clydeport (Hunterston) and Immingham. The demand for imported coal from Clydeport to the Aire and Trent Valley power stations has, ironically, proved the value of both the Glasgow & South Western and Settle & Carlisle lines, which have seen significant investment to handle the coal trains. Similarly, coal from Immingham has led to investment in the Brigg line between Barnetby and Retford, to avoid a flat crossing of the ECML.
- **Containers:** The huge increase in imports from the Far East and Asia, and the development of Felixstowe and Southampton, in particular, as container ports has led to significant growth in demand for rail movement inland to the West Midlands, the Northwest, Yorkshire & Humber and Strathclyde. Significant investment is being undertaken on the routes from Felixstowe to Peterborough and Southampton to the West Midlands, to provide the capacity required.

The competitive threat from bigger, heavier lorries remains today. European Commission proposals include longer, heavier and higher (two-tier) lorries and road trains, and the DfT held a consultation on this in 2011. The Netherlands propose to move to 'mega-trucks' 25m long, with weights up to 60 tonnes, which would have a serious effect on the competitiveness of rail.

The Northern Rail review

The financial impact of the Hatfield accident in 2000 and its aftermath led to financial pressures on the Strategic Rail Authority to look for savings. In secret, studies were undertaken on the costs and benefits of a number of rural lines.

The focal point was the Northern franchise, formed in 2004 by the merger of the North West and North East Regional Railways' franchises which were believed by the Department to be 'unaffordable'. A review was commissioned from Steer Davies & Gleave which looked at options including increasing fares, bus substitution of rail services and line closures. No closures or bus substitutions were recommended, but the case studies proposed for further evaluation were:

A. Possible service withdrawal:
- Stockport-Stalybridge
- Sheffield-Cleethorpes (Brigg line only)
- Knottingley-Goole
- Morpeth-Chathill
- Lancaster-Heysham Port (leaving other services Lancaster to Morecambe)
- Helsby-Ellesmere Port
- York-Sheffield (stopping services).

B. Possible line closure:
- Settle Junction-Carnforth and withdrawal of the Leeds-Morecambe service.

Unsurprisingly, little scope for savings was identified as the lines in A would be retained for other freight or passenger services. Savings for the route closure in B were seen as small in relation to the political problems of implementing it.

Indeed, the conclusions of the review were unambiguous and made it clear it would not be possible to make significant inroads into required levels of support by trimming services and routes at the margin. Northern itself wisely recognised its position and built strong, effective links with its stakeholders, particularly the five PTEs it served. In doing so, it managed to attract further funding by delivering on a number of their objectives and becoming part of the thriving economies of cities like Leeds and Manchester, notching up higher percentage growth of passenger numbers than achieved elsewhere on Inter City or London and South East services. In particular, the review concluded it would not even be possible to reduce the fleet size without withdrawing or reducing the length of trains that were already well loaded. It was an absolute endorsement of the efficient way in which Britain's local railways use their resources:

> The findings of the review are that the Northern Rail franchise is an efficient and well managed operation and that there are no obvious and acceptable 'quick wins' to improving value for money.[2]

Thereafter, there were no more proposals for retrenchment of the network.

Passenger service requirement

Each passenger franchise specifies in some detail the level of train service to be provided, including frequency, journey times, stopping patterns and first/last trains. This specification is set by government, not by the rail industry, and the relevant information is not only published but is the subject of consultation prior to invitation to tender. The whole process is now admirably open, which means that 'closure by stealth' is not a practical approach either for government or train operators. It also precludes pruning services on cost grounds, bus substitution or cutting out Sunday services. (The closure procedure is now quite onerous and is described in Chapter 19.)

In short, rail passenger services now have an unprecedented degree of protection and security, guaranteed by government for the duration of the franchise. The short-term approach of managed decline, which has been a feature of so much of the last 60 years, has now been replaced by a framework that gives confidence to passengers in using the trains and train operators in running them efficiently.

---

1 A 'parliamentary' service represents the bare minimum number of trains to avoid the need to go through the closure process. The term originates from the Railway Regulation Act 1844, which required railways to run at least one train a day on each route at a third class fare of no more than a penny (1d) a mile.

2 *Northern Rail Review*, summary report, March 2006, Steer, Davies & Gleave, paragraph 6.1.

XIX

RAIL'S NEW ROLE

Now is the time to reaffirm commitment to the railway, not to lose faith …
Britain needs its railways now more than ever before.

RICHARD BOWKER, SRA CHAIRMAN AND CHIEF EXECUTIVE, *EVERYONE'S RAILWAY*
– THE WIDER CASE FOR RAIL, 2003

Future reopening?
The Lewes-Uckfield line is a strong contender for reopening and would serve a developing corridor, as well as
providing an alternative route to Brighton, Newhaven and Eastbourne. Seen here in August 1956, before the East Sussex
network had been drastically cut down, a local afternoon train from Tonbridge to Brighton approaches Lewes.

By the time the Labour Party returned to power in 1997, rail as a mode was in a considerably stronger position, with an established growing market and an understanding by Government that it could no longer build its way out of road congestion. All of this was reflected in John Prescott's[1] integrated transport White Paper of 1998, which offered a glowing prospectus for rail.

However, the planning capability had been lost during the previous five years, during which all available resources were devoted to restructuring and privatisation. Dissatisfaction with the railway, the traumatic effect of the Hatfield accident and the chaos that ensued as speed restrictions paralysed the network all served to stifle a golden opportunity. Costs increased as companies became more risk averse and available resources were concentrated on maintaining and renewing the existing railway, rather than expanding it. This discouraged local authorities from considering rail-based schemes, as did the problems of dealing with a fragmented industry.

Table D shows the effect of privatisation on the opening of new stations as negotiations became more complex, costs rose and timescales extended.

Table D: Number of stations opened in Great Britain, 1990 to 2010[2]

Year	No of stations	Year	No of stations	Year	No of stations	Year	No of stations
1990	20	1996	4	2002	3	2008	11
1991	5	1997	3	2003	2	2009	6
1992	15	1998	7	2004	Nil	2010	5
1993	15	1999	5	2005	8		
1994	17	2000	5	2006	1		
1995	9	2001	1	2007	5		

The idea of devolving responsibility for local train services was resurrected in 2000, when the DETR was preparing the Transport Act 2000, and for the same reasons as in 1977 and 1982. In the 'Balkanised' railway of the time, this too was an abrogation of responsibility for strategic planning of the national network, but again the proposition never gained momentum and the issue was passed to the Strategic Rail Authority.

Community rail development

In the early 1990s, some local authorities and rail user groups were encouraging people to use their local railways, in part to prevent future service reductions or even closures. Some of the most effective ideas, and much of the drive to make things happen, came from Paul Salveson,[3] formerly a BR guard and signalman but by then a consultant with innovative practical ideas on how to get more out of underused rural and local lines. In 1996, he formed the Association of Community Rail Partnerships to draw together these local initiatives and to encourage best practice and extension of the concept to other routes.

Starting with some simple concepts on the Penistone line (see Chapter 17), these partnerships encouraged better use of the lines with more effective local publicity and by running some high-profile special events, notably 'jazz trains', to attract people to very lightly used evening services. Local volunteers then turned to improving stations – via landscaping, gardening, painting and basic facilities such as seats – or providing better information, particularly at unstaffed stations. Others found new uses for redundant buildings which sometimes added a shop or café to the station, and in some cases included a station agency to sell tickets, a facility lost many years before.

The success of the partnerships did lead to increased usage, and train operators increased services, as on the Bittern line in Norfolk

(Norwich-Sheringham), where traffic has almost doubled since the partnership was established.

ACoRP was supported by the Strategic Rail Authority where, in 2004, a small team led by Chris Austin produced a community rail development strategy which forms the basis of today's Government policy. A total of 63 routes are now community rail lines or services and many hundreds of stations have been adopted by their local communities.

These lines consistently show above-average growth and attract volunteer input assessed in 2009 at £27m a year. As a consequence, earnings have risen, costs have been restrained, subsidy levels per passenger-km have fallen and there are local economic benefits. One can only speculate what a difference this might have made had such an approach been encouraged 40 years earlier.

The gaps in the network

The closure of routes in the 1960s and 1970s left gaps in the network which either require extended train journeys to circumnavigate or make rail journeys a practical impossibility. Many examples could be cited, but some are perhaps more important because of demographic changes that have taken place since the closures and the growth in both population and employment in the corridors concerned. These are summarised below:

- **The Borders:** Closure of the Waverley Route in 1969, following Tweedmouth Junction-St Boswells in 1964 and Peebles in 1962, left a huge tract of country miles from the nearest railhead and towns such as Galashiels and Hawick completely isolated. This isolation accelerated the decline of Galashiels, with the loss first of its textile industry and then its high-tech manufacturing capacity. An attempt was made to plug the gaps with bus links from Carlisle and Berwick as well as the 30-mile bus trip to Edinburgh, but this proved unsatisfactory and a skilled workforce remained isolated from job opportunities in the capital. An attempt was made immediately following closure to reopen the line by a private company, but this was inadequately planned and resourced and came to nothing – as did a subsequent attempt in the 1990s to reopen the southern part of the route for timber traffic. Local campaigners, together with local authorities, have now persuaded Scottish ministers of the need to do better and the Borders rail link has been approved, running south of the suburban branch to Newcraighall (opened in 2002) to Stow, Galashiels and Tweedbank, just short of Melrose and the future railhead for Hawick. Work is expected to be complete in 2014.

- **East-West:** There are no east-west routes linking the main lines heading north from London between the Birmingham-Leicester-Peterborough route in the north and the North London Line in the inner London suburbs. The proposed reopening of the East-West rail link between Oxford and Bedford, perhaps extending to the East Coast Main Line and Cambridge or Peterborough, would fill this gap and make many more rail journeys possible, relieving the chronic congestion that plagues roads such as the A421 and the A14. Chiltern Railway's Evergreen project also makes use of the western end to provide an alternative route from London to Oxford via Bicester. Chiltern has also proposed making use of the new link by extending Marylebone-Aylesbury Vale services to Milton Keynes.

- **Dunstable:** With the closure of the line through Dunstable, there is no rail route allowing travel between Milton Keynes and Luton Airport or Hatfield and St Albans, the latter being a very congested corridor by road.

- **Didcot, Newbury & Southampton:** The vast fortune spent on the A34 between Southampton and the M40 underlines the need for capacity in this corridor, as do the significant sums spent on upgrading the rail-freight route between Southampton and the West Midlands, including the provision of grade-separated junctions at Reading. The Didcot, Newbury & Southampton line could have provided some of this capacity and, indeed, it was doubled between Didcot and Newbury in 1942, with longer loops installed on the remaining single-line section – investment that was thrown away in 1964.

- **March-Spalding:** The closure of the line in 1982 forced the growing container traffic from Felixstowe to the north to run via Peterborough and created a new bottleneck, particularly for traffic using the 'joint line' via Lincoln. This now needs to be dealt with through multimillion-pound grade-separated junctions at Peterborough or a new avoiding line. Both will be far more expensive than continued operation of March-Spalding would have been.
- **Tavistock:** Extension of the Tamar Valley line by six miles to Tavistock is a proposal put forward by developers Kilbride, with considerable local support. It would be the first substantial reinstatement of an abandoned railway funded by associated property development. Given the state of local roads and congestion approaching Plymouth, the development could only work with a rail link to support it. Once opened, only 15 miles would separate the new railhead at Tavistock from the end of the Dartmoor Railway at Meldon near Okehampton, with restoration of this section creating an alternative route from Exeter to Plymouth and avoiding the vulnerable coastal stretch of the Great Western main line through Dawlish (although also avoiding the population centres of Torbay and South Hams).
- **Lewes-Uckfield:** Reopening a similar short link between Lewes and Uckfield would provide an alternative route between Eastbourne/Newhaven and London. It has widespread local support, but financing it would depend on housing development in the open country between the two towns to be linked, something which the district council has resolutely opposed.
- **Skipton-Colne:** Strong and effective lobbying has highlighted the benefits of closing the gap between the electrified route from Leeds at Skipton and the Colne-Burnley line, using a route lost in 1970 which would give a new link between West Yorkshire and Lancashire. While the campaign has been effective in raising awareness, further progress will be difficult unless financial support from local authorities or Government can be secured.
- **Stratford-Honeybourne/Cheltenham:** Much of the southern part of this route is now operated by the Gloucestershire & Warwickshire Railway as a heritage line. While the formation survives tantalisingly as a cycleway in Cheltenham itself, its restoration is compromised by road development near the site of St James station. The Honeybourne-Long Marston section remains as a siding to serve a Ministry of Defence depot and local campaigning continues over restoration of the missing link between Long Marston and Stratford, where the encroachment of roads serving a new development to the south of the town would make restoration difficult. If restored, it could provide a useful link from Leamington, Warwick and Stratford-upon-Avon to Worcester, Cheltenham, Gloucester and Bristol, as well as an alternative route for freight trains avoiding the Lickey incline.
- **Matlock-Buxton:** The former Midland main line route to

Manchester closed in 1968, following electrification of the West Coast Main Line. A single line now supports an hourly local service from Derby as far as Matlock, where an interchange station offers connection to Peak Rail – a heritage railway using the old route as far as Rowsley South, with plans to extend to Bakewell. Further north, the route extends south from Manchester and Chinley to Tunstead for freight. The gap between the two of just 10 miles remains intact as a popular walking trail and bridleway. Opposition may be expected from those who enjoy the peace of the footpath and from those living nearby, who may react much as Ruskin did in 1877 (see Introduction). The value of such a line would be substantial, however. It would provide an outlet south from the Peak Forest quarries for aggregates to the East Midlands and East Anglia. At present, such flows either go by road or via a circuitous rail route through the congested Manchester hub. It would also provide a more direct route to Manchester from Leicester, Nottingham and Derby, as well as sustainable access to the wonderful Peak District National Park.

Connecting communities

In 2009, the Association of Train Operating Companies published a report written by Chris Austin, which recommended further research into reopening 14 lines that served towns no longer connected by rail. This followed a review of some 75 towns no longer served by rail where the population was 15,000 or more. In many cases, demographic changes and road congestion meant that circumstances were very different from those 40 years previously, when the lines concerned had been closed.

Some failed to make the business case because the numbers of potential passengers were too low, but most fell short because the capital cost of reconnecting was too high, even though they would cover operating costs. In many cases, much of the route was intact but a few key sites were now blocked, typically by housing development on former station sites or new roads blocking the formation at a strategic point where diversion would be difficult and costly. In some corridors substantial numbers of people would be served, such as that between Bury and Rawtenstall (94,000), now served by the East Lancs Railway, and the Ivanhoe line between Leicester and Burton (95,000). While noting that the report made a contribution to understanding the costs and benefits of such schemes, the Government made it clear they would expect them to be driven forward locally in response to an identified problem for which the railway provided the most cost-effective solution.

The McNulty Report

Sir Roy McNulty[4], former Chairman of the Civil Aviation Authority, was asked by Labour minister Lord Adonis in 2010 to conduct a review of the railway costs which had given Governments cause for concern since Railtrack went into administration in 2001. His report was delivered to Philip Hammond, Conservative Secretary of State in the coalition Government, in May 2011. It focused on further development and growth, as evidenced by the report's title, *Realising the Potential of GB Rail.* While he made it clear that he had not considered closures, he indicated at the outset that this might not be the case in the future:

As the Study has said on numerous occasions over the past year, this is Plan A. Only if all concerned fail to deliver the improvements which the Study judges to be both necessary and possible, would consideration conceivably have to be given to a Plan B – a smaller railway.[5]

With advice from experienced civil servants, Sir Roy wisely chose not to put maps in his report – the fundamental presentational error made by Beeching and Serpell – but nonetheless fell into the trap of presenting some misleading comparisons on the finances of local and rural train services. These are shown in Table E below (Table 6.1 of the McNulty Report).

Table E: Difference in the net cost to Government and passengers of the three categories of franchise

	Passenger miles (bn)	Net cost to Government (£m)	Net cost pence per passenger mile	Net cost to Government as a proportion of total cost
Long distance franchises	9.4	693	7.3	25
L&SE franchises	15.7	760	4.8	19
Regional franchises	6.0	1,873	31.1	61

The figures do not show passenger journeys, nor do they differentiate between local and rural services, PTE services with lower fares and the busy interurban routes such as Liverpool-Norwich and Cardiff-Manchester, where costs are high but so are passenger numbers. They were also based on allocated rather than actual costs incurred on local and rural services, which tend to be lower. Inevitably, the network of regional services attracts a high proportion of allocated infrastructure costs. The two key questions are: how much of that would be reallocated to long-distance services if the regional services were removed?; how much long-distance revenue would be lost if connecting regional services did not exist? The cost to the NHS of more road accidents, the economic costs of congestion and expenditure on new roads and higher road maintenance are questions begged by such a table.

Nevertheless, the report had some valuable structural proposals for reducing costs, in particular proposed lower cost solutions for regional railways which would include:

- Different service levels
- Different equipment
- Lower-cost infrastructure
- Different working methods
- Different standards.

It also recommended that a number of lines should be identified as pilot studies to establish benchmarks, and was altogether a much more realistic and positive approach than many reports of past years, pointing out ways to improve the finances rather than assuming that 'unprofitable' services should be eliminated. The change in approach and understanding over the 50 years since Beeching is clear for all to see.

As the reference to 'Plan B' and the thinking behind Table E

demonstrate, threats to the integrity of the network remain and are easily supported by spurious statistics. Continued vigilance is required both to protect the local and rural network and as part of the constant effort to reduce costs and account properly for those incurred.

The reality of such a threat was underlined by Philip Hammond in an interview with *The Guardian,* published on 19 May 2011. He was reported as saying that above-inflation fare rises could disappear within four years if reforms set out (in the McNulty Report) are implemented. But he also ruled out fare cuts, as he warned that the £5.2bn-a-year state subsidy for the 'relatively small' and 'better off' proportion of the population that uses trains is unsustainable at current levels (overall, fare payers currently spend £6.2bn a year):

> In the long term the taxpayer will not be prepared to just continually increase the level of subsidy that they give to the relatively small number of people who ever use trains – something like only 12% of the population. And of course those who use trains tend to be better off anyway.[6]

The erroneous assumptions made by Crosland in 1977 are still being repeated well over 30 years later.

The closure criteria today

The Railways Acts of 1993 and 2005 together set out the basis on which passenger rail services may be discontinued and passenger rail infrastructure may be closed.

The operator or sponsor of the service has to give notice of any proposal to withdraw or close to the Secretary of State, or Scottish ministers, and the minister has to consult if he agrees the process should go ahead.

In a vain attempt to make this an administrative process rather than a highly charged political one, it is the Office of Rail Regulation (ORR) that has to issue the Closure Ratification Notice if satisfied there has been proper compliance with the procedure laid down in the Act. In doing so, the ORR may impose requirements on the operator or the Secretary of State. There is provision in the Act to require replacement bus services to be run if required and for PTEs to establish quality service contracts, if they are what is needed to provide an adequate replacement service.

'Closures' are interpreted rather widely and may even be required where stations are relocated or important facilities for passengers removed. In other cases, changes to station facilities are deemed to be minor modifications and are dealt with through the licence agreement.

There is no equivalent for the closure of freight depots or freight infrastructure – although any line closure, however small, would be subject to approval by the ORR following consultation through the network change procedure, involving all operators who might want to use the line.

Despite the involvement of the ORR, it is well understood that closures remain a political decision for ministers and the procedure is quite tight, discouraging any closure without a very sound basis. The days of closure by stealth or in piecemeal are over.

1   John Prescott (born 1938) was the Labour Party's Deputy Prime Minister from 1997-2007; MP for Hull East, 1970-2010; Deputy Leader of the party, 1994-2007; Secretary of State for Environment, Transport and the Regions, 1997-2001; and First Secretary of State, 2001-07. Ennobled as Lord Prescott in 2010, he is the son of a railway signalman, himself a waiter and steward in the Merchant Navy before becoming an activist in the National Union of Seamen.
2   *Britain's Growing Railway,* Railfuture, 2010.
3   Professor Paul Salveson, MBE, FCILT, is a career railwayman, author, lecturer and community rail pioneer who formed the Association of Community Rail Partnerships and became their first General Manager. He is now General Secretary of the Hannah Mitchell Foundation and visiting professor at the University of

Huddersfield; he was formerly External Relations Manager at Grand Central and Head of Government and Community Strategies at Northern Rail.
4   Sir Roy McNulty CBE (born 1937) was Chairman of the Rail Value for Money Study sponsored by the Department of Transport and the Office of Rail Regulation from 2010-11; Deputy Chairman of the 2012 Olympic Delivery Authority; Chairman of Advantage West Midlands 2009-2012. Previously, he was Chairman of the Civil Aviation Authority 2001-09, Chairman of National Air Traffic Services 1999-2001 and, prior to that, Chief Executive and Chairman of Shorts Brothers plc.
5   *Realising the Potential of GB Rail:* Summary Report, May 2011, DfT p8.
6   *The Guardian,* 19 May 2011.

XX

CONCLUSIONS

Those who cannot remember the past are condemned to repeat it.

GEORGE SANTAYANA, *THE LIFE OF REASON*, 1905

From this extended look at the history of rail closures in Great Britain, some clear conclusions emerge.

There was a view from around 1952 onwards that the rail network needed 'streamlining' to meet changing demands and circumstances. Initially, no clear objectives were set, but absolute clarity was provided in 1963 by Dr Richard Beeching. However, this was based on a narrow view predicated solely on the notional 'profitability' of individual lines and services.

Up to the arrival of Ernest Marples as Transport Minister, rail closures were largely based on commercial decisions by railway managers – although, from 1952 onwards, the BTC had put pressure on the regions to be more radical in their approach. However, from 1960 onwards, closures became a political issue via a determined attempt to shrink drastically the size of the network and diminish the role played by rail in meeting the nation's transport needs.

There was clearly a conspiracy between ministers, senior civil servants and the road lobby, particularly from 1960 to 1965, to shift investment from rail to road and disinvest in a substantial proportion of the rail network. Surprisingly, a number of Labour ministers were captured by the policy and failed to stop this disinvestment, or even defer it pending development of an overarching transport strategy – which would not come for another 40 years.

At various key stages during the 50 years of nationalisation, a toxic combination of very strong or very weak ministers and senior civil servants combined to the detriment of the railway, its customers and its staff. Marples as Minister had a very clear agenda to eliminate a large proportion of the network, ably supported by Serpell and, of course, by Beeching. At a time when decisive action could have changed the course of history and developed the social railway a decade earlier, this was thwarted by the combination of a Minister whose heart was not in the job (Fraser) and a Permanent Secretary (Padmore) whose passion as an amateur musician was greater than his commitment as a senior civil servant.

On the other hand, Peter Parker worked well as BR Chairman and achieved much with his Ministers, particularly Norman Fowler, while the working relationship between Sir Robert Reid and Nicholas Ridley brought tangible benefits in terms of stability and approval of significant investment, including electrification of the East Coast Main Line.

Railway closures were highly contentious and people felt passionately about the dramatic changes. The huge reduction in track and signalling capacity was highly visible, with removal of station facilities, many stations reduced to the status of unstaffed halts,

closure of goods yards and the depressing image of lines of steam locomotives and wagons awaiting scrapping. Perhaps the nadir of the fortunes of Britain's railways was 1965, from which they took many years to recover.

The overriding lessons from the history of rail closures can be summarised as:

- There has never been a good understanding of the costs of lines and services, or of the residual liabilities which may mean that cost escapement will be years behind the running of the last train.
- In short, do not trust the statistics. At best, they tell only half the story; at worst, they can be manipulated to support any argument. Figures are no substitute for a proper management assessment of the issues, including consultation and the deployment of common-sense practicality in preference to more theoretical management techniques.
- The real damage was done by combining a formulaic approach and cod economics to make judgements about a complex series of financial and social interactions. This was made worse by the huge number of lines and stations concerned and the political pressures to make economies quickly. When such a process is rushed, it tends to produce the wrong results.
- The speed of closure gave little time for reflection or consideration of alternatives. Indeed, it would now take longer to plan for a weekend possession for track renewal, than it did to close some lines completely.
- Much planning for reduction of the network was carried out in great secrecy and requests for public information were routinely denied. Governments, the British Transport Commission and the BR board, in its early days, failed to deal with the (accurate) charge from campaigners that closures were implemented without any attempt to reduce costs or raise revenue, and that the information on which decisions were based was flawed.
- Scandalously, there was no back-checking to confirm whether the savings claimed from closures had actually been achieved. To their credit, BRB did commission work on the social effects of rail closures, but the financial effects were not assessed. Nor was there any attempt to assess the economic effect on the communities served.
- The combination of secrecy, limited data and the lack of accountability meant that lines were lost which were making a positive economic contribution and many were closed prematurely.
- Public perception of the inevitability of closures undermined confidence in the railway as a whole. The juggernaut rolled on long after it was clear that it would not meet the cost-saving objectives.

The effect on public confidence in the railway was felt for a generation and still has echoes today.

- Ironically, if time pressures had not demanded a rapid programme of closures, graphically illustrated by the maps in the Beeching Report that showed the extent of the devastation being wrought, many closures could have been achieved over time with less public controversy. Organised opposition would not have taken place so early, or on such a scale.

- It was assumed that overall demand was limited and that the choice lay in meeting it by road or rail. There was no concept of the burgeoning demand for transport that would overwhelm the road system, or that expanding the road network would itself generate yet more demand.

- It was assumed that bus and rail were alternatives for any given journey. They are actually different modes of transport with different characteristics. Some passengers, happy to use rail as an alternative to the car, would not consider using the bus.

- The closure programme entrenched the popular view that rail had outlived its usefulness and gave it a downbeat image which damaged its commercial prospects for a decade. Local closures accelerated the rate at which people turned to cars and, in some cases, never used the railway again.

- The 'accepted view' that railways no longer had a contribution to make led to their potential being ignored in national and local planning terms. New developments were planned around motorway junctions, not railheads, and even new towns such as Basildon and Milton Keynes were initially developed without a railway station. It also led to an unbalanced approach in allocating national resources to road 'investment' rather than rail 'subsidy.'

- The belief by Government that further savings were to be achieved by reducing the size of the network continued long after BR had demonstrated clearly that this was not the case. The issues are deceptively simple: the majority of costs on the railway are staff costs; rural railways employ very few staff compared with InterCity and commuter services.

- The big costs are not on the rural network, but on the busy urban and interurban networks which also carry a lot of people and make a major contribution to both congestion reduction and increased mobility.

- As a general rule, the later closures were probably mistaken, while the earlier ones tended to be those with the weakest case for retention. There was no socio-economic case for lines like the Ventnor West branch or the Newburgh-St Fort line, both closed in 1952. However, had lines like Lewes-Uckfield (closed in 1969), Exeter-Plymouth via Okehampton (1968/72) or the Woodhead route (1981) survived, they would be useful and effective parts of the national network today.

- A whole lexicon of euphemisms was developed to counteract the blunt words of the Beeching Report, from 'rationalisation' of the network to 'unremunerative passenger services' and 'cost ineffective' passenger services. McNulty's interim report speaks ominously of the need to deliver the savings he proposes, as the alternative is 'much less investment and/or a radically smaller network'.[1]

- No strategy was developed to ensure that diversionary routes ensured the flow of traffic between key centres during maintenance or renewals, or as a result of natural disasters such as flooding. Most significantly, no alternative route at all exists to Plymouth and Cornwall, and no reasonable alternative route remains to Aberdeen or between Leeds and Newcastle. Alternative routes from London to Exeter and South Wales, and between Carlisle and Glasgow, are limited by sections of single line. Shorter routes such as Edinburgh-Perth via Kinross, Manchester-Sheffield via the Woodhead Tunnel and Malton-Whitby were sacrificed to save money, leaving longer routes in place with longer journey times.

Postscript

From all the evidence collected in this book, we can see the immense damage caused by a concerted attempt to shrink the network and the role it played in meeting Britain's transport needs. With this came the bad planning, dogmatism, political chicanery, ineptitude and lack of imagination that characterised rail policy in the middle of the 20th century.

In particular, we can see the problems in trying to disaggregate the national rail network, to identify the 'profitable' parts and to devolve or dispose of the rest. Subsequently, we have seen the gradual development of a political pragmatism which accepts the difficulty of demonstrating or disproving the net costs and the inevitable political opprobrium in forcing through a closure. In political terms, what Minister of Transport would want to be remembered for depriving a community of its rail service?

This more pragmatic approach seeks to close the gap between costs and revenue, and to maximise the value of the financial support required by encouraging significantly greater ridership, reducing the subsidy per passenger mile dramatically as well as bringing a number of external benefits.

This book is about the lessons of history. Its authors hope that by setting these out for a new generation of railway managers and policymakers, it will help them avoid the devastating mistakes of the past and focus on the future development of the railway. The need to travel and move freight around, and to do so in a sustainable way, ensures that the railway still has a great future – one of expansion rather than contraction.

---

1 *Rail Value for Money Report*: interim submission to Secretary of State, September 2010.

APPENDICES

Appendix A

4   SECRET

ANNEXE II
PROPOSED PUBLICITY PROGRAMME
1.   A comprehensive publicity programme has been worked out by the Ministry of Transport and the British Railways Board. The programme is outlined below.
2   The Minister and Dr. Beeching will jointly brief Ministry and Board Press Officers (including the Board's Regional Press Officers) at 10.30 a.m. on Monday, 25th March
3.   Publicity Initiated by Railways Board
(a) Advance copies of the Report, together with a Press notice will be issued to the Press under embargo at noon on Monday, 25th March.
(b) Members of the Board, but not the Chairman, will be available on Tuesday, 26th March, to brief individual correspondents. Particular attention will be paid to the two London evening newspapers whose treatment of a report often sets a tone which the national dailies follow.
(c) Dr. Beeching will hold a Press conference at 11 a.m. on 27th March followed by television news interview. Regional Press conferences will be held around noon on 27th March.
(d) The Board have produced a film which will be shown to railwaymen throughout the country. This film has been offered to the B.B.C. as a basis for a television programme which would include also an interview with Dr. Beeching. The B.B.C. are considering the proposal.
(e) The Report will be distributed to the Board's staff down to district officers (around 4000). A special poster addressed to all railwaymen is being prepared. This will contain a short summary of the Report. The proposal to provide each railwayman with an individual copy of a summary of the Report has been abandoned.
(f) Other members of the Board besides the Chairman will be available to appear in television programmes. Similarly, regional chairman will be available to appear in television programmes outside London.
4.   Ministry Publicity Arrangements
(a) A "fact sheet" of background information already on the record will be issued to Lobby journalists by the Public Relations Adviser to the Prime Minister on Thursday 21st March.
(b) The Minister and the Parliamentary Secretary (Mr. Hay) will meet selected journalists on Tuesday 26th March for background briefing.
(c) The Minister will make a statement in the House of Commons at 3.30 p.m. on 27th March. Copies will be given to the Press Gallery in the usual way.
(d) The Minister will hold an open, i.e., attributable, Press conference at 4.30.p.m. on Wednesday 27th March. A Press notice will be issued which will incorporate the Minister's statement in the House and background information of events leading up to the Beeching Report. This will be followed by television news interviews.
(e) Granada television will network a programme on the railways from 9.45 to 10.30 p.m. on Wednesday 27th March. It will include interviews with the Minister and Dr. Beeching.
5.   Other Publicity Arrangements
(a) The Minister of Transport, in conjunction with the Minister without Portfolio and the Chief Whip, will establish a panel of backbench M.Ps. who will be briefed in advance and be available to take part in regional television programmes.
(b) The Minister of Transport, in conjunction with the Minister without Portfolio and the Chief Whip, will arrange to address Government supporters in the House of Commons on the evening of 27th March. A brief for use in speeches would be supplied to them.
(c) A meeting to be addressed by the Minister of Transport will later be offered to the Parliamentary Labour Party.

SECRET

Appendix B

Services listed in the Beeching Report

Section 1
PASSENGER SERVICE, LINE AND STATION CLOSURES
Passenger Services to be Withdrawn
Glasgow Central-Carlisle (local)
Edinburgh Princes Street-Carstairs-Lanark
Glasgow St Enoch-Dumfries-Carlisle (local)
Glasgow St Enoch-Lugton-Kilmarnock (local)
Darvel-Kilmarnock
Stranraer-Dumfries
Dumfries-Castle Douglas-Kirkcudbright
Glasgow St Enoch-Dalry-Kilmarnock
Ayr-Dalmellington
Kilmarnock-Ayr
Kilmarnock-Ardrossan
Lanark-Muirkirk
Glasgow Central-Edinburgh Princes Street
Hamilton-Strathaven/Coalburn
Edinburgh Waverley-Berwick-upon-Tweed (local)
Edinburgh Waverley-Dunbar
Edinburgh Waverley-Hawick-Carlisle
Langholm-Riddings Junction-Carlisle
Thornton-Crail-Dundee
Stirling-Alloa-Kinross
Glasgow Buchanan Street-Stirling-Perth (local)
Gleneagles-Crieff-Comrie
Glasgow Buchanan Street-Stirling-Oban
Killin Junction-Killin
Oban-Connel Ferry-Ballachulish
Craigendoran-Arrochar
Fort William-Mallaig (local)
Ballinluig-Aberfeldy
Perth-Blair Atholl-Struan
Lossiemouth-Elgin
Aberdeen-Inverurie
Aberdeen-Keith-Elgin (local)
Aberdeen-Fraserburgh
Maud-Peterhead
Fraserburgh-St Combs
Tillynaught-Banff
Aberdeen-Ballater
Aviemore-Craigellachie-Elgin
Aviemore-Inverness-Elgin (local)
Georgemas Junction-Thurso
Glasgow St Enoch-Barrhead
Glasgow St Enoch-East Kilbride
Glasgow St Enoch-Kilmacolm
Glasgow St Enoch-Paisley West
Coatbridge-Dumbarton
Edinburgh Princes Street-Kingsknowe
Glasgow Queen Street-Kirkintilloch
Edinburgh Waverley-Musselburgh
Ayr-Stranraer
Inverness-Wick
Inverness-Kyle of Lochalsh
Doncaster-Leeds Central (local)
Selby-Goole
York-Hull
Hull-Hornsea Town
Hull-Withernsea
Driffield-Selby
Leeds Central-Castleford Central-Pontefract
Leeds City-Knottingley

Wakefield-Goole
Bradford Exchange-Batley-Wakefield
Leeds Central-Pudsey-Bradford Exchange
Bradford Exchange-Mirfield-Huddersfield (local)
Bradford Exchange-Halifax-Huddersfield (local)
Huddersfield-Clayton West-Penistone
Leeds City and Bradford Forster Square-Ilkley-Skipton
Leeds City and Bradford Forster Square-Keighley-Skipton (local)
Leeds City-Bradford Forster Square (local)
Leeds City-Cudworth-Sheffield Midland (local)
Leeds City-Cross Gates-Micklefield (local)
Leeds City-Wetherby-Harrogate
Wetherby-Church Fenton
Malton-Whitby
Middlesbrough-Guisborough
Middlesbrough-Whitby-Scarborough
York-Harrogate
Leeds-Harrogate-Northallerton-Darlington
Darlington-Richmond
Darlington-Barnard Castle-Middleton-in-Teesdale
Darlington-Bishop Auckland-Crook
Sunderland-Durham-Bishop Auckland
Sunderland-West Hartlepool (local)
Newcastle-on-Tyne-Washington
Sunderland-South Shields
Newcastle upon Tyne-Hexham (local)
Newcastle upon Tyne-Haltwhistle (local)
Newcastle upon Tyne-Newbiggin
Newsham-Blyth
Monkseaton-Blyth-Newbiggin
Newcastle upon Tyne-Riverside-Tynemouth (local)
York-Sheffield Victoria-Nottingham Victoria-Leicester Central-Banbury
Crewe-Warrington-Preston-Carlisle (local)
Dunstable North-Hatfield
Wolverton-Newport Pagnell
Buckingham-Bletchley
Northampton Castle-Peterborough East
Wellingborough Midland Road-Northampton Castle
Seaton-Stamford
Rugby Midland-Peterborough East
Leamington Spa Avenue-Coventry-Nuneaton Trent Valley
Derby Midland-Tamworth-Birmingham New Street (Local)
Wolverhampton High Level-Burton-on-Trent
Wellington-Shrewsbury (local)
Stafford-Wellington
Crewe-Shrewsbury (local)
Crewe-Chester General (local)
Bangor-Afon Wen
Chester General-Holyhead/Caernarvon (local)
Manchester Exchange-Warrington Bank Quay-Chester General (local)
Llandudno-Blaenau Ffestiniog
Bangor-Amlwch
Wrexham Central-Chester Northgate-New Brighton
Liverpool Lime Street-Chester General
Manchester Piccadilly-Buxton
Stoke-on-Trent-Silverdale
Kidsgrove-Etruria (Stoke loop)
Leek-Uttoxeter
Stockport Edgeley-Stalybridge (local)
Liverpool Lime Street-Tyldesley-Patricroft-Manchester Exchange (local)
St Helens Shaw Street-Earlestown-Warrington Bank Quay
Manchester Exchange-Huddersfield (local)
Wigan Wallgate-Fazakerley-Liverpool Exchange
Wigan Central-Glazebrook
Glazebrook-Stockport Tiviot Dale
Blackpool North-Fleetwood
Manchester Victoria-Bury-Bacup
Manchester Victoria-Bury-Accrington-Colne
Southport Chapel Street-Preston
Earby-Barnoldswick
Rose Grove-Todmorden

Sellafield–Moor Row
Ulverston-Lake Side (Windermere)
Barrow-Whitehaven
Carlisle-Penrith-Workington
Oxenholme-Windermere (local)
Carlisle-Silloth
Kettering-Leicester London Road (local)
Leicester London Road-Nottingham Midland (local)
Manchester Central-Chinley-Derby Midland (local)
Buxton-Millers Dale
Banbury-Woodford Halse
Manchester Central-Chinley-Hope-Sheffield Midland
Kettering-Melton Mowbray-Nottingham Midland
Nottingham Midland-Melton Mowbray
Leicester London Road-Burton-on-Trent
Leicester-Peterborough North
Leicester London Road-Melton Mowbray
Derby Friar Gate-Nottingham Victoria
Derby Midland-Trent-Nottingham Midland (local)
Nottingham Midland-Worksop
Derby Midland-Sheffield Midland (local)
Carnforth-Wennington
Carlisle-Skipton
London Broad Street-Richmond
Watford Junction-Croxley Green
Harrow & Wealdstone-Belmont
Watford Junction-St Albans Abbey
Walsall-Rugeley Trent Valley
Birmingham New Street-Sutton Park-Walsall
Walsall-Dudley
Manchester Exchange-Tyldesley-Wigan North Western (local)
Manchester Exchange-Stalybridge-Greenfield
Manchester Victoria-Newton Heath-Middleton
Manchester Victoria-Horwich
Liverpool Lime Street-St Helens-Wigan North Western
Manchester Victoria-Bury Bolton Street
Royton-Royton Junction
Southport Chapel Street-Crossens
Liverpool Exchange-Southport Chapel Street
Lancaster Castle/Lancaster Green Ayre-Heysham
Manchester Piccadilly-Hadfield/Glossop
Manchester Piccadilly-Romiley-Hayfield/Macclesfield
London St Pancras-Barking (local)
London Marylebone-Leicester Central-Nottingham Victoria
Westerfield-Yarmouth South Town
Shelford-Marks Tey
Saxmundham-Aldeburgh
Audley End-Bartlow
Cambridge-St Ives-March
Swaffham-Thetford
Dereham-Wells-next-the-Sea
Sheringham-Melton Constable
North Walsham-Mundesley-on-Sea
Lincoln Central-Woodhall Junction-Firsby
Firsby-Skegness
Willoughby-Mablethorpe
Lincoln St Marks-Nottingham Midland
Barton-on-Humber-New Holland Town
New Holland Pier-Cleethorpes (local)
Sheffield Midland-Nottingham Midland (local)
St Margarets-Buntingford
Romford-Upminster
Witham (Essex)-Maldon East and Heybridge
Witham (Essex)-Braintree and Bocking
Wivenhoe-Brightlingsea
Peterborough North-Spalding-Grimsby Town
Patney & Chirton-Holt Junction
Chippenham-Calne
Bath Green Park-Bournemouth West
Bristol Temple Meads-Bath Green Park
Taunton-Yeovil Pen Mill

Taunton-Minehead
Tiverton Junction-Tiverton
Taunton-Barnstaple Junction
Liskeard-Looe
Lostwithiel-Fowey
St Erth-St Ives (Cornwall)
Kemble-Cirencester Town
Kemble-Tetbury
Gloucester Central-Hereford
Porth-Maerdy
Abercynon-Aberdare
Barry-Bridgend
Cardiff-Coryton
Caerphilly-Senghenydd
Bridgend-Treherbert
Carmarthen-Aberystwyth
Berkeley Road-Sharpness
Worcester Shrub Hill-Bromyard
Swan Village-Great Bridge
Old Hill-Dudley
Whitchurch (Salop)-Welshpool
Ruabon-Morfa Mawddach/Barmouth
Bala-Bala Junction
Llanymynech-Llanfyllin
West Drayton & Yiewsley-Staines West
Bristol Temple Meads-Portishead
Bristol Temple Meads-Avonmouth Dock
Yatton-Clevedon
Bristol Temple Meads-Patchway-Pilning
Bristol Temple Meads-Clifton Down-Pilning
Cardiff Clarence Road-Cardiff General
Ashford (Kent)-Hastings
Ashford (Kent)-New Romney
Crowhurst-Bexhill West
Haywards Heath-Seaford (local)
Three Bridges-Tunbridge Wells West
Tonbridge-Brighton
Tonbridge-Eastbourne
Brighton-Horsham
Guildford-Horsham
Maiden Newton-Bridport
Brockenhurst-Ringwood-Bournemouth
Salisbury-Fordingbridge-Bournemouth
Okehampton-Plymouth
Barnstaple Junction-Ilfracombe
Okehampton-Padstow
Okehampton-Bude
Barnstaple Junction-Torrington
Yeovil Junction-Yeovil Town
Chard Central-Chard Junction
Axminster-Lyme Regis
Seaton Junction-Seaton (Devon)
Sidmouth Junction-Sidmouth
Tipton St Johns-Exmouth
Exeter Central-Exmouth
Bere Alston-Callington
Halwill-Torrington
Bodmin Road/Bodmin North-Wadebridge-Padstow
Ryde Pier Head-Ventnor/Cowes
Winchester City-Alton
Portsmouth-Botley-Romsey/Andover
Portsmouth-Netley-Southampton-Romsey/Andover (local)
Romsey-Andover
Reading Southern-Guildford-Redhill-Tonbridge (local)
Clapham Junction-Kensington Olympia

Section 2
PASSENGER SERVICE, LINE AND STATION CLOSURES
Passenger Services to be Modified
Newcastle upon Tyne-Berwick-upon-Tweed
Hull-Selby-Leeds City

Hull-Bridlington-Scarborough
Leeds City-Morecambe-Heysham
York-Wakefield Kirkgate-Sowerby Bridge-Manchester Victoria
Newcastle upon Tyne-Carlisle
Alnmouth-Alnwick
Oxford-Bletchley-Cambridge
Birmingham New Street-Barnt Green
Wrexham General-Chester General-Birkenhead Woodside
Manchester Piccadilly-Macclesfield-Stoke-on-Trent
Crewe-Derby Midland
Manchester Victoria-Rochdale-Todmorden
Bolton Trinity Street-Bury Knowsley Street-Rochdale
Manchester Victoria-Wigan Wallgate-Southport Chapel Street
Liverpool Central-Manchester Central
Liverpool Central-Gateacre-Warrington Central
Blackpool Central-Manchester/East Lancashire
Liverpool Exchange-Ormskirk-Blackpool Central
Carnforth-Barrow
Birmingham New Street-Leicester London Road-Nottingham Midland
Derby Midland-Nottingham Midland
London Euston-Watford Junction
London Broad Street-Watford Junction
Birmingham New Street-Sutton Coldfield-Lichfield City
Birmingham New Street-Redditch
Manchester Oxford Road-Crewe
Manchester Victoria-Rochdale/Oldham
London St Pancras-Nottingham Midland
Ipswich-Norwich (local)
Cambridge-Ely-King's Lynn
Bishops Stortford-Cambridge
Ely-Norwich
Cambridge-Ipswich
Ely-Newmarket
Norwich-Dereham-King's Lynn
Norwich-Sheringham
Grantham-Boston
Grantham-Nottingham
Lincoln Central-Market Rasen-Cleethorpes
Didcot-Swindon
Swindon-Bath Spa-Bristol Temple Meads
Bristol Temple Meads-Taunton
Chippenham-Trowbridge-Westbury (Wilts)
Reading General-Westbury (Wilts)
Bristol Temple Meads-Bath Spa-Westbury (Wilts)-Weymouth Town
Taunton-Exeter St Davids
Exeter St Davids-Kingswear
Plymouth-Penzance
Par-Newquay (Cornwall)
Cardiff General-Carmarthen
Carmarthen-Neyland/Milford Haven
Carmarthen-Fishguard Harbour
Swindon-Kemble-Gloucester Central
Cheltenham Spa-Cardiff General
Whitland-Pembroke Dock
Didcot-Oxford-Leamington Spa
Oxford-Worcester Shrub Hill
Stratford-on-Avon-Honeybourne
Stourbridge-Worcester-Hereford
Birmingham New Street-Worcester Shrub Hill
Worcester Shrub Hill-Gloucester Eastgate
Gloucester Eastgate-Bristol Temple Meads
Shrewsbury-Welshpool-Aberystwyth
Tunbridge Wells Central-Hastings
Sheerness-on-Sea-Dover Priory (local)
Brighton-Ore (local)
Basingstoke-Salisbury
Salisbury-Exeter Central
Exeter Central-Okehampton
Exeter Central-Barnstaple Junction

Appendix C

The Beeching Maps

The map from the Reshaping Report that showed the extent of disinvestment. Closures are spread liberally around the country, but the gaps left in Scotland, Wales and the West Country are particularly evident. Some of the lines retained are surprising, such as Alnwick, Neyland and Fawley.

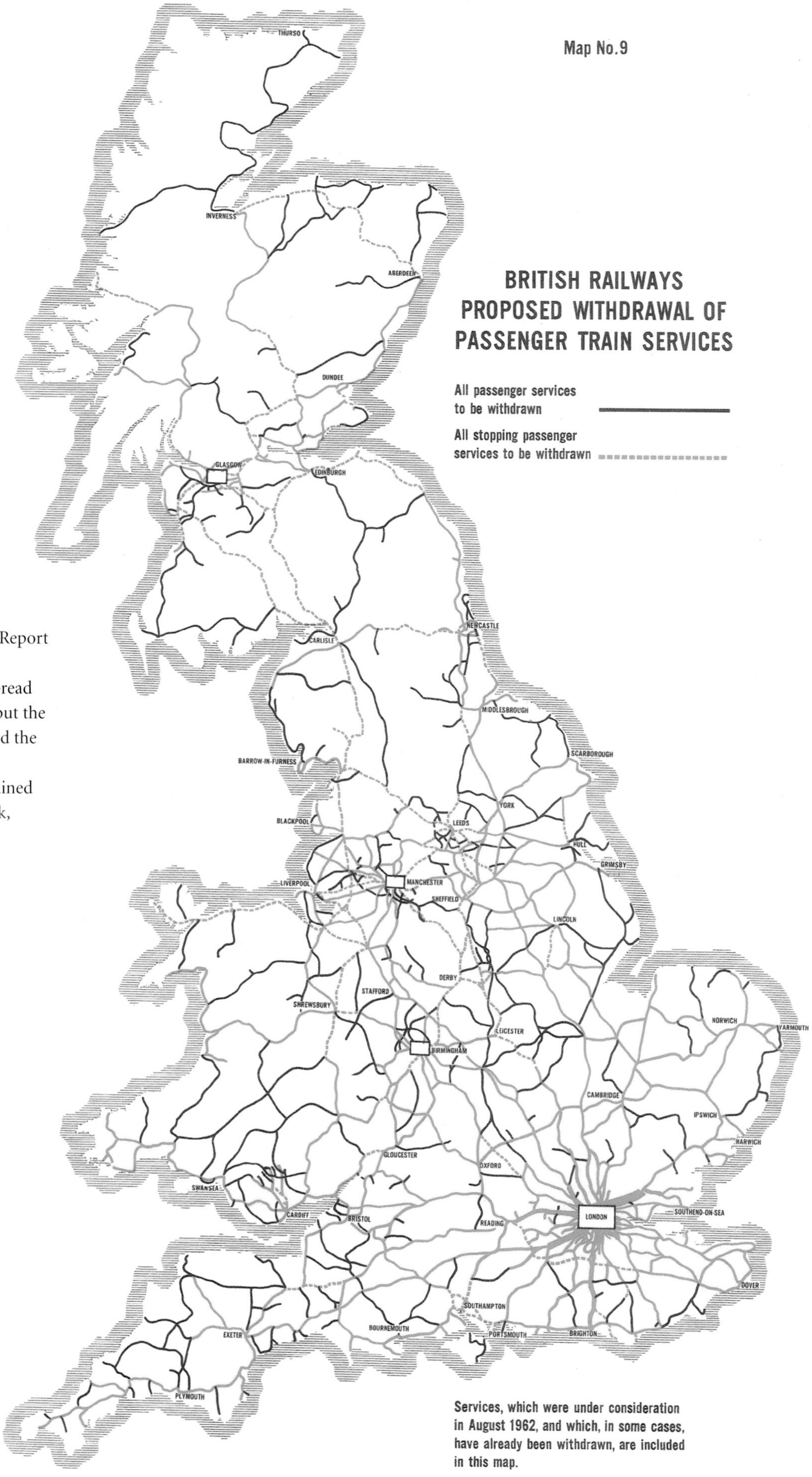
Map No.9
BRITISH RAILWAYS
PROPOSED WITHDRAWAL OF
PASSENGER TRAIN SERVICES
All passenger services
to be withdrawn
All stopping passenger
services to be withdrawn
THURSO
INVERNESS
ABERDEEN
DUNDEE
GLASGOW
EDINBURGH
NEWCASTLE
CARLISLE
MIDDLESBROUGH
SCARBOROUGH
BARROW-IN-FURNESS
YORK
LEEDS
BLACKPOOL
HULL
GRIMSBY
LIVERPOOL
MANCHESTER
SHEFFIELD
LINCOLN
DERBY
STAFFORD
SHREWSBURY
NORWICH
YARMOUTH
LEICESTER
BIRMINGHAM
CAMBRIDGE
IPSWICH
HARWICH
GLOUCESTER
OXFORD
SWANSEA
CARDIFF
BRISTOL
LONDON
SOUTHEND-ON-SEA
READING
DOVER
SOUTHAMPTON
BOURNEMOUTH
EXETER
PORTSMOUTH
BRIGHTON
PLYMOUTH
Services, which were under consideration
in August 1962, and which, in some cases,
have already been withdrawn, are included
in this map.

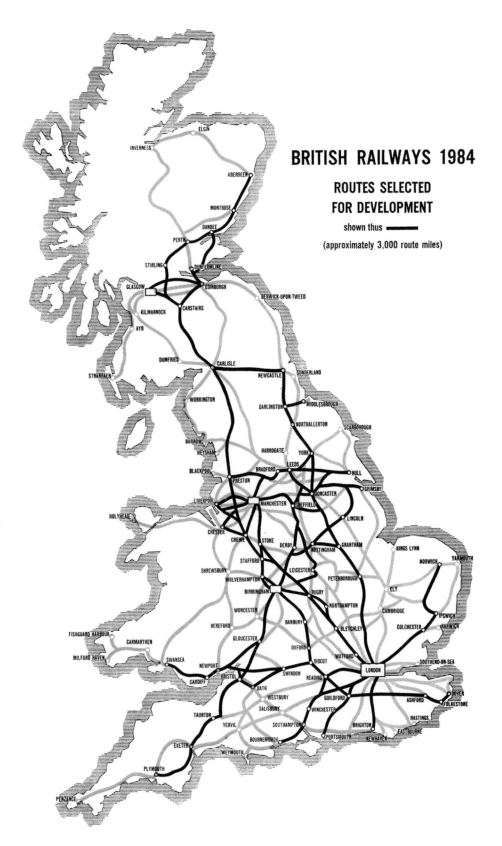

BRITISH RAILWAYS 1984

**ROUTES SELECTED
FOR DEVELOPMENT**

shown thus ▬▬▬▬

(approximately 3,000 route miles)

Map from the Second Beeching Report showing trunk routes selected for development. The network for development was quite small at 3,000 route miles and there are some notable omissions, compared with the trunk network today, apart from the lack of a Channel Tunnel or a high-speed line connecting it to London. The East Coast main line stops at Newcastle, the busy trans-Pennine route via Huddersfield is omitted and the Midland main line is missing. Also left out are routes to Cambridge, Chiltern Railways and the Berks & Hants line. *BR*

Appendix D

The 135 lines listed for grant aid from 1 January 1969, in the statement by the Rt. Hon. Richard Marsh MP as Transport Minister dated 15 November 1968 (*Hansard volume 773*, cc172-80W).

Eastern Region of British Railways
King's Cross-Peterborough/Grantham (local service)
Norwich-Yarmouth (via Acle and Reedham)
Norwich-Lowestoft
Ipswich-Lowestoft
Cambridge-Norwich
Ipswich-Cambridge
Ipswich-Colchester (local service)
Manningtree-Harwich
Witham-Braintree
Wickford-Southminster
Newcastle-Alnmouth-Berwick-Edinburgh (local service)
Newcastle-Sunderland-Middlesbrough
Newcastle-South Shields
North Tyneside services (including Riverside loop)
Newcastle-Hexham-Carlisle
Haltwhistle-Alston
Darlington/Northallerton-Hartlepool
Darlington-Saltburn
Darlington-Bishop Auckland
Middlesbrough-Whitby
York-Scarborough
York-Selby-Doncaster/Hull (local service)
York-Harrogate
Leeds-Harrogate
Leeds-Bradford
Huddersfield-Clayton West/Penistone
Huddersfield-Wakefield
Leeds-Goole
Hull-Doncaster
Sheffield-Doncaster
Sheffield-Chesterfield (local service)
Doncaster-Cleethorpes
Cleethorpes-Newark
Retford-Cleethorpes
Sheffield-Retford
Retford-Lincoln
Lincoln-Nottingham
Grantham-Nottingham
Lincoln/Grantham-Boston
London Midland Region of British Railways
Birmingham-Redditch
Birmingham-Lichfield
Birmingham-Stourbridge/Stourbridge Town-Kidderminster
Birmingham-Leamington Spa
Birmingham (New Street)-Wolverhampton (High Level)
Birmingham-Leicester-Nottingham

Birmingham-Walsall (via Aston)
Birmingham-Walsall (via Soho)
Birmingham-Derby (local service)
Birmingham-Lapworth/Leamington Spa-Stratford-upon-Avon
Stafford-Birmingham
Rugby/Coventry-Birmingham
Rugby-Nuneaton-Stafford
Wolverhampton-Shrewsbury-Chester
Shrewsbury-Aberystwyth
Llandudno-Blaenau Ffestiniog
Leicester-Peterborough
Derby-Manchester
Derby-Nottingham
Derby-Matlock
Crewe-Chester (local service)
Crewe-Derby
Liverpool-Rock Ferry
Liverpool-New Brighton
Liverpool-West Kirby
Liverpool-Ormskirk
Liverpool-Southport
Liverpool-Runcorn-Crewe
Rock Ferry-Helsby/Chester
Runcorn-Helsby-Chester
Liverpool-Warrington-Manchester
Liverpool-Patricroft-Manchester
Manchester-Colne (via Blackburn)
Manchester-Altrincham
Manchester-Northwich-Chester
Manchester-Bury
Manchester-Oldham-Rochdale
Manchester-Preston-Blackpool
Manchester-Buxton
Manchester-Warrington-Chester (General)
Manchester-Stockport-Crewe
Manchester-Styal-Crewe
Manchester-Stafford (via Stoke)
Manchester-Wigan-Southport (via Bolton and Atherton)
Manchester-Chinley-Sheffield (Midland)
Manchester-Romiley-New Mills
Stockport-Stalybridge
New Mills-Sheffield
Bury-Rawtenstall
Preston-Blackpool
Preston-Windermere
Blackpool-Blackburn-Colne
Lancaster-Morecambe

Barrow-Whitehaven
Whitehaven-Carlisle
Scottish Region of British Railways
Glasgow North Suburban Electric Service
Glasgow South Suburban Electric Service
Springburn-Cumbernauld
Glasgow-Lanark
Glasgow-Hamilton
Glasgow-Barrhead
Glasgow-Paisley-Kilmacolm
Glasgow-East Kilbride
Glasgow-Edinburgh (via Shotts)
Glasgow-Ayr
Dalry/Kilwinning-Largs
Ayr-Stranraer
Glasgow-Oban
Glasgow-Fort William
Fort William-Mallaig
Glasgow-Dundee
Glasgow-Perth-Inverness
Edinburgh-Dundee-Arbroath (via Dunfermline)
Edinburgh-Dundee-Arbroath (via Kirkcaldy)
Montrose-Dundee-Perth (local)
Aberdeen-Inverness
Inverness-Kyle of Lochalsh
Inverness-Wick/Thurso
Southern Region of British Railways
Ore-Brighton
Brighton-Portsmouth
Portsmouth-Fareham-Eastleigh/Southampton-Salisbury
Ryde-Shanklin
Western Region of British Railways
Paddington-Bedwyn (local)
Oxford-Worcester
Bristol-Weston-super-Mare-Taunton (local)
Cardiff-Merthyr
Cardiff-Rhymney
Cardiff-Penarth
Cardiff-Coryton
Barry Island-Treherbert
Swansea-Carmarthen-Milford Haven (local service)
Maiden Newton-Bridport
Plymouth-Gunnislake
Exeter-Exmouth
Liskeard-Looe
St Erth-St Ives

Also listed in the statement were 56 services to which the Minister expected to grant aid, but where examination of the applications had not yet been completed.

Eastern Region of British Railways
Cambridge-Peterborough
Cambridge-King's Lynn
East Anglia-Midlands/North England
Colchester-Clacton/Walton (local)
Leeds-York
York-Newcastle (local)
Newcastle-Liverpool
Bradford-Manchester
Bradford-Blackpool
Leeds-Huddersfield
Leeds-Skipton-Morecambe
Leeds-Barnsley-Sheffield
Leeds-Rotherham-Sheffield
Leeds-Doncaster
Sheffield-York (local)
Leeds-Liverpool
Leeds-Hull
Ipswich-Felixstowe
London Midland Region of British Railways
Euston-Northampton-Birmingham
Birmingham-Kidderminster-Worcester
Birmingham (Snow Hill)-Langley Green
Birmingham (Snow Hill)-Wolverhampton (Low Level)
Crewe-Shrewsbury
Chester-Llandudno-Holyhead
Machynlleth-Pwllheli
Liverpool-St Helens-Wigan
Liverpool-Fazakerley-Wigan-Bolton
Manchester-Hadfield/Glossop
Leeds-Carlisle-Scotland
Preston-Barrow
Keswick-Carlisle
Scottish Region of British Railways
Glasgow-Stirling-Dunblane (local)
Glasgow-Fife
Edinburgh-Kirkcaldy
Edinburgh-Dunfermline-Cardenden
Edinburgh-Falkirk-Stirling-Dunblane (local service)
Edinburgh-Glasgow via Falkirk (Grahamston)
Glasgow-Gourock-Wemyss Bay
Euston-Stranraer
Carlisle-Dumfries-Glasgow (local)
Southern Region of British Railways
Reading-Basingstoke-Salisbury
Bournemouth-Weymouth
Western Region of British Railways
Paddington-Reading-Didcot-Oxford
Oxford-Leamington
Worcester-Hereford
Birmingham-Worcester (via Bromsgrove)
Hereford-Shrewsbury
Bristol-Westbury-Salisbury
Bristol-Westbury-Weymouth
Bristol-Worcester (local)
Bristol-Newport (local)
Salisbury-Exeter
Exeter-Barnstaple
Plymouth-Saltash-Liskeard
Truro-Falmouth
Par-Newquay

Appendix E

The 41 Lines

Service	Beeching Report	1968 Grant £000	Blue Book 1972	BR/DoE List 1975	Bus subs studies	Closure proposed	Serpell Option C3	Current position	CRP?	Notes
Wrexham to Bidston	√	155[1]	√		1987		√	Electrification proposed by Merseytravel	√	
Hooton to Helsby	√	190[2]	√					Part electrified within Merseyrail electrics network		
Lancaster to Morecambe	No	69					√		√	
Aylesbury to Princes Risborough	No	Yes[3]	√							
Bristol to Severn Beach	√	81[4]	√		1987 1988		√	Severnside partnership	√	90% growth 2007/11
Harrogate to York	√	172	√	√			√	Half hourly service now runs from Leeds to Knaresborough		
Darlington to Bishop Auckland	√	120	√		1982 1985 1989		√		√	Serves Locomotion at Shildon and links with Weardale Railway
Sinfin to Derby	Not open	Until 1974	n/a		1987 1988	1997	√	Closed		Job losses and factory closures reduced demand
Clayton West to Shepley	√	140[5]	√			1981	√	Closed 1983		PTE support not given
Watford to St Albans	√	45	√				√	Electrified. Conversion to tram/train in hand with Herts CC	√	

Service	Beeching Report	1968 Grant £000	Blue Book list 1972	BR/DoE List 1975	Bus substitution studies	Closure proposed	Serpell Option C3	Current position	CRP?	Notes
Bletchley to Bedford	No	89	√	√		1959 1964 1973	√	Extension to Oxford proposed as part of East - West	√	Closure consent revoked 1974
Stourbridge to Stourbridge Junction	No	30	√				√	Run with Parry People Mover		Part of Centro network
Oldham to Rochdale	No	454[6]	√				√	Converted to light rail		Part of Metrolink network
Stratford to Leamington	√	73	√		1982		√	Through trains to London run by Chiltern		
Colchester to Sudbury	√	61	√			1965 1969	√		√	1969 list for closure
Norwich to Sheringham	No	44[7]	√		1982 1987 1989		√	Passenger numbers doubled since CRP set up	√	
Peterborough to Spalding	√	See below	√		1987	1969	√	Closed 1970 Reopened 1971		
March to Doncaster	No	363[8]	√		1982 1987* 1989#	1981 (March-Spalding)	√	March – Spalding closed 1982		Upgrade as freight alternative to ECML
Grantham to Skegness	†	10[9]	√	√			√	Promoted as Poacher Line.	√	
Retford to Barnetby	No	70[10]	√		1985@ 1988@			Limited service on Saturdays only	√	
Par to Newquay	No¶		√		1987 1989		√	Service doubled, summer London train restored	√	53% growth 2007/11

*   Peterborough-Gainsborough
#   Sleaford-Lincoln and Gainsborough-Doncaster
†   Boston – Skegness included. Grantham – Boston to be retained.
@   Gainsborough-Barnetby proposed for bus substitution
¶   Local services to be withdrawn
CRP   Community Rail Partnership

Service	Beeching Report	1968 Grant £000	Blue Book list 1972	BR/DoE List 1975	Bus substitution studies	Closure proposed	Serpell Option C3	Current position	CRP?	Notes
Falmouth to Truro	No	89	√		1987 1989		√	New crossing loop at Penryn. Train frequency doubled to half hourly	√	91% growth 2007/11
Exeter to Barnstaple	No	148	√		1987 1989		√	Train service increased to hourly	√	47% growth 2007/11
Plymouth to Gunnislake	√	82	√		1987 1989	1965	√		√	22% growth 2007/11
Ashford to Hastings	√	140	√	√		1969	√	Through service Ashford to Brighton.	√	Closure approved 1970 Closure consent revoked 1974
Lowestoft to Ipswich	√	173	√	√			√	Beccles loop planned to enable hourly service to run	√	
Lowestoft to Norwich	No	141	√				√		√	
Shrewsbury to Hereford	No	81	√				√	Key strategic link in Wales rail network used by hourly Manchester – Cardiff – Milford Haven service		
Worcester to Hereford	No¶	319	√							
Ardrossan to Largs	No	285	√				√	Electrified. Part of Strathclyde network		
Stranraer to Ayr	√	213	√		1985 1987	1963	√	Ships moved to Port Ryan Limited Stranraer service More trains to Girvan		'Fast track' closure proposed 11/63 (see Chap 4)
Markinch to Cowdenbeath	No	98¹¹	√				√	Part of Fife Circle. Half hourly service		

Service	Beeching Report	1968 Grant £000	Blue Book list 1972	BR/DoEList1975	Bus substitution studies	Closure proposed	Serpell OptionC3	Current position	CRP?	Notes
Fort William to Mallaig	No¶	176	√	√	1987		√	Major tourist attraction	√	Scheduled summer steam service for tourists
Dingwall to Kyle of Lochalsh	√	177	√	√	1985 1987	1963, 1970 Consent 1971 Revoked 1974	√	Major tourist attraction	√	
Crianlarich to Oban	√	275¹²	√	√			√			
North Berwick to Drem	No	55¹³	√				√	Electrified. Edinburgh commuter route		
Machynlleth to Pwllheli	No	232	√		1987	1967 1971	√		√	Closure consent refused 1974
Milford Haven to Clarbeston Road	No	295¹⁴	√				√	Regular service to Cardiff and Manchester		
Pembroke Dock to Whitland	No	72	√		1987	1967	√		√	
Shrewsbury to Llanelli	¥	110¹⁵	√	√	1987	1962 1968	√	Promoted as Heart of Wales line	√	
Barrow to Whitehaven	√	185	√		1987 1989		√	Strongly promoted by Cumbria	√	

¶	Local services to be withdrawn	4	Grant for part year.
¥	Under consideration prior to Beeching report	5	Huddersfield – Clayton West
CRP	Community Rail Partnership	6	Manchester Victoria – Oldham – Rochdale
1	Wrexham – New Brighton. Part year grant.	7	Part year grant
2	Rock Ferry – Helsby/ Chester	8	'East Lincolnshire services.' Part year grant.
3	Grant of £518,000 paid for whole of Marylebone – Aylesbury service. Princes Risborough – Aylesbury not separately identified.	9	Boston – Skegness. Part year grant.
		10	Retford – Cleethorpes
		11	Edinburgh – Dundee – Arbroath via Dunfermline

12	Glasgow – Oban service
13	Edinburgh – North Berwick. Part year grant.
14	Swansea – Carmarthen – Milford Haven
15	Part year grant

Appendix F

The Serpell Maps

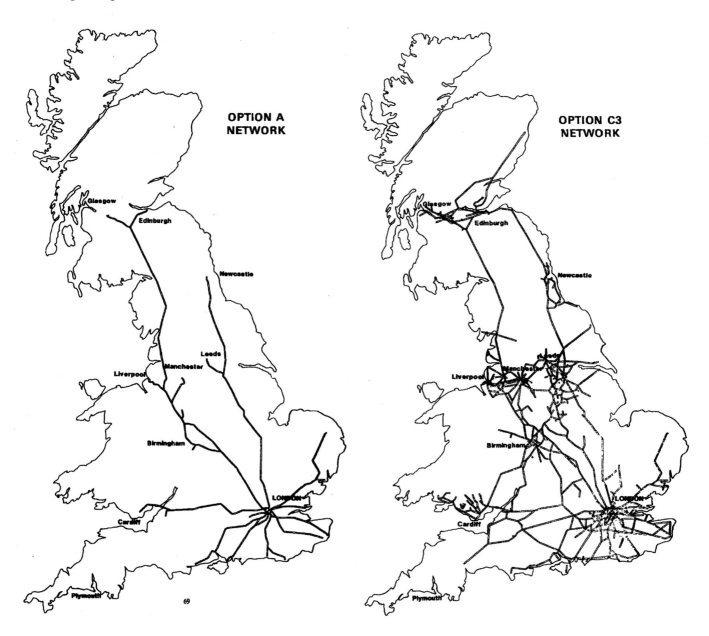

Serpell Option A. The Doomsday Scenario.

This is all that might have been left had the proposals not been comprehensively leaked and the arguments destroyed with withering criticism by the press prior to publication. A 'bare bones' network of just 1,630 route miles, euphemistically titled the 'commercial railway' in the report. No lines serve Scotland, other than from the border to Edinburgh and Glasgow. Wales has only the 22 miles from Cardiff to the Severn Tunnel. There are no railways in Somerset, Devon, Cornwall, Worcestershire or Northumberland. Many major towns and cities are no longer rail connected including Exeter, Leicester, Derby, Sheffield and Cambridge. *BR*

Serpell Option C3.

The network of 6,120 route miles, criticised by the *Guardian*. Two lines converge on Taunton and continue to Exeter, but the traffic centres of Torbay, Plymouth and Cornwall have been severed. Some surprising lines remain, including the Isle of Wight, Uckfield, the Sudbury branch and Oxford to Bletchley, with a branch to Aylesbury!

Appendix G

Transport Ministers with rail responsibilities: 1945 – 2012

Date	Name	Party	Designation	
1945-51	Alfred Barnes	Labour	MT	
1951-52	John Scott Maclay	Conservative	MT	
1952-54	Alan Lennox – Boyd	Conservative	MT/MTCA	
1954-55	John Boyd – Carpenter	Conservative	MTCA	
1955-59	Harold Watkinson	Conservative	MTCA	
1959-64	Ernest Marples	Conservative	MT	
1964-65	Tom Fraser	Labour	MT	
1965-68	Barbara Castle	Labour	MT	
1968-69	Richard Marsh	Labour	MT	
1969-70	Fred Mulley	Labour	MT	
1970-74	John Peyton	Conservative	MT/MTI	
1974-75	Fred Mulley	Labour	MT	
1975-76	John Gilbert	Labour	MT	
1976-79	William Rodgers	Labour	SST	
1979-81	Norman Fowler	Conservative	MT/SST	
1981-83	David Howell	Conservative	SST	
1983	Tom King	Conservative	SST	
1983-86	Nicholas Ridley	Conservative	SST	
1986-87	John Moore	Conservative	SST	
1987-89	Paul Channon	Conservative	SST	
1989-90	Cecil Parkinson	Conservative	SST	
1990-92	Malcolm Rifkind	Conservative	SST	
1992-94	John MacGregor	Conservative	SST	
1994-95	Brian Mawhinney	Conservative	SST	
1995-97	Sir George Young	Conservative	SST	
1997-98	Gavin Strang	Labour	MST	
1998-99	John Reid	Labour	MST	
1999	Helen Liddell	Labour	MST	
1999-01	Lord Macdonald of Tradeston	Labour	MST	
2001-02	John Spellar	Labour	MST	
2002-06	Alistair Darling	Labour	SST	
2006-07	Douglas Alexander	Labour	SST	
2007-08	Ruth Kelly	Labour	SST	
2008-09	Geoff Hoon	Labour	SST	
2009-10	Lord Adonis	Labour	SST	
2010-11	Philip Hammond	Conservative	SST	
2011-12	Justine Greening	Conservative	SST	
2012-	Patrick McLoughlin	Conservative	SST	

Analysis:

Total – 38
Average tenure of office: - 19.5 months
Average tenure of office since privatisation in 1997 – 14 months
Longest in office – Alfred Barnes, six years five months
Shortest term in office – Helen Liddell, three months

Notes:

This table shows the ministers with direct responsibility for railways. In general, Ministers of Transport up to 1969 and Secretaries of State for Transport had a seat in the Cabinet and reported directly to the Prime Minister. From 1970 to 1976, transport was represented by a junior minister reporting to the Secretary of State for the Environment. From 1997 to 2001, transport ministers reported to Rt Hon John Prescott MP as Secretary of State for Environment, Transport and the Regions (he was also deputy Prime Minister). However, Gavin Strang also had a seat in the Cabinet. From 2001-02, John Spellar reported to Stephen Byers as Secretary of State for Transport, Local Government and the Regions, and also attended Cabinet meetings.

Designation codes:

MT	Minister of Transport
MST	Minister of State for Transport
MTCA	Minister of Transport and Civil Aviation
MTI	Minister for Transport Industries
SST	Secretary of State for Transport

INDEX